READING RODNEY KING

READING URBAN UPRISING

READING RODNEY KING

READING URBAN UPRISING

EDITED AND WITH AN INTRODUCTION BY

ROBERT GOODING-WILLIAMS

ROUTLEDGE · NEW YORK & LONDON

Published in 1993 by

Routledge, Inc.
29 West 35 Street
New York, NY 10001

Published in Great Britain by

Routledge
11 New Fetter Lane
London EC4P 4EE

Library of Congress Cataloging-in-Publication Data

Reading Rodney King/reading urban uprising / edited by Robert Gooding-Williams.
     p.   cm.
Includes index.
ISBN 0-415-90734-9. — ISBN 0-415-90735-7 (pbk.)
  1. Los Angeles (Calif.)—Race relations. 2. Los Angeles (Calif.)—
    Ethnic relations. 3. Riots—California—Los Angeles—History—20th
    century. 4. United States—Race relations. 5. United States—
    Ethnic relations. I. Gooding-Williams, Robert.
    F869.L89A26   1993
    305.896'073079494—dc20   92-43381
                                            CIP

British Library cataloging in publication also available.

For Talia

Contents

Part Four: ON THE STREETS OF LOS ANGELES

Part Five: IDEOLOGY, RACE, AND COMMUNITY

Part Six: THE FIRE THIS TIME

Introduction

On Being Stuck

Robert Gooding-Williams

If we want to be instructed by events,
then we must not be in a hurry to solve them.
—Paul Ricoeur

God gave Noah the rainbow sign. . . .
—James Baldwin

When an event becomes news, it acquires the aura of the extraordinary. News events are new events that the news represents as nonroutine. Television news, for example, when it highlights an event, tends to obscure the quotidian setting of that event's occurrence. What Stanley Cavell characterizes as "the theatricality of scripted news recitation" helps to explain this tendency.[1] Theatricality, here, pertains to the emphasis the news places on events themselves, treating them as intrusions upon ordinary situations, but rarely acknowledging the complicated ways in which events develop out of the situations which engender them. The drama of the news constructs social events as transient curiosities that have accidently supervened on the circumstances of day-to-day life.

Events that have ceased to be news we call "old news." Old news consists of news events that we remember to have been news. A news event that has become old news, though we remember it as something extraordinary, is no longer new,

In the course of editing this book I have benefited from the advice and encouragement of Judy Butler, Tom Dumm, Sara Gooding-Williams, Maureen MacGrogan, and Lorenzo Simpson, all of whom I thank for their support. I wish also to thank the many contributors to this volume, both for their enthusiasm and for the timely completion of their essays. Finally, I wish to thank Nancy Board, to whom I owe an immense debt of gratitude for her unfailing efforts to coordinate a project that would not have been possible without her.

1

and so no longer qualifies as news. Old news is no longer news, because it is no longer current.[2]

By the time this book is published, the beating of Rodney King, the subsequent trial in Simi Valley, and the fiery uprising in Los Angeles will have become old news in the minds of most Americans. Less than a year from this writing, all of these events will have gone the way of all news events. The conversations I imagine transpiring then—not in L.A., and perhaps not in California, but surely elsewhere in the United States—will sound something like this: A: "A book about Rodney King? That trial—the first one I mean—was a long time ago." B: "Not really, Los Angeles was burning just last April." A: "You're right, but it still feels like a long time ago. I'm almost sure that it was before the election. But was it before or after the war in the Gulf?" Receding into the foggy background of a picture of the world that the news media, especially the television news media, creates for us, old news—be it yesterday's famine, yesterdays' war, yesterday's police brutality, or yesterday's trial verdicts—slowly but surely ceases to command our attention, as we are set upon relentlessly by the insistent and dramatic intrusions of today's and tomorrow's news. When the beating of Rodney King, the trial in Simi Valley, and the uprising in Los Angeles became news events, they acquired the aura of the extraordinary. When these same incidents become old news, they will strike most Americans as distant oddities whose auras bear little, if any, connection to their present circumstances.

A central purpose of this book is to challenge the construction of the Rodney King incidents (the beating, the trial, and the uprising) as *old news*, though not by transforming these incidents yet again into new and dramatic news events. *Reading Rodney King/Reading Urban Uprising* contests the representation of the Rodney King incidents as *news*, viz., as new and dramatic news events, no less than it contests the remembrance of these incidents as old news. By stripping these incidents of the aura of the extraordinary, this book attempts to recover and to explicate their connections to the uneventful and ordinary realities which, while ignored by the news, persistently affect life in urban America. The uneventful is what the news coverage of "current events" lets disappear from view. It is, more exactly, that complex network of conditions—social, economic, political, and ideological—that enable, influence, and shape the character of events, before they become news events. An explication of the uneventful factors and situations which gave rise to and determined the character of the Rodney King incidents is essential to any attempt to preserve these incidents as objects of public scrutiny and debate—a theme to which I will return below. Only by engaging the complicated contingencies which permitted and gave rise to the Rodney King incidents; and only, therefore, by resisting the construction of them as news and old news, will it be possible, as Paul Ricoeur puts it, to be instructed by them.[3]

When he spoke to the press during the Los Angeles uprising, Rodney King, in his own way, alluded implicitly to the limitations of the news format. "We're all stuck here for awhile," King said, in the course of his call for peace.[4] Although he did not elaborate on his conception of what it is to be stuck, the generality of King's remark, with its unspecified "we" and its unspecified "here," suggested that being stuck is so basic and universal a condition as to be part of the essence of the uneventful. We are all stuck, but only for awhile, because we all eventually die. But before we die and wherever we are, we are prey to the world, routinely and relentlessly bound to circumstances and situations that lack the charisma essential to the news event.

Less well remembered than his T-shirt-commodified and much more newsy query, "Can we all get along?" Rodney King's reference to being stuck identified a condition that is at once ontological and social.[5] Being stuck is an ontological condition (a condition constitutive of human existence), because each of us is, as existentialists insist, forever finding him- or herself saddled with a world that is not wholly a product of his or her creation. But being stuck is also a social condition, since the world and worlds which impinge on us are always and everywhere the products of social histories and ongoing social practices.[6] Being stuck, then, is a matter of being inexorably caught up in a network of political, economic, and cultural legacies that escape the aura of the extraordinary. Neither news nor old news, these legacies constitute the uneventful conditions of social existence which useful analyses of the Rodney King incidents cannot possibly ignore. By calling our attention to the facticity of being stuck, Rodney King's own words provide an appropriate point of departure for such analyses.

Since being stuck is a many-dimensional social phenomenon, *Reading Rodney King/Reading Urban Uprising* addresses a number of topics, ranging from America's history of racial violence to the effects of capital accumulation on the inner cities. Written by philosophers, social scientists, literary critics, and legal scholars, the essays included here discuss the devastating impact that Federal public policy has had on urban America; the creation of suburban geographies that have helped to sequester and to "normalize" communities like Simi Valley; the conflict in Los Angeles between African Americans and Korean-American shop owners; and the repressive activities of the LAPD in the wake of the uprising. More generally, these essays raise a variety of questions regarding the relationships between race and power in American society. What, they ask, is the connection between the bludgeoning of Rodney King and the presence of racism in America? How, they wonder, could a jury come to doubt that the videotape it saw depicted an excessive and unjustified use of violence? And what role, they wish to know, did racial ideology play in bringing about the burning of Koreatown? By addressing these and many other issues, the contributions to this volume explore the multiple connections between the Rodney King incidents and the quotidian exercise of political, economic, and cultural power throughout the United States. The following discussion of these contributions, though it hardly does justice to their complexity and diversity, attempts to identify some thematic affinities between them.

Reading Rodney King / Reading Urban Uprising begins its analysis of the Rodney King incidents by focusing on the ruthless bashing of Rodney King in Lake View Terrace, California. Entitled "Beating Black Bodies," Part One of this volume contains three essays that, notwithstanding the differences between them, all suggest that the attack on Rodney King was the product of a violent racism that is a characteristic feature of ordinary life in America. Judith Butler, for example, in her "Endangered/Endangering: Schematic Racism and White Paranoia," highlights the paranoia which the Los Angeles police enacted in the battering of Rodney King, and which, she maintains, the Simi Valley jurors and President Bush (in a statement he made on the day after the verdict) reenacted. This paranoia, Butler argues, reduced Rodney King to "a phantasm of white racist aggression," while expressing a mode of perception that insists always and everywhere on seeing black bodies as dangerous bodies.

Ruth Gilmore, in her "Terror Austerity Race Gender Excess Theater," also intimates that white violations of black bodies are nothing extraordinary in the United States. Gilmore reminds us, in fact, that the beating of Rodney King was an act of "civilized terror" belonging to a firmly established American tradition of white-on-black violence, the most prominent examples of which are racial lynchings. She also reminds us of the connections between the King beating and America's ritual brutalization of black women, as she suggests that both phenomena need to be seen as quotidian modes of performance that have functioned typically to reinforce a conception of the American nation as a white, male, heterosexual enterprise. The horror of the uneventful looms large in Gilmore's essay: "terrorism, imprisonment, deportation, sterilization, state-supervised death. All of these features are everyday elements of life in California, in Arkansas, in Texas, New York, you name it. This is where we're at; where are we headed?"

Historicizing the picture which Butler and Gilmore begin to draw, Houston Baker, in his "Scene . . . Not Heard," shows that "the classic American 'scene of violence' " to which Rodney King was subject has its origins in American slavery. Turning in particular to Frederick Douglass's 1845 slave narrative, Baker identifies the essentials of this "scene of violence" in Douglass's depiction of an overseer's murder of a slave. Arguing in a more general vein, he also claims that the " 'scening' of the African presence in America—its literal desubjectification and silencing—is in a cogent sense a *local* scene of violence that overdetermines a vast, outgoing scene of American national violence." For Baker, America's relentless objectification and silencing of black bodies cannot be neatly separated from its vaster and bloodier rituals of collective brutality. It can be resisted, however, by a humane hearing of black urban voices (including, especially, a hearing of "rap's multiple . . . soundings") that hearkens to "what precisely it *sounds* like to be violently *scened* in the United States."

In Part Two of this volume, "Acquitting White Brutality," Patricia Williams, Kimberlé Crenshaw, and Gary Peller focus on the trial of the white policemen who beat Rodney King. Williams, in "The Rules of the Game," discusses the change of venue to Simi Valley, the rhetorical strategies of the lawyers who defended King's assailants, and the ways in which, in the course of the trial, "concepts of individualism and group, society and chaos were played against one another." "In summary," she writes, "it is possible to see the King verdict as not merely rational, but as the magnificently artful product of an aesthetic of rationality—even to the extent it rationalized and upheld an order of socialized irrationality." Crenshaw and Peller, in "Reel Time/Real Justice," contend that "law, in general, and the courtroom, in particular, are arenas where narratives are contested, and the power of interpretation exercised." In order to illustrate this claim, they explore the connections between the narrative representation of the King beating in the Simi Valley trial and the narrative representation of race relations in the Supreme Court's opinion in *Richmond v. Croson*. In general, Crenshaw and Peller stress "the ideological and symbolic intertwining of race and power in American culture," and thus address a number of issues that also provide the foci for Part Five of this volume.

Parts Three and Four of *Reading Rodney King / Reading Urban Uprising* examine the King beating and the Los Angeles uprising from a political-economic perspective. Part Three, "Assaulting America: A Political Economy Begets Ruin," considers both events in light of the political economy of the nation as a whole. Cedric Robinson, for example, in his "Race, Capitalism, and the Antidemocracy," stresses the connections between the beating of Rodney King and the Reagan/Bush attacks on America's "liberal social contract." Summarizing his view of the King beating, he insists that the "brutality of the racial drama was a reenactment of a multiplicity of brutalizations inaugurated by the ruling elite. . . . The daily occurrences of street executions, the cruel and indiscriminate arrests and harassment conducted under the authority of law which form the immediate context for Rodney King's experience are the local reiterations of a national social agenda." Focusing more narrowly on economic conditions, Rhonda Williams identifies the macroeconomic developments of the 1980s that ravaged black and Latino communities of color, and that help to explain the "bread riot" character of the postverdict Los Angeles rebellion. The central thesis of her "Accumulation as Evisceration: Urban Rebellion and the New Growth Dynamics" is that these developments, notwithstanding the tendency of mainstream economists to repress the discussion of "socioeconomic agency," should be seen as resulting from the strategic decisions of profit-seeking capitalists to increase their use of foreign labor and to create a two-tiered wage system. In Williams's view, "declining wages, rising wage inequality, and increasing racial inequality [must be located] within the context of dynamic and ruthlessly competitive capitalist accumulation."

Cedric Robinson's and Rhonda Williams's essays remind us that capitalist competition and the implementation of public policy are day-to-day social phenomena that can cruelly shape the character of other social events. Michael Omi and Howard Winant echo this insight in their "The Los Angeles 'Race Riot' and Contemporary U.S. Politics," especially when they describe the L.A. uprising as an act of resistance to state coercion and as "a . . . desperate effort to respond to the impoverishment, not only of the ghetto poor, but of U.S. society as a whole." Omi and Winant also aver that the L.A. riots challenged "the new convergence in mainstream racial politics" and that it testified "to the complexity of contemporary racial dynamics." Paying careful attention to the conjunction of class and racial dynamics, as well as to the politically significant cleavages which qualify panethnic racialized identities (e.g., "Hispanic/Latino" and "Asian-American"), they persuasively argue that a "monumental event like the L.A. riot . . . recasts racial-group identities." More generally, Omi and Winant insist on linking the L.A. riot "to the continuing presence of race in the social structures and meaning systems which organize the U.S. social order and identify its members."

Like Part Three of this book, Part Four—entitled "On the Streets of Los Angeles"—places the uprising in a political-economic context. As distinct from Part Three, however, Part Four examines some of the social forces that were present and active in Los Angeles itself, both before and after the uprising, while giving less attention to the macroeconomic and macropolitical tendencies which Robinson, Rhonda Williams, and Omi and Winant emphasize.

Part Four begins with "Anatomy of a Rebellion: A Political-Economic Analysis" by Melvin Oliver, James Johnson, and Walter Farrell. In this essay, the authors interpret the Los Angeles uprising in light of recent demographic, social, and economic changes occurring in Los Angeles society. They note, for example, that during the last two decades, South Central Los Angeles has been transformed from a predominantly black to a mixed black and Latino area. They likewise report that "the traditional Mexican-American community of East Los Angeles" did not participate in the rebellion (though the participation of South Central L.A.'s Central American Latino population was substantial); that racial tensions between Latinos and Koreans were no less significant than those between blacks and Koreans in precipitating the rebellion; and that prominent among the seeds of the rebellion were structural transformations of the Los Angeles economy and "nearly two decades of conservative policy making and implementation at the federal level." Oliver, Johnson, and Farrell conclude their essay with a critique of the Bush administration's plan to revitalize the South Central Los Angeles community.

Mike Davis's contribution to Part Four, "Uprising and Repression in L.A.," takes the form of an interview that originally appeared in the *CovertAction Information Bulletin*. Concentrating on the repressive aftermath of the uprising, Davis calls attention to INS (Immigration and Naturalization Service) and Border Patrol incursions into South Central L.A. "Very clearly," says Davis, "the INS and Border Patrol have used the uprising to vacuum up people in the community. More than just taking the opportunity to deport large numbers of people, they have used the situation to instill fear. It's been a reign of terror followed by political attacks not only on the Black community, but to a surprising degree on Central Americans." Davis also discusses the LAPD's extensive efforts to disrupt the "gang-unity process" which was one result of the uprising, as well as its ongoing compilation of computerized data bases to facilitate the surveillance and management of criminalized black and Latino youth. "In Los Angeles," Davis claims, "we are beginning to see a repressive context that is literally comparable to Belfast or the West Bank, where policing has been transformed into full-scale countersurgency (or 'low-intensity warfare,' as the military likes to call it), against an entire social stratum or ethnic group."

Part Five of *Reading Rodney King / Reading Urban Uprising*, "Ideology, Race, and Community," augments the political-economic analyses of Parts Three and Four by investigating the role of racial ideology (that is, the representation and interpretation of racial identities) in the Rodney King incidents. Like the exercise of political power and the competitive pursuit of economic profits, racial ideology harshly conditions day-to-day life throughout the United States, persisting in its own way as an essential feature of the ordinary in America. In my own contribution to Part Five, "Look, a Negro" I elaborate a concept of racial ideology that I use to discuss both the trial of Rodney King's assailants and the television media's representations of the L.A. uprising. In my view, courtroom and media representations of black bodies grow out of a long and ongoing tradition of racial ideology that, following Toni Morrison, I call "American Africanism." Such ideology needs to be read allegorically, I argue, in order to expose and to criticize its interpretations of the sociopolitical status of blacks in America. In the second essay of Part Five, "The New Enclosures: Racism in the Normalized Community," Thomas Dumm develops an interpretation of racial representations that stresses the interplay of "scientific " racism, the deployment of monitoring techniques to discipline visual observation, and the use of strategies of normalization to intern black minorities. These factors function conjointly, Dumm argues, to frame and sustain the sense of "normality" that is constitutive of communities such as Simi Valley: "[A] system of streets encloses Simi Valley from the dangerous people of the outside world. People feel safe because they are surrounded with a familiar sameness. Those who are different are far away, spatially. Those who invade will be contained and removed."

The final essay of Part Five, Sumi Cho's "Korean Americans vs. African Americans: Conflict and Construction," investigates the role of racial ideology in urban conflicts between Korean Americans and African Americans. Challenging African-American stereotypes of Korean Americans, as well as Korean-American stereotypes of African Americans, Cho sees both sets of images as having helped to cause the looting and burning of Koreatown and Korean-owned stores during the Los Angeles uprising. Criticizing the tendency to stereotype Korean Americans and other Asian Americans as model minorities, she likewise argues that "the embrace of Asian Americans as a model minority is an embrace of 'racist love.' The basis of that love has a racist origin: to provide a public rationale for the ongoing subordination of non-Asian people of color." When Cho addresses theoretical issues, she boldly challenges race-relations theorists to eschew the traditional interpretation of American race relations in terms of a black/white binary opposition that "misses many of the factual complexities in contemporary, urban politics." Cho also insists on the need to construct race-relations theories that "emphasize the experiences and conditions of the oppressed and of those working directly to improve those conditions."

The sixth and last part of this volume, "The Fire This Time," consists of a group of essays that I read as democratically inspired meditations on the chasm separating the promise of American democracy from the social reality illuminated by the Rodney King incidents. Reminiscent of James Baldwin's *The Fire Next Time*, the contributions of Elaine Kim, Jerry Watts, Henry Louis Gates, Jr., and Cornel West insist that we acknowledge the depths of that chasm, even as we imagine that someday Americans could learn to bridge it. Elaine Kim, for example, in her "Home Is Where the *Han* Is: A Korean-American Perspective on the Los Angeles Upheavals," argues that Korean Americans experienced April 29th and 30th of 1992 as "a baptism into what it really means for a Korean to 'become American' in the 1990s." The absence of genuine democracy could not have been clearer: "When the Korean Americans in South Central and Koreatown dialed 911, nothing happened. When their stores and homes were being looted and burned to the ground, they were left completely alone for three horrifying days. How betrayed they must have felt by what they had believed was a democratic system that protects its people from violence." Korean Americans had to learn, says

Kim, that "protection in the U.S. is by and large for the rich and powerful. If there were a choice between Westwood and Koreatown, it is clear that Koreatown would have to be sacrificed."

For Kim, the contradiction between the American dream and American reality became even more explicit when she began receiving racist hate mail after penning an essay for the "My Turn" section of *Newsweek*. "How many Americans migrate to Korea," asked one *Newsweek* reader, who then added: "If you are so disenchanted, Korea is still there. Why did you ever leave it? Sayonara." Responding to the vicious American reality which statements such as these reveal, Kim recalls Rodney King's remark about being "stuck here for awhile," awaiting "our day in court," and insists that Korean Americans need "tools and weapons" to resist subjugation, just as long as that day and its dream remain deferred. Paramount among those weapons, Kim suggests, is Korean national consciousness.

Like Kim, Jerry Watts knows just how remote now, for many Americans, is the prospect of participating in the dream of American democracy. In his "Reflections on the Rodney King Verdict and the Paradoxes of the Black Response," Watts even warns black Americans against their sometimes "naive faith in America." Such faith, he contends, led some blacks to believe, prior to the Rodney King verdicts, that the criminal-justice system in Los Angeles would "convict white cops for beating a black man when the very same system did not convict white cops for killing blacks." Given the evidence of the videotape, claims Watts, "blacks expected whites to be appalled by the divergence between professed American democratic values and the black urban reality." But, he argues, an honest assessment of the condition of the black urban poor requires the scuttling of such expectations, as well as the sober recognition that poor blacks living in our cities have become "hyperpariahs in American society."

Though the black urban poor have become outcasts in American society, African America's affluent elite, writes Henry Louis Gates, Jr., "is larger than it ever has been." Thus, Gates insists, in his "Two Nations . . . Both Black," black America in the 1990s is having "the worst of times . . . and the best of times." Since 1965, he claims, African Americans' progress has been in many ways "astonishing, something we need to be reminded of even in the wake of the Rodney King riots and the stark statistics that measure the gap within our community between the haves and have nots." And yet, Gates seems to suggest, the black bourgeoisie is still victim to a racism that reared its batons above Rodney King's head and that continues to thwart our democratic ideals: "We are isolated from the black underclass and yet still humiliatingly vulnerable to racism, in the form of random police harassment, individual racial insults from waitresses and attendants in stores, the unwillingness of taxi drivers to pick us up, systematic discrimination by banks and bank loan officers, wage discrimination in the workplace, and our perception of a 'glass ceiling' in the corporate world. . . . The most pernicious forms of racism—the stereotyping of an individual by the color of her skin—still pervade white America. And caught in this no-man's-land of alienation and fragmentation is the black middle class.'' According to Gates, ''fighting the power'' in post–civil rights America must involve the recognition that ''the causes of poverty within the black community are *both* structural and behavioral.'' Rather than scapegoat ''Koreans, Jews, or even Haitians,'' he argues, the black elite must demand a ''structural change in this country'' and take on the task of ''moral leadership.'' ''For them,'' writes Gates, ''the challenge awaits of healing the rift within black America, and the larger nation as well.''

In the concluding essay of this volume, ''Learning to Talk of Race,'' Cornel West suggests that American political culture lacks the conceptual resources it needs to grapple intelligently with issues of race. Liberals and conservatives both, he argues, ''fail to see that the presence and predicaments of black people are neither additions to nor defections from American life, but rather *constitutive elements of that life.*'' A serious discussion of race in America, he adds, ''must begin not with the problems of black people but with the flaws of American society—flaws rooted in historic inequalities and longstanding cultural stereotypes.'' Addressing those flaws, West claims, requires that we look to new frameworks and languages, focus our attention on the public square, and generate new leadership. We need leaders, he insists, who can invigorate all of us with the ideals of ''freedom, democracy, and equality.'' Explicitly echoing Baldwin, West warns us of the peril which awaits us if we *do not* succeed in creating a genuine multiracial democracy in America: ''Let us hope and pray that the vast intelligence, imagination, humor, and courage in this country will not fail us. Either we learn a new language of empathy and compassion, or the fire this time will consume us all.''

By sounding the theme of America's flawed democracy and still-deferred dream, Kim, Watts, Gates, and West remind us that the plight of being stuck can prompt the assumption of responsibility. Here, again, they recall James Baldwin, whose words of thirty years ago remain as relevant today as they were then: ''And here we are, at the center of the arc, trapped in the gaudiest, most valuable, and most improbably water wheel the world has ever seen. Everything now, we must assume, is in our hands; we have no right to assume otherwise.''[7] For Baldwin, being stuck—what he describes as being ''trapped''—was not tantamount to being paralyzed. Rather being stuck, he believed, could be the beginning of an effort to take the world into our hands—to assume responsibility for it. Part of assuming responsibility for a postmodern and post–civil rights America, Kim, Watts, Gates, and West suggest, is committing ourselves to the difficult task of transforming a nation in which large numbers of citizens see peoples of color, *not* as fellow citizens, but as "throwaways" (Watts), as "robotic aliens" (Kim), or worse. The task cannot be an easy one, since so many Americans would delightfully dispose of the cultures and the lives of *all* peoples of color. As one of the *Newsweek* readers who responded to Elaine Kim put it, "I'm from a culture, Ms. Kim, who put a man on the moon 23 years ago, who established medical schools to train doctors to perform open heart surgery, and . . . who created a language of music so that musicians, from Beethoven to the Beatles, could easily touch the world with their brilliance forever and ever and ever. Perhaps the dominant culture, whites obviously, 'swept aside Chicanos . . . Latinos . . . African-Americans . . . Koreans,' because they haven't contributed anything that made—be mindful of the cliche—a world of a difference."

In its own way, *Reading Rodney King / Reading Urban Uprising* is an attempt to heed Kim's, Watts's, Gates's, and West's calls to the cause of a genuine and multiracial American democracy. While the essays included here represent a variety of perspectives, all were inspired by a feeling that the Rodney King incidents had raised a number of issues that deserved a more careful scrutiny and reading than their constitution as news would permit. Each of these essays *reads* (interprets) the Rodney King incidents, by placing them within some political, economic, and/or cultural context. If, taken collectively, they help to keep public debate centered on these events, it will be because they show that the beating, the trial, and the uprising implicated so much of what is repugnant, though ordinary, in postmodern and post–Civil Rights America: the racist abuse of black bodies; the use of the law to advance racial domination; the deployment of public policy and economic power contributing to the devastation of America's cities; the dissemination of racial ideologies that denigrate peoples of color; and, not least of all, the perpetuation of a contradiction between the practice and the promise of American democracy—a persistent and painful consequence of these many other causes for repugnance. By highlighting the connections between ordinary American life and the Rodney King incidents, *Reading Rodney King / Reading Urban Uprising* attempts to keep this contradiction in view, and so to keep alive the hope of surpassing it.

Notes

The first passage cited in epigraph comes from Paul Ricoeur, "The Political Paradox," in *Existential Phenomenology and Political Philosophy*, ed. Hwa Yol Jung (Chicago: Henry Regnary Company, 1972), 337. The second passage comes from James Baldwin, *The Fire Next Time* (New York: Dell, 1981), 141.

1. Stanley Cavell, *Themes Out of School* (Chicago: University of Chicago Press, 1984), 262. See also p. 258.

2. My discussion of old news, here and in the next paragraph, was inspired by Michael Ignatieff, "The Ethics of Television," *Daedalus* 114 (Fall 1985): 70–71.

3. A discussion of the ordinary as the uneventful that I found helpful in formulating my thoughts is present in Cavell, *Themes Out of School*, 184–94.

4. "Rodney King's Statement," *Los Angeles Times*, 2 May 1992, 3.

5. Ibid.

6. For a similar point, see Marcuse's critique of Heidegger's fundamental ontology in the former's "Contributions to a Phenomenology of Historical Materialism," *Telos* 4 (Summer 1970): 21–22.

7. Baldwin, *The Fire Next Time*, 141.

Part One

Beating Black Bodies

1

Endangered/Endangering: Schematic Racism and White Paranoia

Judith Butler

———————

The defense attorneys for the police in the Rodney King case made the argument that the policemen were endangered, and that Rodney King was the source of that danger. The argument they made drew from many sources, comments he made, acts he refused to perform on command, and the highly publicized video recording taken on the spot and televised widely before and during the trial. During the trial, the video was shown at the same time that the defense offered a commentary, and so we are left to presume that some convergence of word and picture produced the "evidence" for the jurors in the case. The video shows a man being brutally beaten, repeatedly, and without visible resistance; and so the question is, How could this video be used as evidence that the body being beaten was *itself* the source of danger, the threat of violence, and, further, that the beaten body of Rodney King bore an intention to injure, and to injure precisely those police who either wielded the baton against him or stood encircling him? In the Simi Valley courtroom, what many took to be incontrovertible evidence *against* the police was presented instead to establish police vulnerability, that is, to support the contention that Rodney King was endangering the police. Later, a juror reported that she believed that Rodney King was in "total control" of the situation. How was this feat of interpretation achieved?

That it *was* achieved is not the consequence of ignoring the video, but, rather, of reproducing the video within a racially saturated field of visibility. If racism pervades white perception, structuring what can and cannot appear within the horizon of white perception, then to what extent does it interpret in advance "visual evidence"? And how, then, does such "evidence" have to be read, and read publicly, *against* the racist disposition of the visible which will prepare and achieve its own inverted perceptions under the rubric of "what is seen"?

In the above, without hesitation, I wrote, "the video shows a man being brutally beaten." And yet, it appears that the jury in Simi Valley claimed that what they "saw" was a body threatening the police, and saw in those blows the reasonable actions of police officers in self-defense. From these two interpretations emerges, then, a contest within the visual field, a crisis in the certainty of what is visible, one that is produced through the saturation and schematization of that field with the inverted projections of white paranoia. The visual representation of the black male body being beaten on the street by the policemen and their batons was taken up by that racist interpretive framework to construe King as the *agent* of violence, one whose agency is phantasmatically implied as the narrative precedent and antecedent to the frames that are shown. Watching King, the white paranoiac forms a sequence of narrative intelligibility that consolidates the racist figure of the black man: "He *had* threatened them, and now he is being justifiably restrained." "If they cease hitting him, he *will* release his violence, and now is being justifiably restrained." King's palm turned away from his body, held above his own head, is read *not* as self-protection but as the incipient moments of a physical threat.

How do we account for this *reversal* of gesture and intention in terms of a racial schematization of the visible field? Is this a specific transvaluation of agency proper to a racialized episteme? And does the possibility of such a reversal call into question whether what is "seen" is not always already in part a question of what a certain racist episteme produces as the visible? For if the jurors came to see in Rodney King's body a danger *to* the law, then this "seeing" requires to be read as that which was culled, cultivated, regulated—indeed, policed—in the course of the trial. This is not a simple seeing, an act of direct perception, but the racial production of the visible, the workings of racial constraints on what it means to "see." Indeed, the trial calls to be read not only as instruction in racist modes of seeing but as a repeated and ritualistic production of blackness (a further instance of what Ruth Gilmore, in describing the video beating, calls an act of "nation building"). This is a seeing which is a reading, that is, a *contestable* construal, but one which nevertheless passes itself off as "seeing," a reading which became for that white community, and for countless others, the same as seeing.

If what is offered here over and against what the jury saw is a different seeing, a different ordering of the visible, it is one that is also contestable—as we saw in the temporary interpretive triumph of the defense attorneys' construal of King

as endangering. To claim that King's victimization is *manifestly* true is to assume
that one is presenting the case to a set of subjects who *know how to see*; to think
that the video "speaks for itself" is, of course, for many of us, obviously true.
But if the field of the visible is racially contested terrain, then it will be politically
imperative to read such videos aggressively, to repeat and publicize such readings,
if only to further an antiracist hegemony over the visual field. It may appear at
first that over and against this heinous failure to see police brutality, it is necessary
to restore the visible as the sure ground of evidence. But what the trial and its
horrific conclusions teach us is that there is no simple recourse to the visible, to
visual evidence, that it still and always calls to be read, that it is already a reading,
and that in order to establish the injury on the basis of the visual evidence, an
aggressive reading of the evidence is necessary.

It is not, then, a question of negotiating between what is "seen," on the one
hand, and a "reading" which is imposed upon the visual evidence, on the other.
In a sense, the problem is even worse: to the extent that there is a racist organization and disposition of the visible, it will work to circumscribe what qualifies
as visual evidence, such that it is in some cases impossible to establish the "truth"
of racist brutality through recourse to visual evidence. For when the visual is fully
schematized by racism, the "visual evidence" to which one refers will always
and only refute the conclusions based upon it; for it is possible within this racist
episteme that no black person can seek recourse to the visible as the sure ground
of evidence. Consider that it *was* possible to draw a line of inference from the
black male body motionless and beaten on the street to the conclusion that this
very body was in "total control," rife with "dangerous intention." The visual
field is not neutral to the question of race; it is itself a racial formation, an
episteme, hegemonic and forceful.

*   *   *

In the white world the man of color encounters difficulties in the development
of his bodily schema. Consciousness of the body is solely a negating activity.
It is a third-person consciousness. The body is surrounded by an atmosphere
of certain uncertainty. I know that if I want to smoke, I shall have to reach
out my right arm and take the pack of cigarettes lying at the other end of the
table. The matches, however, are in the drawer on the left, and I shall have
to lean back slightly. And all of these movements are made not out of habit
but out of implicit knowledge. A slow composition of my *self* as a body in the
middle of a spatial and temporal world—which seems to be the schema. . . .
Below the corporeal schema I had sketched [there is] a historico-racial schema.
The elements I had used had been provided for me . . . by the other, the white
man, who had woven me out of a thousand details, anecdotes, stories. I thought
that what I had in hand was to construct a physiological self, to balance space,
to localize sensations, and here I was called on for more.

"Look, a Negro!" It was an external stimulus that flicked over me as I passed by. I made a tight smile.

"Look, a Negro!" It was true. It amused me.

"Look, a Negro!" The circle was drawing a bit tighter.

I made no secret of my amusement.

"Mama, see the Negro! I'm frightened!" Frightened!"

Frightened! Now they were beginning to be afraid of me. I made up my mind to laugh myself to tears but laughter had become impossible.[1]

Frantz Fanon offers here a description of how the black male body is constituted through fear, and through a naming and a seeing: "Look, a Negro!" where the "look" is both a pointing and a seeing, a pointing out what there is to see, a pointing which circumscribes a dangerous body, a racist indicative which relays its own danger to the body to which it points. Here the "pointing" is not only an indicative, but the schematic foreshadowing of an accusation, one which carries the performative force to constitute that danger which it fears and defends against. In his clearly masculinist theory, Fanon demarcates the subject as the black male, and the Other as the white male, and perhaps we ought for the moment to let the masculinism of the scene stay in place; for there is within the white male's racist fear of the black male body a clear anxiety over the possibility of sexual exchange; hence, the repeated references to Rodney King's "ass" by the surrounding policemen, and the homophobic circumscription of that locus of sodomy as a kind of threat.

In Fanon's recitation of the racist interpellation, the black body is circumscribed as dangerous, prior to any gesture, any raising of the hand, and the infantilized white reader is positioned in the scene as one who is helpless in relation to that black body, as one definitionally in need of protection by his/her mother or, perhaps, the police. The fear is that some physical distance will be crossed, and the virgin sanctity of whiteness will be endangered by that proximity. The police are thus structurally placed to protect whiteness against violence, where violence is the imminent action of that black male body. And because within this imaginary schema, the police protect whiteness, their own violence cannot be read as violence; because the black male body, prior to any video, is the site and source of danger, a threat, the police effort to subdue this body, even if in advance, is justified regardless of the circumstances. Or rather, the conviction of that justification rearranges and orders the circumstances to fit that conclusion.

What struck me on the morning after the verdict was delivered were reports which reiterated the phantasmatic production of "intention," the intention inscribed in and read off Rodney King's frozen body on the street, his intention to do harm, to endanger. The video was used as "evidence" to support the claim that the frozen black male body on the ground receiving blows was himself producing those blows, about to produce them, was himself the imminent threat of a blow and, therefore, was himself responsible for the blows he received. That body thus received those blows in return for the ones it was about to deliver, the blows which were that body in its essential gestures, even as the one gesture that body can be seen to make is to raise its palm outward to stave off the blows against it. According to this racist episteme, he is hit in exchange for the blows he never delivered, but which he is, by virtue of his blackness, always about to deliver.

Here we can see the splitting of that violent intentionality off from the police actions, and the investment of those very intentions in the one who receives the blows. How is this splitting and attribution of violent intentionality possible? And how was it *reproduced* in the defense attorneys' racist pedagogy, thus implicating the defense attorneys in a *sympathetic* racist affiliation with the police, inviting the jurors to join in that community of victimized victimizers? The attorneys proceeded through cultivating an identification with white paranoia in which a white community is always and only protected by the police, against a threat which Rodney King's body emblematizes, quite apart from any action it can be said to perform or appear ready to perform. This is an action that the black male body is always already performing within that white racist imaginary, has always already performed prior to the emergence of any video. The identification with police paranoia culled, produced, and consolidated in that jury is one way of reconstituting a white racist imaginary that postures *as if* it were the unmarked frame of the visible field, laying claim to the authority of "direct perception."

The interpretation of the video in the trial had to work the possible sites of identification it offered: Rodney King, the surrounding police, those actively beating him, those witnessing him, the gaze of the camcorder and, by implication, the white bystander who perhaps feels moral outrage, but who is also watching from a distance, suddenly installed at the scene as the undercover newsman. In a sense, the jury could be convinced of police innocence only through a tactical orchestration of those identifications, for in some sense, they *are* the white witness, separated from the ostensible site of black danger by a circle of police; they *are* the police, enforcers of the law, encircling that body, beating him, once again. They are perhaps King as well, but whitewashed: the blows he suffers are taken to be the blows they *would* suffer if the police were not protecting them from him. Thus, the physical danger in which King is recorded is transferred to them; they identify with that vulnerability, but construe it as their own, the vulnerabilty of whiteness, thus refiguring him as the threat. The danger that they believe themselves always to be in, by virtue of their whiteness (whiteness as an episteme operates despite the existence of two nonwhite jurors). This completes the circuit of paranoia: the projection of their own aggression, and the subsequent regarding of that projection as an external threat.

The kind of "seeing" that the police enacted, and the kind of "seeing" that the jury reenacted, is one in which a further violence is performed by the disa-vowal and projection of that violent beating. The actual blows against Rodney King are understood to be fair recompense, indeed, defenses against, the dangers that are "seen" to emanate from his body. Here "seeing" and attributing are indissoluble. Attributing violence to the object of violence is part of the very mechanism that recapitulates violence, and that makes the jury's "seeing" into a complicity with that police violence.

The defense attorneys broke the video down into "stills," freezing the frame, so that the gesture, the raised hand, is torn from its temporal place in the visual narrative. The video is not only violently decontextualized, but violently recon-textualized; it is played without a simultaneous sound track which, had it existed, would have been littered with racial and sexual slurs against Rodney King. In the place of reading that testimony alongside the video, the defense attorneys offered the frozen frame, the magnification of the raised hand as the hyperbolic figure of racial threat, interpreted again and again as a gesture foreshadowing violence, a gesture about to be violent, the first sign of violence, violence itself. Here the anticipatory "seeing" is clearly a "reading," one which reenacts the disavowal and paranoia that enable and defend the brutality itself.

Over against this reading is required an aggressive coutnerreading, one which the prosecutors failed to perform, one which might expose through a different kind of reiteration of what Fanon called "the historico-racial schema" through which the "seeing" of blackness takes place.[2] In other words, it is necessary to read not only for the "event" of violence, but for the racist schema that orches-trates and interprets the event, which splits the violent intention off from the body who wields it and attributes it to the body who receives it.

If the raised gesture can be read as evidence that supports the contention that Rodney King is "in control," "totally" of the entire scene, indeed, as evidence of his own threatening intentions, then a circuit is phantasmatically produced whereby King is the origin, the intention, and the object of the selfsame brutality. In other words, if it is *his* violence which impels the causal sequence, and it is his body which receives the blows, then, in effect, he beats himself: he is the begin-ning and the end of the violence, he brings it on himself. But if the brutality which he is said to embody or which the racial schema ritualistically fabricates as the incipient and inevitable "intention" of his body, if this brutality is that of the white police, then this is a brutality that the police enact and displace *at once*, and Rodney King, who appears for them as the origin and potential instrument of all danger in the scene, has become reduced to a phantasm of white racist aggression, a phantasm that *belongs* to that white racist aggression as the externalized figure of its own distortion. He becomes, within that schema, nothing other than the site at which that racist violence fears and beats the specter of its own rage. In this sense, the circuit of violence attributed to Rodney King is itself the circuit of white racist violence which violently disavows itself only to brutalize the specter that embodies its own intention. This is the phantasm that it ritualistically produces at the site of the racialized other.

Is it precisely because this black male body is on the ground that the beating becomes intensified? For if white paranoia is also to some degree homophobia, then is this not a brutalization performed as a desexualization or, rather, as a punishment for a conjectured or desired sexual aggression? The image of the police standing over Rodney King with their batons might be read as a sexual degradation which ends up miming and inverting the imagined scene of sexual violation that it appears to want and to loathe; the police thus deploy the "props" and "positions" of that scene in the service of its aggressive denial.

The reversal and displacement of dangerous intention mentioned above continued to be reiterated after the verdict: first, in the violence that took place in Los Angeles in which the majority of individuals killed were black and in the streets, killed by the police, thus replaying, intensifying, and extending the scope of the violence against Rodney King. The intensification of police violence against people of color can be read as evidence that the verdict was taken as further state sanction for racist police violence; second, in remarks made by Mr. Bush on the day after the verdict was announced in which he condemned public violence, noting first the lamentability of public violence against property(!), and holding responsible, once again, those black bodies on the street, as if the figure of the brutalized black body had, as anticipated, risen and raised its forces against the police. The groups involved in street violence thus were construed paradoxically as the originators of a set of killings that may well have left those very bodies dead, thus exonerating the police and the state *again*, and performing an identification with the phantasmatic endangerment of the white community in Simi Valley; a third, in the media scanning of street violence, the refusal to read how and where and why fires were lit, stores burned, indeed, what was being articulated in and through that violence. The bestialization of the crowds, consolidated by scanning techniques which appeared to "hunt down" people of color and figure their violence as "senseless" or "barbaric," thus recapitulated the racist production of the visual field.

If the jury's reading of the video reenacted the phantasmatic scene of the crime, reiterating and re-occupying the always already endangered status of the white person on the street, and the response to the reading, now inscribed as verdict, was to re-cite the charge and to reenact and enlarge the crime, it achieved this in part through a transposition and fabrication of dangerous intention. This is hardly a full explanation of the causes of racist violence, but it does, perhaps, constitute a moment in its production. It can perhaps be described as a form of white paranoia which projects the intention to injure that it itself enacts, and then repeats that projection on increasingly larger scales, a specific social modality of repetition compulsion, which we still need to learn how to read, and which as a "reading," performed in the name of law, has obvious and consequential effects.

Note

1. Frantz Fanon, "The Fact of Blackness," in *Black Skin; White Masks*, trans. Charles Lam Markmann (New York: Grove Press, 1967), 111–12.

2. I do not mean to suggest by "white racist episteme" a static and closed system of seeing, but rather an historically self-renewing practice of reading which, when left uninterrupted, tends to extend its hegemonic force. Clearly, terms like "white paranoia" do not describe in any totalizing way 'how white people see,' but are offered here as theoretical hyperboles which are meant to advance a strategically aggressive counter-reading.

2

Terror Austerity Race Gender Excess Theater

Ruth Wilson Gilmore

[A] civilization maddened by its own perverse assumptions
and contradictions is loose on the world.
—Cedric Robinson

Civilization is nothing but the glory of incessant struggle.
—Gabriele D'Annuziato

The day before I performed this paper at Berkeley, I was driving the 60-mile breadth of L.A. County—my regular commute to UCLA. When I hit the radio button to get a traffic report I found instead, at the middle of the AM band, gavel-to-gavel, opening-day coverage of the trial to determine whether four LAPD cops used excessive force against Rodney King. The prosecutor devoted nearly a third of his 35-minute opening argument to establishing that King had indeed committed several crimes—speeding, driving while intoxicated, failing to yield. As I traveled west on the Foothill Freeway, passing Altadena Avenue at about 55 miles per hour in my Subaru, the prosecutor described how King entered the Foothill Freeway at Altadena Avenue and traveled west, achieving more than

This paper was originally presented 6 March 1992 in slightly different form at a daylong conference at U.C. Berkeley arranged by James Turner, Judith Butler, et al., entitled *Performing: Deforming: Inversions: Subversions* (or something like that). I have not rewritten in light of the 29 April 1992 verdict and ensuing rebellion—in part because I was not the least surprised by either event. I am trying to figure out *how* what is happening works in the minds of mine enemies and by extension, quite literally, on me. That is, I am treading the precipice of my fear while also trying to avoid the trap that held Harriet Jacobs in check for so long 150 years ago. "Both pride and fear" she wrote, "kept me silent." We have not, as she discovered she had not, time for the luxuries of pride and fear. Thanks to friends in the struggle: Saidiya Hartman whose intervention inspired and occasioned the paper; Gilbert McCauley for listening; *always* C.G. for patient reading and passionate talk at any hour (especially the eleventh).

twice my rate of speed in his Hyundai (yes, Hyundai). Listening to the people's attorney describe the long, high-speed chase, in which the California Highway Patrol unit at maximum speed could not catch up, I looked around, expecting to see that the CHP had traded in the force's low-performance Chevrolet V6 and Straight-8 megacube cruisers for speedier, energy-efficient, four-banger imports: a publicly funded endorsement of the Korean manufacturing miracle and American assembly-line decline.

While I do listen to the radio a lot, I don't watch much TV. This austerity in my habits has relatively little to do with moral indignation at stupidifying stuff, and perhaps even less to do with an addiction, as long as memory, to print. Rather, my TV-free living results from the material conditions of my house (its situation in a narrow mountain canyon precludes regular broadcast reception) and my income (I can't afford a satellite dish) and, I confess, the cultural politics of front-yard decor (a dish in the front yard would signify an excess of meaning I am not prepared literally to live behind). When the cable crew came to wire Palmer Canyon, they pretended there was not one last house way up the ridge beyond the rickety, 12-inch, single-plank "footbridge," and we never called to complain that our municipally guaranteed right to consume through the tube had been violated. It is astonishing to think there hasn't been a project of cablizing scale in my corner of L.A. County since the 1930s when the Rural Electrification Act compelled SoCal Edison to install three poles to run two wires up to one glorified cabin in the live oaks.

As a result of a lengthy separation from television in the living room, effected when I went off to college in 1968, I am still surprised to see what has happened in that medium which, among other events, brought the brutality of the anti–Civil Rights movement, Lee Harvey Oswald's murder, and the horrors of Vietnam into the everyday experience of people who, a half generation earlier, had to go to the movies and catch the newsreels to see this stuff in motion—from life but not, as we say, "live." Nowadays, new brutalities, murders, horrors defy surprise, normalize excess, present terror as entertainment; there are not any limits when it comes to picturing death in motion and its melodramatically visible consequences.

My students insist that I cannot teach them adequately if I do not understand how television affects their consciousnesses—their timing and codes canonized, I can only surmise, in MTV. I recognize their appeal in my own intergenerational battles with professors: the men who told us in 1969 that we do not know real danger as they had in the 1930s and 1940s doing real oppositional work which we students in our acting out only insubstantially performed. I knew I was right (as my students know they are) because around me my family and friends went to jail, were assassinated by agents of the FBI, came home from Nam strangers;

those unfettered by prison or trauma spent all their nonwaged time in meeting after meeting after meeting. But then, in 1969, I was not, in the raced (white), gendered (male) institutions I attended, simply, transparently a "student." When Jerry Farber published *The Student as Nigger*, I was taken aback for the first of many times, as a substantive category of my political identity became overtly and publicly metaphorical, symbolic, comparative, abstract.

Toward the end of my sophomoric encounter with God and Man at Yale, I had this exchange with my father (organic intellectual/labor and community organizer/Ivy League drag) after he sat through what was doubtless a dreadful production of Sophocles's *Antigone* (starring you know who/hair bushed halfway to Manhattan/maroon lightweight wool sleeveless bellbottomed jumpsuit/4-inch platform sandals):

> RJW: Daddy! Did you like the show?
> CSW: Are you going to act or are you going to work?

I've never figured out the answer to his retort. Indeed, he knew his question was unanswerable. The substance of the distinction—between drama and realness, between repetition and invention, between spectator and actor, between invention and work, between Fordism and Americanism, between economy and culture—the substance is dialectical, and the tendencies along which the tension both pushes and pulls me are what inform the semiotics and histrionics of my critical performance. So far, I've learned to describe the tension according to this scheme, loading the action (provisionally) into the work: Who works and what works, for whom, and to what end?

Terror Austerity Race Gender Excess Theater

Who works and what works, for whom, and to what end? For the project at hand the question turns toward this particularity: What work do certain kinds of acting—of performance—do, especially when the venue straddles the chasm of a crisis of the crisis state? The crisis state is the warfare state. Toni Negri wrote in 1980 from Trani Special Prison (Italy):

> By transition from "welfare" to "warfare" state I am referring to the internal effects of the restructuration of the state machine—its effect on class relations. . . . Development is now planned in terms of ideologies of scarcity and austerity. The transition involves not just state policies, but most particularly the *structure* of the state, both political and administrative. The needs of the proletariat and of the poor are now rigidly subordinated to the necessities of the capitalist reproduction. . . . The state has an array of military and repressive means available (army, police, legal, etc.) to exclude from [the arena of bargaining or negotiating] all forces that do not offer unconditional obedience

to its austerity-based material constitution and to the static reproduction of
class relations that goes with it.[1]

The "static reproduction of class relations" is a complicated enterprise. It is
hardly accomplished simply from the top down, even with the might of the state's
coercive apparatus. A significant proportion of the people whose relations are
reproduced must concretely consent to the arrangement, however displaced their
understanding. In the U.S., where real and imagined social relations are expressed
most rigidly in race/gender hierarchies, the "reproduction" is in fact a *production*
and its by-products, fear and fury, are in service of a "changing same"[2]: the
apartheid local of American nationalism.[3]

Terror Austerity Race Gender Excess Theater. What kinds of terror are enacted by
and on behalf of the U.S. Crisis State, both as response to *and* mystification of
power shifts occasioned by the new international economic order during the past
decade? How do local—that is, *intra*national—forms of state terrorism work to
create and maintain alienated publics in the current crisis, publics who are *con-
tingently* united, if at all, in cul-de-sacs of identity politics, most frighteningly
realized locally as resurgent American nationalism? By American nationalism I
mean an allegedly restorative tendency (back to family values and all that), normatively white, in patriotic revolution against the "stark utopia"[4] of both late
capitalism's exportation and the state's domestic squandering of the possibilities
of household-based economic security. What's at issue is not simply that things
are getting worse (and they are) but that they are getting worse in stark contradiction to still-rising expectations—the ideology of progress embedded in American commonsense consciousness. In no way an anticapitalist movement per se,
this revolution seeks to explain contemporary disorders and structural adjustments
in U.S. political, cultural, and libidinal economies in natural terms, as though a
transcendent discourse would guarantee the transcendent innocence of the richest,
most powerful, most technologically advanced nation-state in the history of the
world. The contradictions of fascism deny the social but not the constructed
character of U.S. hierarchies. For the new American nationalist, hierarchy is
naturally a result of specific "work," the glory of constructing world power
(identical with household-based progress toward the good life) in the empty yet
threatening wilderness of continental North America. In this formulation, the
U.S. is a muscular achievement of ideological simplicity: "White men *built this
nation!! White men are* this nation!!!"[5] Antonio Gramsci reminds us that work
mediates society and nature. The hierarchical divides of who performs what work
define cultural tendencies of gender, race, sexuality, authority; the divides also
enforce multiple and, in this moment of danger, *competing* economies of being.
When all this identity chat is en route somewhere beyond "self" toward subjec-

tivity, in motion from object to agency, its politics are about these competitions and their possible outcomes.

Terror Austerity Race Gender Excess Theater. First a definition of terrorism from the official U.S. Code:

> "[A]ct of terrorism" means an activity that (A) involves a violent act or an act dangerous to human life that is a violation of the criminal laws of the United States or any State, or that would be a criminal violation if committed within the jurisdiction of the United States or of any State; and (B) appears to be intended (i) *to intimidate or coerce a civilian population*; (ii) to influence the policy of a government by intimidation or coercion; or (iii) to affect the conduct of a government by assassination or kidnapping [emphasis added].[6]

"To intimidate or coerce a civilian population"; which civilians? War, the State of World War, the World Warrior State, is the theater of operations for the production of new American nationalism, the post-Vietnam syndrome, the idea and enactment of winning, of explicit domination set against the local reality of decreasing family wealth, fear of unemployment, threat of homelessness, and increased likelihood of early, painful death from capitalism's many toxicities. Arthur MacEwan writes:

> U.S. business and the U.S. government are still an extremely powerful set of actors, but the era of U.S. hegemony is past. U.S. corporations have felt the impact in numerous ways, losing their dominant role in many world markets and experiencing substantially lower profit rates in the 1970s and 1980s than in the preceding decades. Capital, however, is highly mobile, and in many instances U.S. firms have been able to detach themselves from the fate of the U.S. economy and, indeed, have been able to use the structures of the international system to shift the burdens of adjustment onto the backs of labor. Working people in the United States have borne a considerable burden from the emergence of a "new international economy" in the post-hegemony era.[7]

One of many debtor nation-states in the world economy, the post-hegemony U.S. is in process of structural adjustment—the sine qua non of all debt service. In everyday life, enforcement of the structural adjustment increasingly takes the form of local and international war. How come that Hyundai beat out the Chevy? Maybe because American workers are on drugs. The War on Drugs will take care of that, doubling the prison population every few years, unless adoption of Charles Murray's starkly utopian recommendations for market regulation (through voucher power) results in more barricaded, death-soaked ghettos à la Warsaw (1940) or Pico Union and Westside and North Las Vegas (1992).[8] Warfare: "Civilization is nothing but the glory of incessant struggle." War is accepted, in common sense, as the principal medium of power, prestige, and means to explain all structural adjustments, including the "fatalities" Benedict Anderson isolates as crucially accounted for in *pre*-national ideological systems: "death, loss and servitude."[9] What this all means for us at this historical moment can be summarized as follows: The ideology of nation demands sacrifice; the enactment of the warfare state demands human sacrifice. And further, both the forces and the relations of ideological production in the warfare state—in other words the crisis state—require an excess of accused, of enemies, especially if the state is successfully to exact austerity from an economy whose polity expects, as a right, indulgence (transcendent, TV-reified innocence), prosperity, excess. Such as the case fifty years ago, with the internment of the Japanese, and the centrally coordinated attacks on U.S. blacks who began many franchisement actions during the war against racism.[10] Such is the case today.

Play according to the drama of the moment.

The long-dong batons of the LAPD gangstas who beat Rodney King as he writhed on the ground are too obviously priapic to withstand much discussion. What interests me here are the theatrical venues for the repetition of that act of state terror and the subsequent configuring of the enemy, the accused—the dramturgical roles of both George Holliday, the "neighbor" cameraman who brought the secret act to light, *and* of television, which brought the secret to "the world," and finally of the courts, which decide how secret the secret must be. Through what work does the "mass mediated society"[11] intertwine local terror with beliefs contrary to what the society is able to know about the system which produces and directs the terror. How, for example, could/have any number of people, including perhaps the jury sitting in judgment of the performance, determine that King deserved, earned, needed what he got? Central to the mission, a massive willing suspension of disbelief, is a dramatic clue: "Arrest is the political art of individualizing disorder."[12] I'd thought to show the video, Holliday's representation of political artists at work—have it loop silently in the background as I describe the meanings of King's torture. But, frankly, I can't display the act as artifact: whether or not it might *be* otherwise, it *was* not. Instead, let's try to summon within the confines of orality a picture of the terror, an image of the enemy, the accused, to "see it and say it . . . in theory."

We can propose as explanatory hypothesis Ketu Katraks' description from her study of Wole Soyinka's drama: "The protagonist's personal history is intertwined inextricably with his people's history, which, at any given time embodies the totality of his community's present-past-future. The personal and the historical come together in the actions of the protagonist. . . ."[13] Katrak's excursus through Soyinka requires many mappings, not the least of which are routings of her own and Soyinka's active consciousness as "post-independence"[14] historical subjects. The confusion of *American* protagonists in the King/LAPD video is multiple. Who *is* the accuser, who the accused? King? The cops? The busybody Holliday? Dangerously available technology? We who watched the tape on television (I was called from the mountain to witness) over and over and over and over? And what do I mean by "we"? The tangle of violence we encounter in sorting out the "accused" emphasizes layers and layers of effective Americanness as white maleness. The violently abstract work of blackness in the U.S., the growing proportion of guard-duty (cop, etc.) work in the sum of all U.S. employment, the violence of being a stoolie, all propel the question at the heart of the post-Grenada, "when-hegemony-fails-give-'em-a-dose-o'-dominance" ideological enterprise, democratically domesticated as state terror: Is or ain't an "American" a contender? Doesn't a contender have to protect as well as beat up? Two bits of evidence: First, Holliday's video cassette, which the prosecutor showed to the jury during his opening argument, has a length of "extraneous footage" at the beginning: Holliday's "wife" and her "girlfriend" hanging out in the living room, American girls having American fun. Segue to the beating. Second bit of evidence: California Highway Patrolwoman Melanie Singer, on patrol with her husband (!) Tim, was the in-charge officer at the scene until LAPD Sergeant Koon told her to back off. Taking the stand against the LAPD officers, she tells us that King was acting silly, that he did a little dance. Stacey Koon's defense attorney tells it differently, citing Koon's deposition: King was "on something"; "I saw him look through me," and, when Singer told King to take his hands away from his butt, "he shook it at her [dramatic pause]. he shook it at her." The women, of course, are what makes the nation possible (and Melanie should give up that job to a man), the "class," as Brackette Williams says, that produces for and serves a "race of men."[15] Here, the protection of womanhood is actually the reassertion of race/gender in the national hierarchy: to keep Singer from being accused (in austere times of having a man's job; of trying to do a man's work without succeeding), King must stand in for both Willie Horton *and* for Melanie Singer. He must become the accused, in service of the rehabilitation of the nation.[16]

Frantz Fanon writes that violence "binds [the oppressed] together as a whole, since each individual forms a violent link in the great chain, a part of the great organism of violence which has surged upward in reaction to the settler's violence in the beginning. The groups recognize each other and the future nation is already indivisible."[17] Manthia Diawara comments:

> There we have it: violence is a system or a machine, or, yet, a narrative, of which the individual desires to be a part in order to participate in the (re) construction of the nation. Furthermore, in order to be actualized, violence "introduces into each man's consciousness the ideas of common cause, of a national destiny, and of a collective history." Violence—"this cement which has been mixed with blood and anger"—in this sense becomes the founding basis of the nation, the process through which the individual articulates his/ her relation with the nation.[18]

For good reason we tend to think of this "cement mixed with blood and anger" in terms of the not-white, not dominant, and in fact the topic of Diawara's essay is Black British cinema. But what Stuart Hall calls "new ethnicities," cementing into solidarity in fear of power shifts, include, of course, "Americans." Hall's proposal of such groupings centers on Black diaspora formations.[19] The conceptual extension of new ethnicities to the United States, and to the normatively white U.S. at that, signifies this: the very crisis which we must exploit—the raw materials of profound social change—is tending toward fascism through the brutal romance of identity, forged in the always already of the American national project. Our work is to rearticulate our own connections in new (and frightening) forward-looking moves in order to describe, promote, organize, bargain in the political arenas.

In a sense, 1992 is the year of the rehabilitation of white, male heterosexuality: its return to sites of centeredness, beauty, prosperity, power. Such a rehabilitation is central both to the European community and to the Columbian quincentenary. The rehabilitation extends to resurrections of some of those legendary dead white men—JFK, Columbus—as well as those who are trying to stay undead: from WAR's Tom Metzger on the ultra "Right" to name your pundit on the other side. Metzger's laissez-faire terrorism, stage-managed for spontaneous, natural effect, is of a piece with the nationalist power theater which the U.S. tuned in to with the invasion of Grenada in 1983. The shifts in the production of profit in the U.S. during the several years immediately preceding that invasion reflect how the circulation of value was less and less a function of productive labor and more and more the direct transfer of capital among competing traders—investment bankers, corporate raiders—and the exportation of labor relations. The major warfare matériel and engineering transnationals are located in the U.S.—the principal but by no means only state to which the transnationals pay tribute in exchange for defense, both for protection and for patronage. By 1983 they needed the kind of ideological zap (and subsequent funding spurt) which Sputnik provided the military-industrial complex in 1958. (The historical connection between the military-industrial complex and contemporary U.S. white-racist nationalism is explicit, and current; for example, Richard Butler, founder of the Aryan Nation, is an engineer and retired military man who worked in aerospace before he recolonized northern Idaho to maintain and produce the pure.)[20] These ideological zaps are certainly a function of the "I'm proud to be an American" rah-rah, but *more*, they work—they dramatically arouse the sorts of sensations that last even unto the voting box and other fora where Americans are emptying their pockets into the valises of the rich—if cemented by blood and anger. Thus the need for an enemy whose threat obligates endless budgetary consideration ("I could see him look through me." "He was on something.") and who can perhaps be found and fought as well by the brave American nationals who are sacrificing all for the sake of the nation-state: the dead and undead white men and their cadres who, Tom Metzger's windshield flyers assure us, built and (therefore) *are* this nation. Contenders.

A final accusation, expanding the ranks of the potentially accused, is that of being a spectator: only a watcher, a critic, a conscientious objector, gay, lesbian, unwaged, a blackteenagewelfaremother, a supernumerary who fails to exit on cue. These performances of inadequacy are incompatible with the demands of the crisis state—or so terror teaches. Spectators in judgment, the judge and jury of the LAPD trial, are already notorious as the result of an alleged jury-tampering attempt by a member of the Ventura County NAACP. One prospective juror told the press: *"I kind of got the feeling that they wanted me to vote a particular way— because I'm black,"* lines repeated over the television, simulcast in idiot-card and voice-over. "See it and say it in American." By the way, the jury has no black members or alternates.

The U.S. Supreme Court, effectively, has no blacks either. To a degree, whether or not one is white and male (in an old-fashioned sense) does not necessarily determine one's ability to perform "American," in the restricted nation, when power relations allow and indeed require the (formal) subsumption of the Other to the . . . Other. Clarence Thomas composed his first dissenting opinion for the case concerning whether prison personnel may beat up a prisoner; he averred they may as long as they don't have so much fun that the stand-in has to go to the hospital. State terrorism, locally defined, is not terrorism at all. State terrorism is the price of misbehavin', of acting out, including acting out in the world in particular mortal casing.

My friend F— tells it this way: she was a teenager in Little Rock, in 1924. The second Klan had reached its apogee: a million white Protestant men and women, organized against the Bolsheviks, the Catholics, the blacks who did not know their place; Kathleen Blee tells us they even tried to enlist "their" blacks to help control the in-migration of black disruptives and other foreigners in an effort to maintain the social order characterized by three generations of Redemption and Jim Crow.[21]

This is the end of the life of a black man F— never knew. The lynchers tied him to the back of their Ford car and dragged him throughout the city streets, through white and black neighborhoods alike. All of his skin scraped off. F— noticed the black man had turned white and she wondered whether that's what they had in mind when they preached in church about how we're all the same underneath. Then the lynchers, some of whom she recognized as prominent members of the Little Rock élite and civil-service cadres, built a bonfire at the intersection where the black part of town abutted the white, out where the pavement ends. They threw the man in the fire. As the acrid smoke of human sacrifice filled the neighborhood, some of the lynchers, especially the men in training showing off for their girls, pulled pieces of burning flesh and smoldering bone from his body, and walked the streets with their trophies. A high-tech lynching, thanks to that Ford car. State-sanctioned terror. Human sacrifice.

My friend F— lived at that intersection. She watched from the porch for a while, and then horror pulled her down the steps to see more closely what was happening to this man so that she would always know it in its particular and repeated terror across the years.[22] *Until 1960, race riots in the United States were these sorts of enactments, staged by a civilization loose upon the world.*

I went down from the mountains, again, to catch part of the Hill/Thomas story, tuning in at the exact moment when "high-tech lynching" entered the popular imaginary. With that plot twist, Thomas regendered himself, transforming Hill's sexist thug to Ida B. Wells's bourgeois truth teller. If the polls are to be believed, the work of anagnorisis is powerful in its capacity to delimit vision. Thomas had already performed class suicide by marrying up. Now he abstracted himself to an important role in the crisis state—that is, he became a stand-in for "progress," just as junk-bond trading becomes a stand-in for production. In both instances, the aftermath of excess—of excessive abstraction of "race" *and* of "value"—produces a remaining austerity, a scarceness of every sort of resource, a disappearance of types of workers, with the notable inclusion of Thurgood Marshall as a worker type.

Anita Hill is mystified as "black woman" such that all-we-all, including Thomas's "arrogant, entitled, dependent" sister, and their mother for whom the sister is the unpaid caregiver, fade into an infinitely regressing chorus line, abstracted to a single gynomorphic silhouette. Hill's "personal" history becomes entwined with that of her "people"—and, her people's with her. Educated in an élite university, Hill worked in DC for the better part of the 1980s dismantling regulations the enabling legislation of which two generations fought to enact. In recent, informal conversation, a noted black feminist journalist asserted that nobody really *knows* what Hill's politics are. In response to my rehearsal of the DC years, my interlocutor curled her lip and said, "But that was her job." This common-sense differentiation of "job" and "politics" reinscribes the fatal space between "work" and "act," or "political" and "economy." The space itself is a result of the disciplinary configurations within and around knowledge-production centers (e.g., the university, *itself* in crisis) that make possible the masking of how we act our politics; of how how we act *is* our politics; that politics is not ultimately derived form nor reducible to our gestures at the ballot box. And further, the willful ignorance demonstrated in the assertion of that distinction by a "feminist" argues exculpation on the basis of equal opportunity—for a woman to undo women: logically extended, we ought to celebrate Lynne Cheney Day. The issue returns us to an aspect of the problematic which my unwieldly title foregrounds: austerity, or scarcity—here, both in availability of types of waged work which an overeducated sister may perform (the government, including the armed services, is our principal employer) *and* in the portion of any person's actions one may politically scrutinize even though these actions in aggregate constitute, in the last analysis, material political performance.

The mystification of Hill, her abstraction to general meaning adequate to critique the performance of "black woman" as a class, entails a general desire by audiences, some black, some female, for black women, in general, to disappear: that is, for us to cease our public performing, to carry on with our mediations as though we are not really here in the *flesh*, as Hortense Spillers would have it, especially when the work is flesh work. How can it be otherwise when in *every* case woman, recast through the antiabortion crusade as national mother, vessel, "fetal container," *is* the performance of (hetero)sex (at whom *should* he have shaken it?) and its consequences: children; and also, when black, addiction ("he was on something") and AIDS. Los Angeles is the site of at least 29 torture murders of poor women, mainly black, many of whom earned their livelihoods (and supported their children) working in the sex industry. The police are prominent in this drama as well. A grass-roots organization trying to bring an end to these deaths and take care of the survivors, Black Coalition Fighting Back Serial Murders testified at the Christopher Commission Hearings. "By labelling all the women prostitutes, the police attempted to segregate them from other women, and at the same time gave other women a false sense of security."[23] The only arrest made in connection with these murders was that of a cop; the forensic evidence that led to his arrest was "reevaluated" by the same lab that found empirical support for his complicity, and he was released shortly thereafter.

Terror Austerity Race Gender Excess Theater

Here, finally, the title fully represents its dramatic possibility, every element functioning to coerce into silence and invisibility poor black women who perform, if at all, as the expendable class but who, at the same time, embody, to the terror of the American nation "the [imagined] totality of our community's past-present-future." *Terror*: murder; torture; what to do with the children? The *austerity* of poverty, of turning finally to the body as the means for daily reproduction. The poverty that attaches to *race*—as Immanuel Wallerstein exposes in "The Myrdal Legacy," racism is a necessary component, rather than a passing phase, of capitalism.[24] The poverty that attaches to *gender*: According to the United Nations International Labor Organisation, women do two-thirds of the world's work for five percent of the income and one percent of the assets; since we know the poorest among us are people of color, these data quantify racism and sexism on a global scale.[25] The *race/gender excess* of these dead women is expendable enough for the LAPD to refuse to state categorically whether or not the murders have ceased. The work of the murdered and their survivors turns on the performance of *excess*, a quick ride on a paying penis—is this the fatal one?—the *theater* of orgasm become Grand Guignol become terror itself become snuff. War is the enemy of the poor.

The attempts to get major, in particular *televised*, coverage of this series of murders, and of deaths in similar circumstances as far away as Kansas City and Florida, encounter no dramaturgical zeal. After all, what work would this revelation do to extend coercion of the least powerful segment of the social formation? And, further, the coverage would result in an excess of something else, of attention paid to black women who are not individually upwardly mobile objects of rape and other male abuses (Hill, Givens, Washington, Winfrey). The coercion is already effectively in place, carried by fear and the antigospel gossip circuit; women get on the phone and talk, like the women who tried to turn in Dahmer before he'd eaten his fill. We talk until we're sure someone is listening—when we know we are performing for the technological apparatuses that turn on a suspect word—and say we'll talk some more when (when?) we meet again. We are the accused (like Anita Hill, who also accuses us), we who conspire to prevent the American nation from regaining its ancient heritage, its accessible white-male identity, clothed in whatever melanogender fits the needs of the political economy of the crisis-capitalist state. Spectators at our own undoing, we are filthy vessels of unwanted offspring, body parts that just won't work in the bodies of those who can afford to buy a spleen, a kidney, a heart—not even Fordism can save us now—separated by the excess of genetics, the fact of race in this era of neo-biologism, from any work/act/performance that does not run up in the face of state terror over and over and over again. I can stay in the mountains for this show; it won't be televised.

Stand-ins. What is so perfect, so perfectly austere in this theater is how nobody is a star—American equality in action. We're stand-ins, as Gloria Anzaldúa says,[26] and so are all the objects of state torture, of state terrorism, targets cast for the fit, the lighting, the camera, the angle, the story, in place of anyone who dares perform a comparable excess of being. But even stand-ins, in times of austerity, might unionize, might move from being objects of organized abandonment, red-lined along with the buildings and neighborhoods, to *subjects* who refuse—who refuse to bear the weight of late capitalism's stark utopia, the abstraction of abandonment, the violence of abstraction.[27] We are poised in a performance I've yet to plot, or map, or systematically to theorize the semiotics and histrionics of, beyond these preliminary remarks. I believe it is too late to fight nationalism with nationalism; that bloodily disintegrating process must result in planetary death. I also believe it is not too late to act, to make work *work*, through rearticulation of the "complex skein of relatedness":[28] organic integrations of the earth, technology, desire.

The Great Leveler Thomas Rainboro said it in 1637: "Either poverty must use democracy to destroy the power of property, or property, in fear of poverty, will destroy democracy."[29] If we start from where we're at, and organize in and for work, conceived in the fullness of our imaginative powers, we might push and pull the current tendency of crisis away from a national resolution in fascism: terrorism, imprisonment, deportation, sterilization, state-supervised death. All of these features are everyday elements of life in California, in Arkansas, in Texas, New York, you name it. This is where we're at; where are we headed?

Notes

The passages cited in epigraph come from Cedric Robinson, *Black Marxism* (London: Zed, 1983), 452, and Colin Mercer, "Fascist Ideology," *Politics and Ideology*, ed. James Donald and Stuart Hall (Philadelphia: Holmes and Meier, 1986), 218.

1. Toni Negri, "Crisis of the Crisis-State," *Revolution Retrieved: Selected Writings on Marx, Keynes, Capitalist Crisis and New Social Subjects, 1967–83* (London: Red Notes, 1988, pp. 181–82. Also particularly helpful to the formulation of this paper's tendency are: Marie-Hélène Huet, *Rehearsing the Revolution* (Berkeley: University of California Press, 1982); Selma James, *Sex, Race and Class* (London: Falling Wall, 1986); A. Sivanandan, *Communities of Resistance* (London: Verso, 1990).

2. The phrase is Amiri Baraka's but Paul Gilroy put it in my vocabulary. See Leroi Jones, "The Changing Same," *Black Music* (New York: Apollo Editions, 1970); see also Paul Gilroy, "Sounds Authentic: The Challenge of a 'Changing Same,' " paper delivered at *The Politics of Identities* conference, 4 April 1991, Claremont, CA.

3. Any who doubt my claim need only study the 1992 Democratic party platform and the party's many pundits whose subtexts resound with the unvoiced but clear desire for black people to disappear so that liberalism can be reborn as a white, working thang. If the Democrats are committed to "distancing" themselves from black people, then the distance will require a material force to maintain it. Doubling the prison populations in the past decade, the reinstitution of the death penalty in many states, combined with recriminalization of practices which had become misdemeanors in the 1970s (e.g., possession of marijuana for personal use) set in motion both the concrete and the ideological forces necessary to dispose of a subset of an entire racially marked group of the population without once using the word "fascism" as a rallying cry in mainstream circles. See Dan Baum, "Just Say Nolo Contendere: The Drug War on Civil Liberties," *The Nation* 25, no. 25 (29 June 1992): 886–88.

4. Karl Polanyi, *The Great Transformation* (New York: Farrar and Rienhart, 1944), p. 3.

5. White Aryan Resistance (WAR) flyer, distributed to windshields throughout the western U.S. WAR's headquarters is about 25 miles from where I live (same area code). Tom Metzger, founder of WAR, and his son John were convicted of inciting Portland, Oregon, skinheads to commit racist acts of terror, which culminated in the murder of the Ethiopian student Mulugeta Seraw. Morris Dees and the Southern Poverty Law Center successfully prosecuted the case. Dees is now on Metzger's hit list.

6. Cited by Noam Chomsky, "International Terrorism: Image and Reality," *Western State Terrorism*, ed. Alexander George (New York: Routledge, 1991), 13.

7. Arthur MacEwan, "What's 'New' about the 'New International Economy'?" *Socialist Review* 21, nos. 3 and 4 (July–December 1991): 112. An example of a U.S. corporation successfully detaching "from the fate of the U.S. economy" (or more, *defining* that fate through its detachment!) is General Motors, which idled tens of thousands of workers and closed 12 plants between 1969 and 1989, one of which was South Gate in South Los Angeles. GM plans to close 21 more plants and lay off an additional 74,000 by 1995; one permanently idled auto worker means two to three layoffs in businesses where the worker spends her pay. But take note: in 1985 the same transnational ranked 13th (right behind Ford and Hughes Medical Institute) among contractors in *arms* exports. See Raúl Madrid et al., *U.S. Arms Exports: Policies and Contractors* (Washington, DC: Investor Responsibility Research Center, Inc., 1987).

8. Charles Murray, "Drug Free-Zones," *Current* 326 (October 1990): 19–24. Thanks to Mike Davis for telling me about this article, originally published in the *New Republic*: *Current* is a reader's digest for the radical right. Also see Mike Davis, "Blacks Are Dealt Out," *Nation* 255, no. 1 (6 July 1992): 7–10.

9. Benedict Anderson, *Imagined Communities* (London: Verso, 1983; rev. 1991), 36.

10. See C. L. R. James et al., *Fighting Racism in World War II* (New York: Pathfinder, 1980) Also, a debate raged in middlebrow and learned journals on this very topic, with not only activists but also "friends of the Negro," and what Ish Reed calls "talking androids" all contributing to the argument. See Virginius Dabney, "The Negro and His Schooling," *The Atlantic Monthly* 169, no. 4 (April 1942): 459–68; Warren H. Brown, "A Negro Looks at the Negro Press," *Saturday Review* 25, no. 51 (19 December 1942): 5–6; John Temple Graves, "The Southern Negro and the War Crisis," *Virginia Quarterly* 18 (1942): 500–518; etc.

11. Robin Erica Wagner-Pacifici, *The Moro Morality Play* (Chicago: University of Chicago Press, 1986), 1–21.

12. Allen Feldman, *Formations of Violence: The Narrative of the Body and Political Terror in Northern Ireland* (Chicago: University of Chicago Press, 1991), 109.

13. Ketu Katrak, *Wole Soyinka and Modern Tragedy* (New York: Greenwood, 1986), 129.

14. Ella Shohat, "War, Sexuality, and the Imperial Narrative," paper presented at the annual convention of the Modern Language Association, San Francisco, 30 December 1991.

15. Personal conversation; see also Brackette Williams, *Stains on My Name, War in My Veins* (Durham, NC: Duke University Press, 1991). See also Anne McClintock, " 'No Longer in a Future Heaven': Women and Nationalism in South Africa," *Transition* 51 (1991): 105–24.

16. All references to the trial are from notes taken on the road listening to the opening remarks by the D.A. and by Koon's defense attorney. KFWB, Los Angeles, 5 March 1992; the information was substantiated in reports in the daily press.

17. Frantz Fanon, cited by Manthia Diawara, "Black British Cinema," *Public Culture* 3, no. 1 (Fall 1990): 33–47.

18. Ibid. Internal citations are Fanon.

19. Stuart Hall, "New Ethnicities," *Black Film, British Cinema* (London: ICA Documents, 1988), 27–31.

20. James A. Aho, *The Politics of Righteousness* (Seattle: University of Washington Press, 1990), esp. ch. 2.

21. Kathleen Blee, *Women of the Klan* (Berkeley and Los Angeles: University of California Press, 1991).

22. Thanks to my friend, Mrs. FVH, an octogenarian who keeps the rest of us in line.

23. U.S. Prostitutes Collective Statement, reported in *Update from the Wages for Housework Campaign/ LA* (Fall/Winter 1991): 3. In fact, the only time there was any major, sustained coverage of these murders as *news* was on the occasion a white woman who had been organizing against the slayings was found dead in San Diego, gravel stuffed in her mouth. Otherwise, the biggest coverage was in the form of a *Los Angeles Times* feature in 1986 which coordinator Margaret Prescod and others fought for to announce formation of the Coalition. Source: Black Coalition Fighting Back Serial Murders.

24. Immanuel Wallerstein, "The Myrdal Legacy," in *Unthinking Social Sciences* (Oxford: Polity, 1991), 80–103.

25. These figures are from the United Nations International Labor Organisation; they are also ten years old. What with all the restructuring in the First through Third Worlds as a result of the debt crisis, these income and asset figures have undoubtedly shrunken, while the proportion of work has certainly risen. Thanks to Krisha Ahooja-Patel, an economist with the UNILO, who worked to produce these data, and the International Wages for Housework Campaign, for both the data and the contemporary critique of the data. See also Maria Mies, *Patriarchy and Accumulation on a World Scale* (London: Zed, 1986), esp. ch. 4.

26. Gloria Anzaldúa, "Theorizing, Mestiza Style," lecture delivered in Claremont, CA, February 1991.

27. See David Harvey, "Crises in the Space Economy of Capitalism," in *The Limits to Capital* (Chicago: University of Chicago Press, 1982), 413–45, and David Harvey, *The Condition of Postmodernity* (Oxford: Blackwell, 1989); see also Derek Sayer, *The Violence of Abstraction* (Oxford: Blackwell, 1989).

28. Charles Johnson, "The Education of Mingo," in *The Sorcerer's Apprentice* (New York: MacMillan, 1986), 19.

29. Quoted by Raphael Samuel, "British Marxist Historians," *New Left Review* 124 (March/April 1980), 28.

3

Scene . . . Not Heard

Houston A. Baker

The Afro-American slave narrative is a classic site of what might be called the "scene of violence" in American discourse. This scene plays itself out, as the scholar Richard Slotkin has demonstrated, with infinite variation in American history. But in slave narratives and Afro-American history in general, it shapes itself according to a unique logic of sound and silence, agency and powerlessness. An example from the 1845 *Narrative of the Life of Frederick Douglass, An American Slave* serves to illustrate. Douglass's narrator begins one of the work's most gruesome scenes of violence as follows: "Mr. Gore [white overseer for Colonel Lloyd] was a grave man, and, though a young man, he indulged no jokes, said no funny words, seldom smiled. . . . His savage barbarity was equalled only by the consummate coolness with which he committed the grossest and most savage deeds upon the slaves under his charge."

Mr. Gore has just commenced beating the slave Demby when the slave flees: "he [Demby] ran and plunged himself into a creek, and stood there at the depth of his shoulders, refusing to come out. Mr. Gore told him that he would give him three calls, and that, if he did not come out at the third call, he would shoot him." The third call yields no response, so "Mr. Gore . . . without consultation or deliberation with any one, not even giving Demby an additional call, raised his musket to his face, taking deadly aim at his standing victim, and in an instant poor Demby was no more. His mangled body sank out of sight, and blood and brains marked the water where he had stood.''

In this horrifying scene of violence, Demby has no interpretive power or authority. He remains conspicuously silent. Others may define him as an emblem of resistance or a site of counterinterpretation. But insofar as he is a slave *in situation*, he has no articulate being for himself. (By *in situation*, I mean the legal, physical, and material constraints of slavery as everyday life.) Like Demby, the black slaves who are also party to the scene remain silently outside the articulate precincts of the law.

In nineteenth-century domains of American slavery, it was unthinkable for a black person to offer testimony against any white act whatsoever. African-American slaves were, thus, literally ''out-lawed.'' And in the 1850s, Chief Justice Taney declared that it was a good law and precedent that a black man had no rights that a white man was ''bound to respect.''

In Douglass's narrative, only Mr. Gore is granted interpretive authority. He is called by Colonel Lloyd to explain Demby's death. Gore's defense is recorded as follows: ''He argued that if one slave refused to be corrected, and escaped with his life, the other slaves would soon copy the example; the result of which would be, the freedom of the slaves, and the enslavement of the whites.'' What this defense amounts to is a sharply abridged version of Hegel's lordship and bondage. Gore argues, in effect, that if ''we'' of the master position *recognize* the slave's ''uncorrected'' right to speech or action then ''we'' shall certainly be enslaved ourselves.

Given the silence of Demby and his fellow slaves and the entailments of Gore's defense, does the slave *in situation* have a voice at all? Yes, says Douglass, there is a rhetoric available to the slave, but it is only one of falsehood.

The narrator recounts an incident in which Colonel Lloyd demands of one of his slaves who does not know the master's identity whether the slave considers himself well treated. The slave answers ''No.'' A brief time afterward, the slave is seized, shackled, and sold to a Georgia trader as a threatening and ''uncorrected'' malcontent. Douglass's narrator comments as follows: ''The slaveholders have been known to send in spies among their slaves, to ascertain their views and feelings in regard to their condition. The frequency of this has had the effect to establish among the slaves the maxim, that a still tongue makes a wise head.''

One might infer from this nineteenth-century tale of surveillance and punishment that ''truth'' can never exist as a token of exchange between wise blacks and their spying masters. A rhetoric of falsehood combines with a white interpretive exclusivity to lock the scene of violence into place. *Slave truth* is, therefore, not only an oxymoron, but an impossibility. Semiotically, the scene of violence seems to reinforce Umberto Eco's definition of that fundamental unit of exchange—the sign. Eco writes:

> Semiotics is in principle the discipline of studying everything which can be used in order to lie. If something cannot be used to tell a lie, conversely it cannot be used to tell the truth: it cannot in fact be used 'to tell' at all. I think that the definition of a 'theory of the lie' should be taken as a pretty comprehensive program for a general semiotics.

(Black folklore tells of David Wharton, a humorless overseer not unlike Mr. Gore. He was never known to laugh. On the first day of his new assignment, he confronts Nehemiah, a slave who is known to avoid work through his wit and humor. Nehemiah has defeated all masters' attempts to make him work. Wharton means to be obeyed and to make the slave work. "Wal, Massa, dat's aw right, but ef Ah meks you laff, won' yuh lemme off fo' terday?" "Well," said David Wharton, "if you make me laugh, I won't only let you off for today, but I'll give you your freedom." "Ah decla', Boss," said Nehemiah, "you sho' is uh good-lookin' man." "I am sorry I can't say the same thing about you," retorted David Wharton. "Oh, yes, Boss, you could, if yuh tole ez big uh lie ez Ah did!")

The key aspects of the "soul-less" state of slavery as Douglass records it in his narrative are: the silent slave, the hermeneutically powerful master, and the semiotically reflexive "rhetoric of falsehood." These aspects of the slave scene of violence are not, however, confined to the South. For the slave—even when he or she is a "fugitive" from southern violence—is expected to remain *silent*. At northern abolitionist rallies, for example, the fugitive becomes the "Negro exhibit." She silently turns her naked back to the audience in order to display the stripes inflicted by the southern overseer's whip. Blacks in white-abolitionist employ were required always to earn the right—by silent display—to tell their stories. And even when blacks were permitted to tell their stories, the *interpretation* of their narratives—no matter how effective a slave's oratory—was the exclusive prerogative of their white-abolitionist employers.

The novelist Ralph Ellison captures the northern-abolitionist inflections of the American scene of violence in his novel *Invisible Man*. After Ellison's black and brilliantly gifted protagonist has roused a Harlem audience with a stunning speech, he is sharply criticized by the white hermeneut "Brother Hambro." Hambro—one of the protagonist's white employers—declares that the invisible man requires a crash course in scientific socialism if he is to speak "correctly." No "uncorrected" black oratorical behavior is allowed in Ellison's ironically named "Brotherhood."

If both North and South are conjoined in silencing black meaning, what expressive alternatives exist for blacks? In Douglass's narrative, we learn the virtues of the slave songs: "Every tone was a testimony against slavery, and a prayer to God for deliverance from chains." Do the songs themselves define interpretive agency? No, says Douglass. *In situation*, as we have already seen, the slave wields no interpretive power: "I [Douglass] did not, when a slave, understand the deep meaning of those rude and apparently incoherent songs. I was myself within the circle; so that I neither saw nor heard as those without might see and hear." But once Douglass the fugitive is in the North, he is able to provide captivating descriptions of the songs. He subjects them to a written, black interpretation in his writings that gives them an authentic group meaning. The slave songs, therefore, have to be *written* before they can become fully agential as interpretive protests or negations. As readers, we do not actually hear the songs. We simply see them. In one sense, then, they too become scenic rather than audible.

Yet, there is a kinship of sorts between John Keats and Frederick Douglass where song, writing, and memory are concerned. The nineteenth-century slave narrator might be seen to emulate the voice of the British romanticist insofar as the two speakers perform acts of interpretive recollection before scenes of "unheard" song. Contemplating the famous Grecian urn, Keats's speaker in the ode proclaims: "Heard melodies are sweet, but those unheard / Are sweeter; therefore, ye soft pipes, play on; / Not to the sensual ear, but, more endear'd, / Pipe to the spirit ditties of no tone." Douglass's narrator similarly urges a spiritual response to "those songs" of slavery that can not actually be *heard* at northern sites of abolitionist employment. Thus, both Keats's speaker and Douglass's narrator assume what can be called a "metasonic" interpretive position that enjoins readers to *hear between the lines*. Effective reading in the hermeneutics of Douglass and Keats is *overhearing*.

The scene of violence in Douglass's writing becomes finally (and finely) heard. The visual and *voiceless* slave is finally set spiritually, meaningfully, and resistantly singing. And what is overheard by effective readers is a lyrical repudiation of the master's exclusive right to meaningful being in the world.

In retrospect, it seems obvious that the implications of Douglass's literate metasonics were not seriously heard or heeded by the United States of his era. At least this is a reading of matters that gestures toward the mighty apocalypse of the American Civil War. That war was, I think, at least in part, a function of nineteenth-century America's refusal truly to grant black men and women a *hearing*. Even in the clamorous beginnings of the conflict that is now read as a "war to end slavery," white men in the North and South agreed that Negroes were to be *scene* and not heard.

"This is a white man's war" was the general interpretive framing of War events until matters grew so burdensome that Negro soldiers were immediately required. The "scening" of the African presence in America—its literal desub-jectification and silencing—is in a cogent sense a *local* scene of violence that overdetermines a vast, outgoing scene of American national violence. And it is normally only at the lugubrious conclusion of such vast, orgiastic bouts of national violence that an ear is tuned to the primal local scene of violence. An "investi-gation" or "hearing" is always commissioned in a belated attempt to grasp the meaning of it all. However, as we know from reading the Civil War, after the event, the *Freedman* in the courts, commissions, or regulative *bureaus* is seldom more meaningfully heard than his enslaved forbears. He remains a visual icon, turning silently on the materialist pedestal of "white events." But, if we shift the scene to a balmy southern-California night in the spring of 1991, do matters appear differently? Can we escape the uncanny silence of that voiceless black icon without agency . . . turning?

It is 3rd March 1991. A speeding car occupied by three black men drives through red lights on California Highway 210. In pursuit . . . not Mr. Gore . . . but a husband-and-wife team of the California Highway Patrol. When the lead vehicle finally pulls over, out jumps a 6'3", 200-pound black man, who, according to witnesses, danced about, grabbed his behind, and laughed crazily. Was this Nehemiah in the face of David Wharton? The police were not amused. Twenty-one Los Angeles city police officers had arrived at the scene along with two Unified School District officers by the time Rodney G. King jumped out of his car. The newly arrived told the husband-and-wife Highway Patrol team that they would handle matters. Fifty-six crushing blows, several stun-gun blasts, and random savage kicks and pushes later, these bold white officers had indeed succeeded in "handling" matters.

The twenty-five-year-old, black Rodney G. King, who suffered the complete weight of the law, was left with a split inner lip, a partially paralyzed face, nine skull fractures, a broken cheek bone, a shattered eye socket, and a broken leg. When called upon to give an explanation, one of the officers at the scene said: "I think he was dusted [under the influence of the drug PCP or "angel dust"]." Is this a postmodern writing of "uncorrected" slave behavior?

Now . . . we all know that, unbeknownst to Officer Laurence Powell and his police brethren, a white plumbing company manager, George Holliday, was trying out his new video camcorder on 3rd March, creating a visual of the King beating that instantly became national media currency. There was virtually no call for the "fugitive" himself to record his story before white audiences. He had merely to be wheeled out for television cameras and turned silently before outraged courts of American opinion in all of his bandaged, swollen, and bruised victimization.

The eighty-one-second video tape captured in lurid, shaking chiaroscuro the "scene of violence." And the tape's circulation made the president of the United

States himself declare that it sickened him. The "fugitive" was silent. New-age teleabolitionist networks played the video for us—night and day.

King was always already *silent*. Moral pundits and paparazzi alike took up his cause. Not only was there a scene of violence, but an *overseen* one in ways unimaginable to Colonel Lloyd and Douglass. The video camcorder seeing of the beating was, quite literally, everywhere.

But as the criminal-justice system geared up to deliver justice, wise white men knew that what was wanted for an *interpretation* of the scene was a site where the compulsive repetition anxiety of lordship and bondship was likely to carry its most effective semiotic weight.

The small town with the unbelievably egotistical name of a valley was chosen as the "change of venue" for the trial against the four white police officers— Stacey Koon, Timothy Wind, Laurence Powell, Ted Briseno—who had beaten the living daylights out of a twenty-five-year-old black man.

"Simi Valley," home to a two percent black population, was, in the judge's estimation, a place where white LAPD officers would not be unfairly treated due to adverse publicity. Of course, Simi Valley resonates in the present reading of Rodney G. King, like the grand, white manor house of Colonel Lloyd in eastern Maryland. The foxes are being chauffeured to Fox Manor for judgment . . . and America, retinally surfeited by the eighty-one-second video imaging of the scene of violence, awaits the verdict.

King is still *silent* and manifestly invisible, in proper person. It is as though he is sickeningly caught forever in the graceless heaviness of his attempts—crudely videotaped—to escape the next crushing blow from the bold officers of the LAPD. He has not been *heard* from as the trial begins. And—stunningly—to the amazement of so very many—he is not called to Fox Manor to testify in his own behalf . . . nor are the two black men who were in the car with him. King is *silent*, and barely seen outside the repetitive scene of video-ed violence.

(Now . . . this *silence* lends . . . in an age where reality is only sound and images marking what Lyotard calls the "postmodern condition" . . . this *silence* lends the possibility of a heroic interpretation of the unheard victim of the videotape. We see him there on the ground, writhing under the baton. Without an opportunity to hear his voice, we make him a new age "Demby." The complete blank victim. But the age of information overwhelms this solacing interpretation. "Instant" analysis and information write that Rodney G. King was a man who had served time for second-degree robbery . . . a young man drunk on Olde English 800 and slowed by marijuana in his blood when tested by police. Two times married, father of three . . . unemployed. So we await the verdict without romanticizing the seen former felon, a fugitive from justice . . . We still believe the prior evidence of our eyes . . . eyes that have witnessed the video and know that *no man* . . . even the mythical *no man* . . . deserves to be so treated by brutal, club-wielding uniforms of violence.)

But we have not heard from Rodney King himself, nor have we been historically or semiotically astute enough to conduct our own hearing of the American scene of violence as it has immemorially sounded itself in the New World. We thus wait in vain for something which a hearing of Rodney King—in all the reverberant energies and echolalic resonances of times and scenes of violence gone by—will never produce. That "something" is, of course, *a scene truly heard.*

In that white, lordly repetition compulsion that now seems eternal, the defense attorneys for the four LAPD officers play the scene of violence in slow, discrete, frame-by-frame analysis for the ten white, one Asian, and one Hispanic juror.

The voice-over for this slow, interpretive semiotics of violence is provided by the attorneys themselves. They demonstrate that Rodney G. King's behavior was clearly "uncorrected." Had this brutish black been allowed to go "uncorrected," why "we" would surely have been enslaved. For he was always threateningly *controlling* the action . . .

The jurors understand the "we" as those who are ensconced compulsively behind the "thin blue line" of policing that protects them from the black horrors of the city. The attorneys' new-critical reading (as my colleague Manthia Diawara has successfully taught me) is like all new-critical readings. That is to say, it is a misreading, a misprision—taking the "scene" and controlling it. It is a policing of images by dissection and tends always to preserve the tale of violence and control in its primal form. Unless the officers had exercised a violent "control" of the scene, that dread black urban animal from South Central Los Angeles might well have enslaved white suburban America. (Never mind, friends, that Demby is cowering, up to his shoulders in an open creek, or that King is decisively writhing in debilitating pain on the ground.)

Douglass's narrator says of Mr. Gore's defense:

> Mr. Gore's defence was satisfactory. He was continued in his station as over-seer upon the home plantation. His fame as an overseer went abroad. His horrid crime was not even submitted to judicial investigation.

In Simi Valley, the verdict came in: NOT GUILTY!

The officers will doubtless be continued in force on the Los Angeles "home plantation" . . . but we do already know the consequences of the unheard *scening* of blackness in America, don't we? The occurrence of such local scenes is the hard semiotic rock in the great pool of American signification. It ripples out into national disaster, a clamorous, destructive uproar that seems bloodily unstoppable.

Los Angeles exploded in a manner that carried the map of California-Highway-

210 violence across South Central, to Simi Valley, which is north and west of South Central. Westwood and Santa Monica were burning along with the flames of Hollywood. Long Beach erupted and the urban reverberations shook America in Seattle, Atlanta, Detroit, and elsewhere. Globally—in Germany, Hong Kong, Japan, Paris, London—images of American urban disaster were projected as proof positive that George Bush and others had no license to babble of "human rights" ever again.

When Los Angeles's streets were once again under police control, more than fifty people were dead. Thousands were injured. The beating of a white truck driver had become the preferred video of the "riot," "insurrection," "rebellion," "anarchic criminal chaos"—call it what you will. Millions of dollars in property had gone up in smoke.

And where was the voice of Rodney G. King?

Well, we all know that it was *heard* in what some called a passionate, moving sequence of sounds:

> People, I just want to say . . . can we all get along? Can we get along? . . . We'll get our justice. They've won the battle, but they haven't won the war. . . . We all can get along. We've just got to, just got to. We're all stuck here for awhile. Let's try to work it out. Let's try to work it out.

American eyes and ears were focused. They were tuned to a black man speaking. Speaking, of course, *after the fact* and beyond the verdict of Fox Manor. He was now allowed to plead—as a witlessly turned icon—for an end to the fire storm spreading outward from the latest local enactment of the great American scene of violence.

It *was* moving. But no heroic interpretation is available after we learn that the main lines of the broken, sweated King plea for pacification were supplied by, respectively, his lawyer, who hopes to clear a couple of million dollars from the civil suit that he has entered on behalf of his client, and James Banks, vice president of Triple-7 enterprises which now owns the rights to Rodney G. King, *tout court*.

Here, once again, was the altogether predictable *ventriloquizing* of the desires of the black man, who remains today, as far as we can ascertain, *in situation* in Ventura County, California.

But what of the possibilities of a hearing of the Rodney G. King scene of violence akin to the hearing Douglass provides for Demby and the nineteenth-century South? Today, what we have available to us for interpretive hearing are not slave songs, but deep-bass black notes of rap expressivity and rap-video production. Suddenly—in the crashing, burning, looting, riotous middle of Los Angeles urban disaster—the national ear perked up. And its eyes focused on young urban black prophets of postmodernity who have been trying to push through for more than two decades what Grandmaster Flash called "The Message."

N. W. A., Public Enemy, Ice-T, Boogie Down Productions, Ice Cube, Poor Righteous Teachers—these are but representative names from rap's multiple sites and soundings of the great black urban scene of violence in America—a scene sponsored on the "home plantation" by Reagan/Bush "colonels" and "overseers" alike. Prime-time media at the Rodney King moment tuned into the sounds and sights of rap with the passion of *discovery*. Of course, what many of the black rap artists were and had been producing, for more than a quarter century, was a contemporary, reverberant echo of historical black soundings of the scene of violence. Rap, in many of its most energetic and popular manifestations, was but an updated song of explanation. It was an articulate cry to the world about the insufferable poverty, relentless police brutality, and frustrated hopes of the black urban scene. It chronicled and catalogued drug wars and the fierce intraracial fury of black-youth homicide. It presented its own clear black understanding of the inner city's economic and political abandonment. It urged the lessons of a "stop the violence movement" and fostered a program called HEAL (Human Education Against Lies).

Rap is a young person's domain, replete with codes of speech, dress, walking, and talking in a world seen as essentially dangerous and only problematically capable of black or holy redemption.

(Now it would be romantic in the extreme to set rap on precisely the same productive, reproductive, and economic axes as the slave songs referenced by Douglass. The world has grown much too technologically complex and globally interconnected by consumer capitalism for that. Rap has been an enormous international and commercial success, especially in its purchase by young white suburbanites. And much of the "product" has been tailored exclusively for sale to the young and the restless, devoid of all hermeneutical or educational intent and effect. The injunction implicit in such rap is solely "dance for me!" But the work of Public Enemy and BDP and other "message" groups—while danceable—is primarily interpretive, if not homiletic, in its effect.)

Despite the resonant soundings—the interpretive and predictive force—of groups such as Public Enemy and N. W. A., all rap has been taken by much of General America as the functional equivalent of songs for happy, illiterate darkies. The educational, pedagogical, prophetic, historical wisdom of the form in its most canny and brilliant manifestations, such as Eric B and Rakim, or A Tribe Called Quest, or Das EFX, has scarcely been attended to. Urban Studies scholars, government officials, and social analysts are so far in arrears vis-à-vis rap that their findings are hardly as significant as Naughty By Nature's perspicacious "Everything

Is Going to Be All Right.'' Surely rap has not been *overheard* in the ways that both Keats and Douglass suggest for effective readers.

Douglass writes of nineteenth-century white hearings of the slave songs as follows: ''I have often been utterly astonished, since I came to the north, to find persons who could speak of the singing, among slaves, as evidence of their contentment and happiness.'' Rather than a *mishearing* produced by incorrect inference, Douglass implies that the attribution of ''contentment'' and ''happiness'' to slaves upon hearing their songs is a deliberative, hermeneutical privilege belonging to white people alone. Such an attribution is always comforting to those who do not wish to be moved to new understandings or transformative action.

Rodney G. King jumped out of that car on 3rd March in the kinesthetic disguise of black minstrelsy. Laughing and grabbing his behind, he hoped to show white folks that he was a contented darky. He was playing the black master of his very own kind of false rhetoric. And he nearly lost his life . . . without a meaningful sound.

What no one has subjected to a hearing, however—at least not an attentive enough hearing—are the sounds of King's situation. Rap has informed America for years that if—as Angela Davis stated it many years ago—they come now to ''get us'' in the morning, they must expect the apocalypse. Because, we have given up on being merely *seen* or *scened* and not heard. Rodney King was a pure product of Reaganomics and Bushian urban abandonment. He was the ghostly shadow of a new black urban personhood, appearing out of the dark night of dreadful neglect.

And while he played the minstrel, his compeers, who have made dramatic and manifold appearances in the provinces of ''Gangster Rap,'' had already moved to a far more sobering and dangerous mood than minstrelsy in the throes of American recession. As one writer for *Newsweek* recorded matters: ''Inevitably, the catastrophe [of the Los Angeles flames] summoned up memories of Watts, but the differences were more striking than the similarities. 'All you had then was bottles and bricks,' said one blood, opening his trunk to show his stash of automatic weapons. 'That ain't it now—this ain't gonna be like the '60s.' ''

And, indeed, it was not like the '60s at all, as Hispanic and black, white and Asian youth and their elders set out on a rampage that rocked and shocked the 1992 spring world, to the beat of a deep-bass, hammering, slamming rap that had, for too many years, been the unheard national anthem of the black inner city.

The lesson of Rodney G. King and the Los Angeles inferno has yet to achieve fully comprehensible form. It has not achieved a form that allows it to provide summary conclusions and predictive readings of postmodern, postindustrial, global urban conditions as a whole. Moreover, so much of the ''Rodney G. King

Affair'' was a matter of media: momentary and sensational scenes of violence compulsively repeated to the point of instant gratification and diurnal desensitization. It was a mere moment in that telesurfeit that makes us all media toddlers at a thousand-and-one-ring circus—always off after the next unfolding teletale of scandalous violence.

And yet we can historicize the Rodney G. King moment as an instance of the classic American "scene of violence." And we can attempt for postmodernity's sake to break dramatically out of the accustomed roles of a racially divided viewing audience seeing, but not hearing, the "other" side of a ruthless mise-en-scène.

In his classic narrative, Douglass suggests a positional relocation as a way of recoding the disastrous semiotics of the American scene of violence:

> If any one wishes to be impressed with the soul-killing effects of slavery, let him go to colonel Lloyd's plantation, and, on allowance-day, place himself in the deep pine woods, and there let him, in silence, analyze the sounds that shall pass through the chambers of his soul,—and if he is not thus impressed, it will only be because "there is no flesh in his obdurate heart."

One hesitates to advocate a similar "assessment," or settling down beside rap in some vast, Olympian auditorium of the postmodern where young black sound blasts the ears like mortar shells. Such a cacophonous site hardly seems to border on spirituality.

Still the expressive economies of *rap*—economies staffed by men and women closer by far to Rodney King's twenty-five-year-old status than most American politicians and social-policy analysts—these expressive economies are, perhaps, far more likely to yield a hearing that forestalls further American urban disaster than any sophisticated and commissioned Los Angeles post mortems that we can presently imagine.

Beyond the rhetoric of falsehood and the hermeneutical exclusivity of some newly commissioned bureau to put Rodney King on the freedman's pedestal, we might actually gain a hearing from rap of what precisely it *sounds* like to be violently *scened* in the United States.

Such a hearing would place us in the metasonic position of Douglass's abolitionist fugitive in the North, hearing between the lines. Furthermore, it would position us to respond as Douglass himself did to his very own times. As politician and orator, as concerned citizen of the public sphere, he responded by *speaking on* his era at the precise sites of its violence against humanity. He thus became an informed and active site of audition.

A *hearing* of Rodney G. King can commence with a hearing of rap.

The rest is history.

Part Two

Acquitting White Brutality

————————————

4

The Rules of the Game

Patricia J. Williams

The last time I had heard from my friend R. was sometime around Christmas, just after the jury found Jeffrey Dahmer's cannibalistic necrophilia the product of a sane mind. R. was in quite a tizzy, and he called all the way from Paris: Exactly how many people *do* you have to eat in the state of Wisconsin, he wanted to know, before they find you crazy?

Fifty-two, I told him.

When R. called this time, one day after the Rodney King verdict, he was waxing philosophical. He wanted to talk about hyperindividualism, the meaning of agency, and the construction of the autonomous subject. He wanted to know, in short, what in hell that juror meant when she described King as being "in complete control" and "directing all the action" and "choosing" the moment when he "wanted" to be handcuffed.

This one was harder to explain, I confess, than Dahmer the sane cannibal, or Goetz the reasonable racist, for that matter, or Donald Trump or Clarence Thomas or even Ronald Reagan. So I tried to make it as simple as possible.

It's a kind of a game we Americans play, I told him, sort of like charades and Candid Camera and a Rorschach test all mixed into one. You just take a big chunk of material reality, freeze it frame by frame, mix all the frames up, and then play

Patricia Williams's "Rules of the Game" is an expanded version of an article by the same title which first appeared in the *Village Voice* on 12 May 1992 and is reprinted here with the permission of the author and the *Village Voice*.

them backward, forward, upside down at randomly varying speeds, for a nice kaleidoscopic effect. When you start to feel a little dizzy, you bring in a team of players, called experts, who interpret the designs as creatively as they can, and then the jury has to pick the meaning that they like the best.

In Paris, I told R., he probably got only the videotape and the verdict; and with nothing more than that, it's sort of like trying to predict the winner of a baseball game without knowing the rules. So I ran through some of the base hits and home runs that preceded the verdict, some of the scoring that had mounted up in the defendants' favor that R. might have overlooked:

1) In the first place there was, as with any important gladiatorial event, a vital little piece of pregame entertainment called "choice of venue." It's like choosing a place for the Olympics. In it, all the courts in California had to compete to hear the trial, based on categories like racial diversity, how many people read the newspaper, what percentage of the population are retired police officers, and whether it's surrounded by a mountain range to protect against random acts of terrorism. In the category of racial diversity, the lowest score wins, and "white" is not included as a "race." Thus, while it's unusually hard to find a place anywhere in California that is not pretty mixed up, Simi Valley had a clear advantage with its population of only 1.5% people of color.

The category of newspaper reading is a kind of complicated surrogate for "being informed," and in jury trials that's scored as a bad thing. My friend kept insisting that anyone within a 9000-mile radius who wasn't too brain-dead to watch TV had seen the Rodney King tape, but I reminded him that this is a game and it has rules that have to be respected and, furthermore, that's why it's so important to find a community with lots of policemen in it and that's why Simi Valley won because, unlike Paris, it's full of race-neutralized people who love the law and understand its order, and besides, there's this really beautiful mountain range right nearby . . .

2) What R. also couldn't observe, not subscribing to Court TV like the rest of us, was how brilliantly the defense played that part of the game that is called "The Clarence Thomas Witch-Hunt/High-Tech-Lynching Memorials/Metaphors-of-Reversal Sweepstakes." Who could not but tingle with admiration as the police officers invoked the goddesses of soft restraint and even sensuality, in their description of the "application" of "departmentally approved" baton "power strikes" to the upside and downside of Rodney King's head. Or the employ of all those terms that turned Rodney King's body into a gun: what to those of us who saw only the plain old normal version looked like King's body helplessly flopping and twitching in response to a rain of blows, became in the freeze-framed version a "cocked" leg, an arm in "trigger position," a bullet of a body always aimed, poised, and about to fire itself into deadly action. What to

some of us looked like King's involuntary motor responses to the multitude of blows (Officer Powell alone struck him over 45 times) became, in the mouth of the defense, evidence of how "anesthetized" he was to pain, and not evidence "that he is going into compliance."

Frame by frame, the videotape was subtitled with the most extraordinary explanations: Sergeant Koon ordering his officers to hit King in the joints— elbows, knees, wrists—in order to get him to "submit" because there was no "nonverbal communication" that he was "ready to comply." Frame by frame, even when King was lying on his back with his arms raised in apparent surrender, the defense voice intoned that his legs were "still cocked," that he still had "access to his hands, access to his legs" and a "visual sight of where the officers" were. A few frames later, he was on his face, looked unconscious and utterly limp. "Now he is in more of a compliance mode." (Nevertheless, Officer Briseno stepped on King's neck while he was in this "compliance mode" because "the heel of King's right foot" began to lift again and Briseno feared that King's hand was headed for his waistband, so stepping on his neck was "perfectly reasonable." This is the same Officer Briseno who testified that, in contrast to these "reason- able" actions, the other officers continued on, after he had stopped, to beat King with a ferocity that made him think that *they* were "out of control." They were doing things, he said, that "didn't make any sense.")

Who could fail to be touched by the inventive whimsy of that police paramedic who described King, hog-tied and admittedly choking, as "belligerently spitting" blood. And let's not forget the general, all-purpose utility of those repeated descriptions of Rodney King as a bear, and of his groans as bearlike. Not only did it engage the hunter sensibility of all those good NRA folks on the jury, this image of a big vicious prey become more dangerous for the wounding, it also set up an innocence of metaphoric allusion, this thing with animals—"He wasn't an animal, was he?" demanded the prosecution in some annoyance; "No, Sir," replied the smooth Officer Powell. "He just acted like one." So when they got to that stuff about gorillas in the mist, it became cast as just another reference to big dark furry creatures. Gorillas as racist?! How annoyed the jury was with *that*. Accusations of racism became just as ridiculous as trying to make a case of bearism.

3) Finally, there was a way in which concepts of individualism and group, society and chaos, were played against one another. The frames of the videotape were played individually, like medieval tableaux, transcendently isolated moments, rather than as part of a motion called history, having a tempo or chronology that meant anything; the deflection by minutiae. The police officers were presented as a group that added up to a single entity, "the Los Angeles Police Department"—the department becoming so monolithic in its replacement of the individual defendants that no one could remember any of their names, and

so authoritative that even the three individual officers who testified *against* the defense became exiled, presumptively other than officers, departmentally ignorant, and unapproved. Rodney King, whose name everyone knew, became in an odd way, the symbolic if not the real defendant in the case, sort of the way that Willie Horton became the Democratic presidential candidate in the 1988 election. In the final argument, the defense parlayed Rodney King the individual into his symbolic groupness quite explicitly, as "the likes of Rodney King." (What is it you want, Officer Powell's defense attorney asked the jurors in his final argument, "as members of the community"? The police do not get paid, he went on to say, "to lose street fights" or "to roll around in the dirt with the likes of Rodney King.")

It is this move that also explains much of the juror—and popular—response to the immediately ensuing riots: "Even if we voted all of them guilty, this would have happened."[1] Despite the fact that only thirty-six percent of those arrested in the riots were African American, most Americans continue to assume that the riots were confined to the peevish discontents and childlike overreactions of African Americans, period. Despite the dramatic intervention of Amnesty International's findings of long-term, grossly excessive police violence directed against all citizens in Los Angeles, but most particularly the African-American community, much of the emerging media historicization has chosen to focus on King as a repeatedly belligerent drunk who deserved a good ass whipping, rather than on the appropriate limits of state force. Riotous chaos became not the result of the verdict, but a local condition preexisting the police encounter, in fact the cause of the beating. (They were just punishing him for Watts, you see, which in turn had been preceded some years before by a very unruly slave rebellion . . .) Thus, Rodney King became both the controlled agent of his own beating in particular and yet, in some more general sense, "indicative of a person who was out of control"[2] (in the words of a juror). King's supposed control was simultaneously reconciled as a subcategory of social chaos; the man turned into gorilla turned into Black power turned into something beyond the border of civil society turned into the chaotic controlling. As the defense's attorneys also argued, there's only a "thin blue line" between "society and chaos" (to say nothing of that thin black ribbon of highway between Simi Valley and South Central L.A.).

In summary, I told R., it is possible to see the King verdict as not merely rational, but as the magnificently artful product of an aesthetic of rationality—even to the extent it rationalized and upheld an order of socialized irrationality. By finding the officers innocent, and, in effect, Rodney King guilty, the jurors were honoring the noble efforts of the Los Angeles Police Department to continue its long and well-documented tradition of keeping at bay "the likes of Rodney King"—Rodney King, from this perspective in the Rorschach test, no less than

Martin Luther King the sane agent of social disorder, a monopolist of control, a thief in the temple of civilizing will; if he is confined, the game card reads, so will be any disorder in our lives. If on the other hand, King had been found not in control of the officers, then society—through the police—would have become the agent of its own degeneracy through its own unwillingness to see. The pervasive denial that allowed the officers to carry on as long as they did, or that allowed the jurors to conclude that King "did not seem to be hurt excessively"[3] despite all those broken bones, if revealed, would implicate the blinding normative power of a whole set of prejudices posing as "reasonable social expectations." It would challenge the presumptive unboundedness of "willed vision" as the central metaphor of what we call the order of things.

"I see," said R. "Now can you explain this little item in the newspaper about how some people are speculating that Daryl Gates may have a good chance at running for mayor in the next election?"[4]

"You read the newspaper?" I said patiently. "There you go breaking the rules again. Now the first thing you have to know about being a good voter in the game of politics is that having a sense of history is scored as a very bad thing . . ."

Notes

1. *International Herald Tribune*, 2–3 May 1992.

2. Ibid.

3. Ibid.

4. *New York Times*, 6 May 1991.

5

Reel Time/Real Justice

Kimberlé Crenshaw
and
Gary Peller

Like the Anita Hill/Clarence Thomas hearings a few months before, the Rodney King beating, the acquittal of the Los Angeles police officers who "restrained" him, and the subsequent civil unrest in L.A. flashed Race across the national consciousness, and the gaze of American culture momentarily froze there. Pieces of everyday racial dynamics seemed briefly clear, then faded from view, replaced by presidential politics and natural disasters.

In this essay, we want to examine in more depth what was exposed during the brief national focus on Rodney King. We take two main events, the acquittal of the police officers who beat King and the civil unrest in Los Angeles following the verdict, as starting points for an analysis of the ideological and symbolic intertwining of race and power in American culture. Along the way, we explicate the outlines of a "Critical Race Theory" focused not solely on the Rodney King "incident," but more broadly on a consideration of how racial power generally is produced, mediated, and legitimated, an approach that seeks to connect developments in diverse arenas in which race and power are contested.

As we see it, there is a deep connection between the various ideological conflicts that become apparent in the way the Rodney King events played in national consciousness. The techniques utilized to convince the Simi Valley jury of the

---

"Reel Time/Real Justice" is a condensed version of a piece forthcoming in the *Denver Law Journal*.

"reasonableness" of the use of force on Rodney King are linked to the struggle, in a quite different legal arena, over whether to permit race-conscious, affirmative-action programs, and both those arenas are in turn related to the conflict over whether to see the events in South Central L.A. as an "insurrection," as Representative Maxine Waters characterized it, or as a "riot" of the "mob," the official version presented in dominant media and by the president of the United States. At stake at each axis of conflict is a contest over which, and whose, narrative structure will prevail in the interpretation of events in the social world. And exposed at each conflict is the inability of concepts like "the rule of law," or "reason," or even the technology of video, to mediate these conflicts in a neutral, aracial way.

We believe that the realm of interpretation, ideology, and narrative is a critical site in the production of American racial domination. The Rodney King episode is particularly challenging for our approach because it seems so easily assimilable to more conventional models of the way that power works. Rather than imagine racial power being produced in the soft space of ideological "superstructure," the world saw it exercised at another point of production—at the material "base" where the nightstick met the skull. And unlike 1980s and 1990s racial controversies over affirmative action, ethnocentrism, and multiculturalism, the King beating bore the familiar markings of the 1950s and 1960s—rather than being encased carefully in definitions of merit and neutrality, old-time white supremacy was boldly and crudely inscribed on the body of King. You don't need any fancy theory to figure out what went on between the L.A. police and Rodney King. That's true. But the Rodney King events are also particularly illuminating for an approach that focuses on the ideological, because part of what was revealed in the Rodney King saga was the need for an account of how racial power continues to work, blatantly in the King case, decades after it has been outlawed as a matter of formal decree, cultural convention, and elite preference.

To get a picture of how various structures of interpretation played out after the verdict, first remember the reaction in most sectors of American culture when the famous videotape of L.A. police officers beating King was initially broadcast on network television. There was a broad national outrage shared by African Americans and most whites and minorities, with the only fairly visible exception being the fringe (but becoming stronger) white protofascists of the Patrick Buchanan/David Duke camps. This was an easy event for the entire mainstream of American culture to abhor; it didn't present any of the "hard questions" of the 1990s' controversies over race—like the "dilemma" of affirmative action, say. And the videotape lent objectivity to the charge of police brutality—there was no question of interpretation and subjective bias clouding the issue.

This wide consensus was actually based on the congruence of various ideological positions around the "proof" of the videotape, as became apparent in the verdict's aftermath. But for most people, including most political conservatives, there was no difficulty "seeing" what the tape represented: old-style, garden-variety racist power exemplified by the Bull Connor/Pretorialike images of heavily armed white security officers beating a defenseless Black man senseless. Part of the progress that African Americans have made in terms of the achievement of formal legal equality and its cultural analogs was manifest in the circumstance that, unlike the 1950s and 1960s, there was no voice anywhere near the mainstream of American life saying that this kind of police practice was legitimate. In the 1990s, the moderate white Right also defines itself in terms of the repudiation of the backward doctrines of white supremacy. The breadth of the wide social consensus over the King videotape was rooted in the sense that how one understood what happened to Rodney King was not linked to how one understood the "murkier" issues of contemporary racial conflict; in political terms, the King videotape gave the moderate Right the opportunity to oppose clear-cut racism and thus to demonstrate that its opposition to affirmative action, say, is not linked to interests in racial supremacy.

But this broad consensus was misleading to the extent it made it appear that the video meant the same thing to everyone; subsequent events would reveal the deep cleavages in how the tape was understood. In our view, the differentiation that underlay the consensus around the King tape—between "old" ideologies of racial supremacy and contemporary "dilemmas" of race—was too quick, and obscured the ways that, in fact, the acquittal of the L.A. police officers of using excessive force was intertwined with narrative structures that prevail in debates about "affirmative action." Part of understanding the failure of the formal legal equality achieved by African Americans to protect Rodney King means understanding how formal prohibitions like those against police brutality and against racial discrimination are necessarily always mediated through narrative structures, of which the Simi Valley jury's verdict is a particularly striking example but not different in kind from the more rarified ideologies of Supreme Court justices— that is, from the racial ideologies of the "moderates." When the cultural consensus over the meaning of the videotape blew apart in the violence of South Central L.A., the limits of formal legal equality also became apparent.

It is useful to pause here to consider how the initial, widespread, "common-sense" consensus about what the King video showed was confronted by the defense attorneys in the courtroom. They had frame-by-frame stills made of the video, which were mounted on clean white illustration board, and then used as the basis for questions to "experts" on prisoner restraint. Each micromoment of the beating of King was broken down into a series of frozen images. As to each one, the experts were asked whether it was clear that King had assumed a compliant posture, or might a police officer have reasonably concluded that he still was a threat to resist. Once the video was broken up like this, each still picture could then be reweaved into a different narrative about the restraint of King, one in which each blow to King represented, not beating one of the "gorillas in the mist," but a police-approved technique of restraint complete with technical names for each baton strike (or "stroke"). The videotape images were *physically* mediated by the illustration board upon which the still pictures were mounted, and in the same moment of *disaggregation*, they were *symbolically* mediated by the new narrative backdrops of the technical discourse of institutional security and the reframing of King as a threat rather than a victim.

The eighty-one-second video was, in short, broken into scores of individual still pictures, each of which was then subject to endless reinterpretation. Then, since no single picture taken by itself could constitute excessive force, taken together, the video tape as a whole said something different—not incredibly clear evidence of racist police brutality, but instead ambiguous slices of time in a tense moment that Rodney King had created for the police.

There are many "explanations" for the King verdict. Most center around the image of jury lawlessness—the idea that what the jury did was in a way corrupt, because they ignored the clear evidence of brutality to acquit the police. They didn't follow the rules. Along these lines, there are some who claim to have expected the verdict, because you just can't get justice out of the "system" controlled by "them." Others have located the pivotal turning point at the granting of the defense motion for a change of venue, resulting in the case being tried in an area dominated by law-and-order white conservatives, and, ironically, an area disproportionately the home of LAPD officers and retirees. Another view places responsibility on an inept (or worse) prosecution that failed to humanize Rodney King to counter the defense continually objectifying him.

There is some truth in each of these explanations. The problem we see, however, is that they either differentiate the King verdict too sharply from the other sites for the production and exercise of American racial power—that is, suggesting that, but for these "quirks" of the case and the irrationality of the jurors, the legal system would respond to an event like the beating of Rodney King—or, at the opposite pole, they too quickly make the particular way that the King judgment was reached subordinate to an overly instrumental view of the way that law and other mediating ideologies serve power.

In our view, law, in general, and the courtroom, in particular, are arenas where narratives are contested, and the power of interpretation exercised. In that sense, the legal realm is a political realm. But it would be a mistake to see narratives simply as some after-the-fact story about events concocted after the *real* power has already been exercised; the story lines developed in law "mediate" power in the sense that they both "translate" power as nonpower (the beating of King becomes the "reasonable exercise of force necessary to restrain a prisoner"); and they also *constitute* power, in the sense that the narrative lines shape what and how events are perceived in the first place. Understanding these relationships between law, power, and ideology is necessary to comprehending that, in many ways, the King verdict was *typical*, not extraordinary.

To develop this idea, it is helpful to turn from the King verdict to a very different legal arena, the issuance of Supreme Court opinions. Our point here is to draw connections between the narrative structure presented by the defense attorneys in the police-brutality trial—breaking the videotape up into scores of single, still images—and the narrative structure utilized in the more academic and "rational" atmosphere of the Supreme Court.

We will discuss in brief outline the case of *Richmond vs. Croson*,[1] where a Supreme Court majority struck down as unconstitutional Richmond, Virginia's municipal policy of awarding construction contracts on a race-conscious, affirmative-action basis. Under Richmond's program, prime contractors were required to "set aside" 30 percent of their work to be performed by minority subcontractors. As matter of legal doctrine, *Croson* is an important refinement of the meaning of "equal protection" in the Fourteenth Amendment; it is the first case in which a majority of the Court applied "strict scrutiny" (meaning stringent requirements of a policy's importance and fit), the traditional test for "malign" racial classifications that burden Blacks, to a "benign" affirmative-action plan burdening whites. The symbolic message of this doctrinal development is that the problem of racism is a symmetrical one—both Blacks and whites can suffer when racial classifications are utilized, and therefore the same level of scrutiny is warranted whether a racial classification benefits Blacks or whites. From this vantage point, racism consists of the failure to treat people on an individual basis according to terms that are neutral to race. In the Richmond context, this embrace of "color blindness" as the norm of equal protection meant that the Court could plausibly equate the legal significance of the City of Richmond benefiting white contractors through the contracting system (say, by excluding Blacks) with the legal consequences of a decision to benefit Black contractors (by requiring set-asides).[2]

In this doctrinal setting, the legal issue in *Croson* was whether the Richmond affirmative-action policy was constitutional—could it survive "strict scrutiny"?—as a policy serving the compelling aim of remedying past discrimination against Blacks. According to the Court such an aim was in fact compelling, but only as the remedy for "particular" discrimination, lest the "remedy" constitute a new instance of racial discrimination. The problem in *Croson* was that there had been no "proof" that there had been significant racial discrimination in the Richmond construction industry that needed remedying.

The analog to the videotape of Rodney King's beating that failed to ''prove'' unreasonable and excessive force was the familiar picture of Black economic exclusion suggested by the formal record before the Supreme Court in *Croson*. The record included: Congressional findings that there had been massive discrimination in the construction industry across the country; the 50 percent Black population of Richmond; the fact that .67 percent of the city's prime contracting dollars went to minority-owned businesses; and the testimony of the mayor, the city manager, and two councilmen as to the long and thorough history of racial discrimination that the City of Richmond had officially sanctioned and practiced in education, voting, and housing.

Like the Simi Valley jury, the Supreme Court was confronted with a picture— the near-total dominance of white firms in the contracting business of Richmond, Virginia, in the one case, the videotape in the other—and asked to determine if illegitimate power had been exercised. And like the attorneys for the L.A. police officers, the Court utilized the process of *disaggregation* to conclude that racial discrimination was not proven to be the cause of the huge disparity between the racial composition of Richmond's population and the racial composition of recipients of prime construction contracts.[3] Just as the defense attorneys directed the jury's consideration from the reel time of the video to the disaggregated stills of the L.A. police and Rodney King, the Court freeze-framed each element of the Richmond setting and isolated it from its meaning-giving context—the history of racial subordination in Richmond, Virginia, the former capital of the Confederacy and one of the central sites of ''massive resistance'' to desegregation orders in the 1960s. The Court's opinion considered each piece of evidence individually, determining that, by itself, each wasn't sufficient to conclude that there had been discrimination, and therefore ruling that there was no ''proof'' that the Richmond construction industry had been the site of racial discrimination that could now be remedied legally by affirmative-action set-asides.

Once the Court disaggregated each factor from its context in the full picture of the racial history of Richmond, it was still left with the glaring statistical evidence that Blacks had been shut out of the construction contracting business. And, as with the L.A. policemen's defense at trial, once meaning was divorced from context, it was possible to weave the disaggregated images together with new, alternative narratives. In the Rodney King brutality case, the stills were reconnected through a story of King's power and agency—his body could become ''cocked'' and could appear ''in a trigger position.'' In the *Croson* affirmative-action case, a new narrative was also created, one which implicitly explained the lack of minority contractors in terms of the (lack of) skill, initiative, and choice of Blacks—rather than the exclusionary power exercised by whites.

Part of the great appeal of what we have been calling ''formal legal equality''— the blanket legal prohibitions against racial discrimination that were achieved in the 1960s—is the belief that the identification of the grossest forms of racial discrimination is straightforward and objective. Rather than leave protection to the whim of politics or the discretion of power, the imagery of the "rule of law" suggests that the prohibition against racial discrimination is clear and determinate. It doesn't depend on "subjective" evaluation. And from this frame, what's so enraging about the King verdict is that it seems to show that even such clear, objective prohibitions can be subverted by racial power, like that embodied in the Simi Valley jury.

Our first point in drawing out the structural similarities in the ways that narratives were constructed in the Rodney King trial and the Supreme Court's *Croson* opinion is to question this kind of thinking about the protections of formal equality. In other words, we are not saying that the Supreme Court is like the Rodney King jury in the sense that they, too, are acting lawlessly or corruptly by violating some objectively identifiable "reality" about race in America, or in Richmond. Rather, our point is to examine critically how ideological narratives work as a form of social power, to show how a belief in formal legal equality, in the objectivity of "the rule of law," can help obscure the everyday character of racial power.

As we see it, an important image underlying the initial consensus in American culture about the videotape and ultimate acquittal of the L.A. police officers who beat Rodney King was that the videotape exemplified an old-style mode of racial domination that, today, virtually the entire American culture opposes. The videotape reverberated with the skeletons of American apartheid. And on issues of "basic civil rights," a wide spectrum has embraced the morality of 1960s race reforms ensuring formal equality "regardless" of race. On the other hand, the "disagreements" over affirmative action, or multiculturalism, seem less clearly focused, less objective, and more political.

But this way of perceiving these two arenas of race is, to our minds, already a product of a particular narrative, a particular way of articulating the meaning of race within which the granting of legal rights to formal equality—to being treated the same as everyone else regardless of race—is taken as an intrinsically meaningful and comprehensible goal separate from the "murkiness" that's supposed to be involved in the morally "tougher" 1990s issues of race. The prohibition of explicit racial discrimination is seen as a formally realizable goal, in the sense that it can be applied without any more elaboration of controversial value choices. That's how come we can be so sure the Simi Valley jury acted "lawlessly," or "fraudulently," in a way that seems at first so different from the careful, reasoned, philosophical arguments of Supreme Court opinions. There appears to be a qualitative difference between what the Simi Valley jury did and what the Supreme Court does. In the cultural imagination, it's like the difference between rednecks and the gentry.

As we have suggested, this contrast between arenas of racial controversy is ideologically constructed: from another perspective, that of "narrative" and "disaggregation," the sharp difference between issues of "formal equality" as opposed to "special treatment" fades as the identification of each is seen to depend, ultimately, on which pictures of the world are believed, and which are disbelieved. The sharp distinction usually drawn between formal equality and affirmative action suggests that formal equality can be achieved outside the realm of power and interpretation because it can be identified objectively by law. But to us, what the King verdict represents is not the corrupt subversion of the values of the rule of law, but rather the ideological power of belief in the rule of law itself.

Through the description of "disaggregation," we have tried to describe features of what we see as the dominant form of contemporary race ideology, linking the Simi Valley jury's acquittal of the police with the race narratives of moderate, mainstream legal culture. Through the typical process of "disaggregation," a narrative is created within which racial power has been "mediated" out, like the anesthetic effect of mounting stills on clinically white illustration board. In both the Simi Valley police-brutality trial and the *Croson* case, a narrative mediates the representation of the world by divorcing the effects of racial power—the number of Black contractors in Richmond, the curled body of Rodney King—from their social context and from their historic meaning. In the compulsive legal search for the clearly defined, objectively verifiable, perpetrating act of illegitimate power— the single, particular offending blow in the frame-by-frame representation of King and the L.A. police; the particular acts of discrimination that directly caused white economic hegemony in Richmond, Virginia—social events are decontextualized in both *space*—where things happened, and between whom—and *time*—what larger forces operated to give events their meaning.

Hence the symmetry of the idea of "racism" in mainstream American culture: once race is divorced from its social meaning in schools, workplaces, streets, homes, prisons, and paychecks and from its historic meaning in terms of the repeated American embrace of white privilege, then all that's left, really, is a hollow, analytic norm of "color-blind"—an image of racial power as embodied in abstract classifications by race that could run either way, against whites as easily as against Blacks. And finally, this kind of disaggregation also, oddly, seems like the very definition of what's neutral and objective, a narrative that doesn't depend on point of view, a tape of the social world with the images so enlarged and slowed down that it could say anything.

Rather than see the jury acquittal as an aberration by some low-down, Simi Valley redneck consciousness, consider it the reigning ideological paradigm of how to identify illegitimate racial power, vivid precisely because of the extremity of the conclusion that only "reasonable force" had been used on Rodney King.

The virtue of formal equality is that there is something important in the fact that power wielders can no longer justify conditions in the social world based on the supposed natural inferiority of Blacks. But the problem of formal equality is that it is appealing precisely because it seems to be able to do what it cannot do— resolve issues of social power, racial power, once and for all, according to some neutral and objective rules.

Our point here is that Rodney King did, in a sense, get the fruits of formal equality. But the terms that embody the guarantee of the rule of law—terms like "reasonable force" or "equal protection"—are necessarily indeterminate. Their meaning must be socially constructed—through narratives of place and time— for there to be any meaning to them at all. What the Simi Valley jury did is not so different from what the Supreme Court does. In neither realm is the rule of law being subverted; the "law" and the "facts" of the social world do not exist in any objective, ready-made form. They must always be interpreted according to politics, ideology, and power.

The belief in what we've called formal equality resulted in one particularly intense set of reactions to the verdict—the extreme disillusionment felt by many (particularly integrationist-oriented) Blacks who had invested more than symbolic meaning in the guarantees of objectivity presented by law, in particular, and the wider cultural rhetoric, in general. Like the white cultural mainstream, many Blacks believed that the baton against the Rodney King's skull would speak for itself, just as many have believed that principles of color blindness and other varieties of formal equality provide a clear, almost self-generating protection against racial discrimination. What many people did not comprehend was that police brutality, just like discrimination, does not speak for itself. This very struggle over meaning is precisely what the intense contestations about race in the law are really about. Rather than providing some kind of firm ground to challenge racist institutional practices, notions of formal equality, objectivity, neutrality, and the like tend to obscure the way that race is experienced by the vast majority of African Americans in this society.

We have described "disaggregation" as a narrative technique that narrows the perception of the range of illegitimate racial power by divorcing particular episodes from their larger social context. We have relied implicitly on a contrast between this kind of "distortion" and "real" time, considering things as they "are" rather than freeze-framing space and time into isolated stills that can be reinterpreted through a benign narrative of justification. The part of our argument that seeks to identify "disaggregation" as part of a conservative ideology is made easier by the image we all share of Rodney King being beaten, and the confident sense we have that we see the *meaning* of the videotape. It is by implicit reference to this "real" time that the disaggregation technique looks like a distortion.

Here we want to question the "real" time we have to this point assumed, and consider the implications of thinking that we can identify the corruption of the Simi Valley jury by contrasting its verdict with the reality depicted on the videotape. Consider the possibility that even the videotape itself has no special, objective status—what we progressives "see" in the images is the product of mediating narratives in much the same way as what the Simi Valley jury "saw" depended on the technique of disaggregation that we have been discussing.

People invested very different meanings in the Rodney King videotape. For many, the existence of the videotape was a source of excitement that technology was finally utilized in service of the masses, so that "they" (the authorities) couldn't say that people were just making up charges of police brutality. The underlying assumption for a lot of people was that such conduct is a more or less regular feature of many police encounters with Blacks, particularly in L.A. The underlying frustration has been over not being able to put a stop to these practices through the creation of formal legal prohibitions because of the inability to "prove" what happened. When the tape was first broadcast, in addition to the pain of seeing such brutality, there was also exhilaration that the videotape would solve the problem of proof so that the police would finally be disciplined. Simply put, the significance of the video was not that it proved to masses of Blacks and others that the L.A. police are brutally racist, but rather that it was projected as what would satisfy "the law" that brutality against Blacks occurred.

But also within the initial national outrage at the King videotape were many who saw the brutality depicted in the videotape as awful but exceptional, as part of another era which reared its ugly head only occasionally and happened to be caught on videotape. The videotape "proved" brutality, but the brutality and the fortuity that it recorded were experienced as popping out of the same random, chaotic sea.

In short, a gulf of incomprehension existed underneath the broad American consensus that the videotape depicted outrageous police behavior. For some, the existence of the videotape was critical to comprehending that this kind of racist brutality "still" occurs in American society, because the videotape presented "objective" proof. In other words, without the tape, they would have had no outrage, indeed no consciousness, of the conditions of police-and-community relations in L.A. For others, the videotape didn't serve to *establish* this kind of police behavior, but rather simply to document it and thus satisfy the powers that be.

There is a deep, ideological connection between the kind of need for, and embrace of, "objective" proof and the more general ways that race is understood in American culture. The special status that was accorded the King videotape as objective proof was, we believe, a social construct, just as the particular interpretation of the tape embraced by the Simi Valley jury was constructed. *Both* the perception of the tape as showing a "reasonable exercise of force" *and* the perception of the tape as showing "racist brutality" depend, not simply on the physiology of visual perception, but rather on *interpretation*, on the mediation of perception with background narratives that give visual images meaning.

Valorizing the so-called "objective proof" of the videotape is problematic, because, to the extent that the videotape was understood to "prove" the racist brutality of the LAPD, such a conclusion implicitly rested on the idea that, but for the tape, no "objective" proof was available. Yet an important piece of the background context to the Rodney King events was that there has always been available the witness and testimony of hundreds of thousands of victims of police brutality who can attest to the practices of the L.A. police, as well as those of many other departments. Typically, such victims are arrested for "disorderly conduct" after they have been beaten, and so deep is the street-level understanding of the uselessness of the processes of the "rule of law" that, in the overwhelming run of cases, no complaint is ever made. The emphasis on the objective proof of the videotape, in short, marginalizes as merely subjective all those whose reality is devalued because there was no tape, only their word and the community's long-standing experience of the LAPD.

Underlying the elevation of the videotape as objective proof of the racist brutality of the LAPD is a hierarchy of evidence and meaning, a hierarchy that distinguishes between objective proof and subjective assertion, fact and opinion, disinterest and bias. These categories are neither natural nor independent criteria with which to evaluate various narratives about the world; they, themselves, form the vocabulary for a particular narrative, one that assumes the possibility of a vantage point of "objectivity" that could exist outside of any particular vision or interpretation, a vantage point that is seductive because it seems to transcend the partialities of history and geography, of time and space. But the images of objectivity and impersonality, like the allied distinctions between fact and opinion, between color blindness and discrimination—and between law and politics—are, in our social context, the terms of a particular discourse of power, here the power that's manifest in the inability of Black people in L.A. to get redress when the police beat them unless they have what will satisfy others as "proof."

To see how the hierarchies of objectivity and subjectivity work as a discourse of power to marginalize the victims of these racist police practices, consider that it is not the videotape, the disinterestedness of technology, that makes us "see" what happened to Rodney King. The videotape images of the L.A. police officers and Rodney King do not mean what they mean for us as a matter of objectivity, but rather as a matter of social construction. We must, necessarily, weave narratives into the images to give them a life in some time and space. Just as the legal concepts of formal equality are indeterminate and only acquire meaning in a social struggle over describing the world, as the *Croson* case reveals, so the video images are clear to us because we bring our own narratives to them, and we see in them the images of Bull Connor and Soweto and various episodes of the long story of racial apartheid being brutally enforced, images and narrative lines that we carry around in our collective memory. In this sense, our judgment, like that of the Simi Valley jury and the Supreme Court in *Croson*, is mediated by background narratives that tie together what otherwise would be a random set of images.

These different images underlying people's first impressions of the King videotape help make sense of the various reactions to the verdict. Of course, the sharpest contrast was between those who responded to the verdict by taking to the streets in Pico and South Central and, at the opposite pole, the police-department personnel who cheered the news. But most across the spectrum of mainstream culture who deplored the "rioting" didn't do so because they agreed with the verdict or with the cheering police. To the contrary, for the most part, they sought to preserve the very value that they thought the Simi Valley jury had impugned—the value of the rule of law. The dominant public discourse of the "L.A. riots" quickly became articulated as an opposition between those urging restraint and advocating respect for the "rule of law" and those articulating an alternative first principle of "no justice, no peace." The contrast between the rhetoric of "rule of law" and "no justice, no peace" was soon translated by the dominant culture into a contest between an objective, reasoned, responsible reaction and an emotional, passionate, irresponsible one. These strands of narrative culminated in the symbolic conflict between whether the people out in the streets should be seen as a "mob" "rioting" or as part of an "insurrection."

It didn't seem ironic that many people who deplored the Simi Valley verdict also deplored the "rioting." In fact, from within the discourse of objectivity and respect for "the rule of law," it seemed obvious that there was a deep link between the jurors who acquitted the police who "restrained" Rodney King and the rioters on the street. In the dominant cultural narrative, both embodied a form of irrationality, of emotion-driven distortion. In the case of the jurors, their irrationality with respect to the videotape was seen in terms of white racism and fear of Black crime. And the people on the streets looked simply like a chaotic, emotional reaction, one without "reason," in the burning of neighborhoods, stores, and the like.

The language of an "insurrection" that Rep. Maxine Waters and others employed suggests, however, a counternarrative, one which implicitly rejects the various rhetorical clusters that came to define the way that the Rodney King events were incorporated into mainstream discourse—including the reference points of objectivity, rationality, colorblindness, and legalism. The narrative of insurrection suggests a competing view of the whole Rodney King episode.

Rather than view the beating of King as an aberration from a legal norm of the "reasonable" use of force, the insurrection narrative implies a focus on the power relations and dynamics that exist between the "rioters" and the police. While the image of the "riot" suggests a kind of instantaneous, emotional reaction to the verdict, the image of an insurrection directs attention from the "shock" of the verdict to the day-to-day subordination of the L.A. African-American community. Rather than see the beating of King as an outrageous deviation from the norm of police objectivity, the image of community subordination comprehends a systematic set of social dynamics—including a geographic context in which a largely Anglo police force with enforcement responsibility for the sprawling metropolis of L.A. speeds through Black neighborhoods in fortified, heavily armed cruisers dispatched from some remote location, and a historical context in which police brutality toward Blacks has been common and repeatedly the subject of investigation, expert commission report, and inaction. In contrast to the image of the uprising as an explosive reaction to a disappointing verdict, the language of insurrection conceives of the uprising as a communal response to a much larger set of issues of social power.

The image of insurrection, in short, is part of a narrative that sees the relations of police and Blacks in L.A., not as the disaggregated diad of state official and private citizen, mediated by neutral legal norms of reasonableness and nondiscrimination, but instead in terms of the power-laden relationship of communities defined by race, within which whites, through the police, exercise a kind of occupying power, and within which Black neighborhoods appear as something like colonies. In these terms, an "insurrection" is not the blindly irrational acts of "rioters" (who, in the dominant narrative, should be expected to protest peacefully), but the concerted action of a community determined to raise the cost of peace to the colonizers, and thereby to increase its leverage on the continuing power relations.

Following the widespread urban unrest of the 1960s the Kerner Commission concluded that the "riots" expressed an angry frustration with the slow pace of racial integration.[4] To reach that conclusion, the Commission had to misinterpret the Black Nationalist rhetoric of many rioters themselves, and impose an integrationist view of racial justice. The dominant reaction to the recent disorder in L.A. evidences the same ideological framing of the issue. But like the disciples of Malcolm X in the 1960s, the narrative of insurrection challenges the vision of race and racial power implicit in the conventional idea that racial justice means the end of "discrimination" and the achievement of formal equality and integration into the dominant community. Instead, the imagery of occupation and sub-

ordination points to a wholly different comprehension of race relations, one which
looks to the power relations between historically defined racial communities,
rather than away from race and toward colorblindness. And accordingly, rather
than see justice in terms of achieving police colorblindness, a race-conscious focus
on power between communities focuses attention on the legitimacy of the dominant community administering the "colony" in the first place. Most who
deplored the L.A. riots assumed a Vegalist model of racial justice in which the
norms of objectivity and neutrality are central to the achievement of racial integration. From within that kind of ideology, there is simply no place for ideas like
community control over police, education, and other public services, because the
Black community, say, is no longer even perceived—there are just people who
"happen to be Black."

Rejecting the proposed "grounds" for determining the "real" in "objective"
and "impartial" fashion, we believe that relations between communities cannot
be mediated in a neutral fashion through the recognition of formal legal rights.
Accordingly, the problem in the Simi Valley verdict acquitting the L.A. police
was not that it deviated corruptly from some objective norm of legality or objectivity; instead, those "norms" themselves constitute a narrative, an ideology for
understanding race that excludes from vision the political and power-laden terms
of race relations.

But believing that issues—like the meaning of the Rodney King videotape or
the racial composition of Richmond's construction contractors—are necessarily
and always subject to interpretation rather than "objective" proof does not mean
that we are any less outraged by the verdict. The identification and enforcement
of legal rights require acts of meaning attribution, of narration. So does comprehending the "meaning" of a videotape. But that doesn't mean that everything is
therefore relative, that anything goes since it's all power anyway. To the contrary,
once the narratives became so disparate between a community and the police, or
the legal system, it seems to us that it is time to recognize that, in a deep sense,
Blacks in L.A. live in a different world from whites, in something like a different
nation. They and the police are like foreigners to each other. And understanding
this distance means comprehending relations, not according to norms of universal
equality and equal treatment, but as the rule of one community over another.

From this counternarrative, what is needed is not color blindness on the part
of the police force, but the redistribution of power so that the police force is not
an outside occupier, but rather a part of the community itself, subject to regulation by the Black community in L.A. The community doesn't need formal
equality from the police, but actual control *over* the police—as well as other
public institutions.

Notes

1. 488 U.S. 469 (1989).

2. The critique of this general norm of colorblindness has been one of the central projects of "Critical Race Theory" scholars, a group of writers informally organized in 1989 to pursue progressive-oriented studies of race, culture, and law. For a description of the group's aims, see Kimberle Crenshaw, "A Black Feminist Critique of Antidiscrimination Law and Politics," *The Politics of Law*, ed. David Kairys (New York: Pantheon, 1990), 195. For citations to the group's work to date, see Richard Delgado and Jean Stenfancic, "Critical Race Theory: An Annotated Bibliography." *Virginia Law Review* 78 (forthcoming, 1992). For examples of criticisms of color blindness from within the critical race theory genre, see Neil Gotanda, "A Critique of 'Our Constitution Is Color-Blind,' " *Stanford Law Review* 44 (1991): 1; Gary Peller, "Race Consciousness," *Duke Law Review* (1990): 758; Patricia Williams, "The Obliging Shell: An Informal Essay on Formal Legal Equality," *Michigan Law Review* 87 (1989): 2128.

3. We borrow the term "disaggregation" from Justice Marshall's dissent in *Croson*. See 488 U.S. at 542 (Marshall, J dissenting): "[T]he majority's critique [of the evidence of racial exclusion] shows an unwillingness to come to grips with why construction-contracting in Richmond is essentially a whites-only enterprise. The majority . . . takes the disingenuous approach of disaggreggating Richmond's local evidence, attacking it piecemeal, and thereby concluding that no single piece of evidence adduced by the city, 'standing alone,' . . . suffices to prove past discrimination. But items of evidence do not, of course, 'stand alone,' or exist in alien juxtaposition. . . ." For a more extended discussion of the manner in which the Court disaggregated causal factors in *Croson*, see Michel Rosenfeld, "Decoding Richmond: Affirmative Action and the Elusive Meaning of Constitutional Equality," *Michigan Law Review* 87 (1989) 1729, 1761–66.

4. See *Report of the National Advisory Commission on Civil Disorders* (New York: Bantam, 1968), 205–38.

Part Three

Assaulting America: A Political Economy Begets Ruin

6

Race, Capitalism, and the Antidemocracy

Cedric J. Robinson

The fear was of a Mandingo sexual encounter.
— Sergeant Stacey Koon

I don't want to see any white people today.
— Herman Collins

In the third year of the reign of King George of Avarice, under the authority of law, a high-tech Los Angeles police mob formed, and with due deliberation, secure in its corporate habits of mind and the perverse soul of the civilization which nurtured it, began the pavement lynching of Rodney King. Preserved at the height of its frenzy by an amateur video-camera operator, the naked images of ''law enforcement'' applying its civilizing discipline to King appeared seductively familiar to the American audience. Indeed, the images of this one brutal moment kaleidescoped backward and forward. The scenes from this unmistakably real cop show cascaded backward to the recent and not-so-distant past as an inadvertent mimicry of the info-tech war in the Persian Gulf and prior instances of Pax Americana. And then ahead, with the less reflexive realization that this repulsive vision of muscular hatred served as well as an anticipation of an inevitable montage of public performances to be orchestrated by the powerful in America.

Among the familiar narrative oppositions, the signature of recent American military history could be discerned almost intuitively in the stark disparity in the techniques of violence, the dissimilarity of numbers, the persistence of the attack, and the presumption of moral authority which obtained between Rodney King and the uniformed predators. The videotape of the beating of King microcosmically rehearsed in specular form and ideology the political character of what Andy

Rooney dubbed "the best war in modern history":[1] the "Desert Slaughter" of the Iraqi masses which the leaders of the most powerful Western/Christian/civilized nation had initiated and choreographed only a few months earlier. And in the original and its copy, in the fevered imagination of the dominant, the horror descending upon the inferior was deserved, the warrant for the act issued by natural law. White-American might was its own raison d'être.

The political rulers and their factoti, self-narcotized by such power and habituated by its display—in Grenada, Lebanon, El Salvador, Nicaragua, the Persian Gulf, Panama, Iraq, and the streets and courts of every American city—demonstrated their conceit and their simultaneous forfeiture of a more authentic legitimacy. Now, more than at any time in American history, societal consent had dissipated, plunging authority into that domain which the French philosopher Merleau-Ponty nominated as "contempt's radical challenge." For the increasing millions of poor and alienated the official distractions of foreign and domestic wars, the pious litanies evoking national security, the scourges of drugs and crime were wearing thin. The state was becoming a transparent instrument of partisan rule, an exposed entrenchment of the privileged. In some anguish, William Greider has proclaimed: "The decayed condition of American democracy is difficult to grasp, not because the facts are secret, but because the facts are visible everywhere."[2]

A few months following the first airing of the King tape, the congressional replica of this recurring audition of oblivious power again seized the national attention in an exhibition staged in a similarly public forum. The Senate Judiciary Committee provided the forum for the defamation of Anita Hill, the Black law professor. Unlike Rodney King, Ms. Hill had been a loyal subject to the reactionary powers that be, a willing participant in the disestablishment of institutions representing liberal democratic values and antiracism (the Department of Education and the Equal Employment Opportunity Commission). As a Black woman in this male legislative locker room, however, she could claim no certain membership. When her professional calling caused her to balk (at first, hesitantly) at the Bush administration's counterfeiting of the Supreme Court by the cynical nomination of Clarence Thomas, she too was debased to King's disinherited status. By a conspiracy of the White House, the Justice Department, and the Senate, Ms. Hill was transformed from an admirable functionary into a political pariah with a flawed memory and an inclination toward sexual fantasies. For three memorable days, the innuendos and character assassinations bombarded the air with the same regularity with which the batons had filled the space above King's prone figure and the phosphorous munitions had rained on Baghdad. When the curtain fell, however, it was not Anita Hill but the powerful who stood in the searchlight of public humiliation.

But as it had for more than a decade, the unrelenting assault against the liberal social contract persisted. From 1980 to 1989, while Ronald Reagan occupied the White House, under the authority of law a multi–trillion dollar national debt was accumulated while billions were cut from social security, unemployment insurance, food stamps, housing assistance, aid for families with dependent children, employment training, nutrition programs for poor children, low-income energy assistance, vocational education, the job corps, and compensatory education for the disadvantaged.[3] Trumpeted by a mass media, itself progressively monopolized by corporate capital, the message of limited government masked an economic revolution in the interests of the most wealthy.[4] Obliterating the historical consciousness that the antitrust legislation of the late nineteenth century, the New Deal programs of the mid-1930s, and the Civil Rights acts of the 1960s had been necessitated by the voracious excesses of capitalism and racism, the reactionaries contained their public recitations to pseudocivic oppositions to big government, judicial activism, social engineering and reverse discrimination (i.e., affirmative action).

In the last months of the Reagan administration, the yield from the debauchery of an unfettered capitalism and political and bureaucratic corruption surfaced with a vengeance: The junk bonds, corporate mergers, and financial mismanagement facilitated by deregulation occasioned the multi–billion dollar Savings and Loan crisis. The unprecedented growth of war production and the anarchy of capitalist development submerged the economy into a depression and massive unemployment. Political and financial scandals stretched from the federal bureaucracy to Wall Street.[5] These were merely the overt concomitants to the achievement of an astounding transfer and concentration of wealth. Between 1977 and 1989, according to the Congressional Budget Office, the wealthiest 1% of American families amassed 60% of the growth in after-tax income while the poorest 40% of families experienced actual income declines (the "superpoor," the bottom 20% of families, suffered a 9% income loss). In the same span of time, chief-executive salaries rose from 35 to 120 times the average worker's pay, and the number of (primarily corporate) lawyers doubled to 740,000. These trends in the concentration of wealth at the top, documented by economic historians as having begun in the 1960s, accelerated in the 1980s. And they mirrored the national income disparities which had marked the late 1800s and early 1900s, a trend halted only by the Great Depression.[6] And for a final indignity, the nation became riveted in 1987 by the revelation of the existence of a secret and unconstitutional government whose activities determined foreign policy in the Middle East and Central America. Headquartered in the Central Intelligence Agency and the National Security Council, "the establishment" had financed itself through foreign potentates and tyrants, and illegal ventures in arms and drugs.[7]

The impoverishment and alienation of the electorate would take their toll on the 1988 presidential election. Only 66.6% of the 178.1 million eligible voters registered; and only 57.4% of the eligible voters participated in the election. George Bush was elected president at the behest of a minority, a mere 30% of those who might have voted.[8] As Reagan had before him, with the supine concurrence of the mass media, Bush pretended his minority constituted a moral mandate. And as with Reagan before him, domestic and international political extremism dominated his agenda. At the end of 1989, contravening international law, Bush ordered the invasion of Panama (Operation Just Cause) and imposed a new government on that American colony; early in 1990, ignoring both domestic and international law, Bush's CIA and its private conduits subverted the election in Nicaragua; that same year, with the complicity of the majority in the Security Council, Bush overrode United Nations regulations in order to organize the modern crusade against Iraq, the campaign which culminated in the 1991 Gulf War.

In the domestic arena, the new administration was equally cavalier with social ethics and the principles of representative government: during the first year of the Bush Administration, 24% of the regulations empowering the departments of Labor, Housing and Urban Development, and Education, the Occupational Safety and Health Administration, and the Environmental Protection Agency were scuttled in the sacred name of deregulation; Bush vetoed civil-rights legislation in 1990 on the basis of "quotas"; in 1991, on the most spurious grounds imaginable, the White House and the Justice Department designated and protected the Thomas nomination; in 1991 and 1992, Bush and his secretary of state, Jim Baker, refused political asylum to tens of thousands of Haitian refugees fleeing from a murderous military dictatorship, preferring to designate them "economic refugees"; and in the federal bureaucracy and the media, the Administration pursued its budgetary and ideological attack on social programs for the disadvantaged. "Twisting the data to fit a desired political conclusion" is how William Greider described the routine of the president's Office of Management and Budget, a key agency in the Executive's shenanigans in domestic affairs.[9] That came as close as any to an apt portrayal of the administration's operational sense of protocol both at home and abroad.

Though embedded in the American racial narrative, the vigilantism of Rodney King's violation extended beyond the political and ideological economies of Black oppression. Race is the signature of the beast marauding America and its empire, but only an aspect of its nature. But this was not meant to be immediately apparent to its victims, whether Black or not. Habituated by the "two nations" thesis first popularized by the Kerner Commission (the National Advisory Commission on Civil Disorders) in 1968, and supplemented by a ration of routine racial constructions in official statistics and the discursive canons of American journalism, the public perception of the increasing stratification of American society is fashioned through a racial screen.

Thus, while one-quarter of Black men in their twenties are under the control of the criminal courts, the United States imprisons Blacks at a rate four times that of South Africa, it is also the case that 1.2 million white males and females (56% of the total incarcerated; and at a rate at least twice as high as Europeans) were in prisons in 1990 and that the prison population of the country had doubled in the decade 1980–1990.[10] By 1991, based on the Sentencing Project annual report, the *Christian Science Monitor* observed, "More people, per capita, are in jail in the United States than in any other country on earth."[11] In 1985, the *Los Angeles Times* estimated that nearly one-quarter (56.1 million) of America was poor, an increase of 11 million since 1978.[12] If all Blacks were poor, one-half of the American poor would still be unaccounted for. As has been the case through-out America's history, the majority of the American poor are white but now they are absent. Andrew Hacker observes:

> Neither sociologists nor journalists have shown much interest in depicting poor whites as a "class." In large measure, the reason is racial. For whites, poverty tends to be viewed as atypical or accidental. Among blacks, it comes close to being seen as a natural outgrowth of their history and culture. At times, it almost appears as if white poverty must be covered up, lest it blemish the reputation of the dominant race.[13]

Rhetorically, in the American Empire, the stigmata of poverty, the "deviancy" of crime—and much of the political responsibilities of critical dissent—have been transferred to Blacks and other "natives."

The beating of King, was, then, a reverberation from the disintegration of civil society in America. The brutality of the racial drama was a reenactment of a multiplicity of brutalizations inaugurated by the ruling elite, historically the most constant source of antidemocratic extremism.[14] The daily occurrences of street executions, the cruel and indiscriminate arrests and harassment conducted under the authority of law which form the immediate context for Rodney King's experience are the local reiterations of a national social agenda. Deliberately obscured, and in part negotiated into a cultural currency by the protogenocidal outrages perpetrated against Blacks, is the habituation of American society to a Hobbesian moral discipline and political order. Under the cloak of "a new world order," an amoral ruling elite has attempted to traduce the historical aspirations for democracy in America: in foreign policy substituting nationalism, militarism, and neoimperialism for international law and the community of nations; conjuring racism, sexism ("family values"), authoritarianism, and an economism of patri-otism to drown out the hopes for equality, justice, and individual dignity.

However, the historical and structural forces behind the transformation of the American political order are neither psychological nor cultural. Notwithstanding the malevolent and avaricious personalities of our executive managers, the banal subordination of their bureaucratic minions, or the mean spiritedness of their functionaries, their dogmatic cultural convictions and rationally sophomoric articulations provide the surface idioms rather than the profound objectives necessitating their conduct. In the wake of the Soviet world system's collapse and the reemergence of Germany and Japan as powerful claimants to American hegemony, the modern world system is experiencing profound structural shocks and there are reasons for its political coordinators to brace for more. Utilizing the ironic voice, Noam Chomsky reports:

> As capitalism and freedom won their Grand Victory, the World Bank reported that the share of the world's wealth controlled by poor and medium-income countries declined from 23 percent to 18 percent (1980 to 1988). The Bank's 1990 report adds that in 1989, resources transferred from the "developing countries" to the industrialized world reached a new record. Debt service payments are estimated to have exceeded new flows of funds by $42.9 billion, an increase of $5 billion from 1988, and new funds from the wealthy fell to the lowest level in the decade.[15]

The social deprivations which are the concomitants to these hemorrhaging transfers of wealth constitute the circumstances which have historically spawned revolutionary movements. Presently, however, largely through the efforts of the Western intelligence community and military agencies, the preferred antitoxin is tyranny: fascist military dictators like Saddam Hussein, Ferdinand Marcos, Anastasio Somoza, and Sese Seko Mobutu. A similar Western strategy has already made its appearance in parts of the former Soviet Union and in Eastern Europe.

In the Third World, where the instability of what Kofi Hadjor[16] characterizes as "Bonapartism" is a constant, and the loyalty of tyrants to their Western benefactors even more mercurial, U.S. power can anticipate occasions when military interventions will be necessitated. Ingratitude appears to be a dialectic of clientelism. Consider, for the moment, that after years if not decades of cultivating and hopefully assuring the loyalties of the Marcos, Noriega, and Hussein, American presidents were compelled to overthrow or destroy them. Nevertheless, such "wars" are morally ambiguous, and, of course, require major historical revision and erasure. On this last score, there are bound to be conflicts and resistance. Ronald Reagan, for instance, was so perplexed by the policy reversal involving the ejection of Ferdinand Marcos that his White House managers were forced to keep him from access to the media and the American public for weeks.[17] And though testimony and documents concerning the troubling relationship between Manuel Noriega, the CIA, and its former director George Bush were never permitted to become a part of Noriega's trial, the American public has access to some of the truth.[18] Similarly, Bush's consort with Hussein has returned to haunt him. And of course the military campaign in the Gulf, like its predecessors in Grenada and Panama, was subject to extreme press manipulation and censorship.[19] Public cynicism accrued, encouraged by the exposures of official deceits, misdeeds, and misjudgments.

In the post–Cold War era, a democratic America, that is to say, an America persistently struggling to vanquish the autocratic tendencies of its governing elites and to reverse the mean consequences of the structural "correctives" of capital, would be ill-suited as a launching site for miliary adventures designed to chastise former allies, recapture markets and human and material resources, and to reimpose American hegemony. Despite the deluge of prowar propaganda during the long run-up to the Gulf War, it should be recalled, substantial opposition developed to a military confrontation. Within days of the bombardment of Kuwait and Iraq, American public opinion was nearly equally divided for and against the war.[20] And earlier, several years into Reagan's poorly concealed war on revolutionary Nicaragua, the majority of Americans still consistently opposed the "secret" but official policy.[21] Alternatively, an America principally driven by nationalism, militarism, and racism, an American majority with a renewed consciousness of its external and domestic enemies, an American majority sobered through a long period of declining incomes and unsatisfied desires might be more appreciative of official alarms and remedies.

Much as during the onset of the Cold War, a radical reconstruction of American political discourse and the bounds of tolerable thought is in progress. In that previous moment, a critical segment of the American people was persuaded that in the name of anticommunism whole portions of the political spectrum would have to be sacrificed. To that end, compelled by the realization that unprincipled, fanatic communists were already within the gates, it became necessary to purge indiscriminately the deceived as well as the truly evil. The inquisition was merciless and unrelenting, and entangled industry, government, education, entertainment; the private, the public, and the personal. Public humiliation, self-confession, denunciations of family, friends, and colleagues were a small cost when the alternative was considered.[22] That earlier repression was ultimately frustrated by Black culture and the emergence of the civil-rights movement. The first provided sanctuary for dissenters, the second, substantially but not entirely, restored a liberal discourse.[23]

In the present moment, perhaps mindful of its history, reaction has placed race in the foreground. And Rodney King was only one of its victims. Thus, in the company of such bizarre phantasmagoria as "political correctness" and "reverse discrimination" are placed the real aspirations of women, workers, the poor, and peoples of color.

Predictably, inevitably, the present machinations of power have inspired their own contradictions. On 29th April 1992, twelve years into the pageantry of the ultra Right's usurpation of the state, the outraged and the betrayed took to the streets of Los Angeles, San Francisco, Las Vegas, and other American cities. And no one living in this America had the right to be surprised. The history of such social rebellions is as old (and current) as poverty and injustice. The classicists inform us that in the sixth century B.C. just such insurrections initiated the process which eventually culminated in Athenian democracy. And in Europe's "Middle Ages," it took the original Inquisition centuries to suppress socialist and democratic movements. It is just as Thomas Rainboro predicted in the seventeenth century: "Either poverty must use democracy to destroy the power of property, or property in fear of poverty will destroy democracy."[24] It is this fundamental opposition which must be concealed. But it was not during the Los Angeles rebellion. The images of the betrayed coalesced; Black, Latino, and white, contradicting and marginalizing the desperate discourses on "race riot" which followed.[25] Ironically, by the very act of racial affirmation which Rodney King's assailants confidently sought in their mob identity, they provided the most certain catalyst for its negation.

Notes

In the first passage cited in epigraph to this essay Sgt. Koon, commander of the Los Angeles Police unit which beat and arrested Rodney King, imagines the reaction of an armed female officer to King's presence. See Richard Serrano, "Koon Pens Blunt Book about Life in LAPD," *Los Angeles Times,* 16 May 1992, B2. In the second passage cited Herman Collins, an unemployed 26-year-old Black man, comments on the acquittal of the four policemen charged in the King beating. See "The Fire This Time," *Time,* 11 May 1992.

1. John R. MacArthur, *Second Front: Censorship and Propaganda in the Gulf War* (New York: Hill and Wang, 1992), 105.

2. William Greider, *Who Will Tell the People: The Betrayal of Democracy* (New York: Simon and Schuster, 1992), 11.

3. Richard Meyer and Barry Bearak, "Poverty: Toll Grows amid Aid Cutbacks," *Los Angeles Times,* 28 July 1985; Andrew Hacker, *Two Nations* (New York: Charles Scribner's Sons, 1992), 98ff.

4. For the concentration of ownership in the media, see Ben Bagdikian, *The Media Monopoly* (Boston: Beacon Press, 1990); for the news media, see M. Hertsgaard, *On Bended Knee: The Press and the Reagan Presidency* (New York: Farrar, Straus and Giroux, 1988).

5. For the history of the Savings and Loan crisis, see Greider, *Who Will Tell the People,* ch. 2.

6. Sylvia Nasar, "The 1980's: A Very Good Time for the Very Rich," *The New York Times,* 5 March 1992. Of course, Nasar reclaimed her loyalty to the established order by prominently displaying Paul Krugman, whose *The Age of Diminished Expectations* (Cambridge: MIT Press, 1992) maintained there was no relationship between the rich getting richer and poor more impoverished (22–23).

7. Holly Sklar, *Washington's War on Nicaragua* (Boston: South End Press, 1988).

8. See Clifford Krauss, "A Bill to Ease Voter Registration Clears House and Pressures Bush,"

New York Times, 17 June 1992, and Rosemary Keane's letter to the *Times,* 9 July 1992. Bush vetoed the 1992 bill, thus ensuring the 60 million voters—disproportionately the poor—would remain unregistered.

9. See Greider *Who Will Tell the People,* 146, and Brian Tokar, "Regulatory Sabotage," *Z Magazine,* April 1992.

10. See David Savage, "1 in 4 Young Blacks in Jail or in Court Control, Study Says," *Los Angeles Times,* 27 February 1990, and Steve Whitman, "The Crime of Black Imprisonment," *Z Magazine,* May/June 1992.

11. Cameron Barr, "U.S.: World's Lock-Em-Up Leader," *Christian Science Monitor,* 7 March 1991.

12. Meyer and Bearak, "Poverty."

13. Hacker, *Two Nations,* 100.

14. M. I. Finley, *Democracy Ancient and Modern* (New Brunswick: Rutgers University Press, 1985), 107.

15. Noam Chomsky, "The Victors II," *Z Magazine,* January 1991, 21.

16. Kofi Hadjor, *A Dictionary of Third World Terms* (New York: Penguin, 1992).

17. Cedric J. Robinson, "The American Press and the Repairing of the Philippines," *Race and Class* 27, no. 2 (Autumn 1986).

18. See Mark Cook, "Scribes in the Courtroom: Controlling the Damage at the Noriega Trial," *EXTRA!,* January/February 1992, and Larry Rohter, "Noriega Sentenced to 40 Years in Jail on Drug Charges," *New York Times,* 11 July 1992.

19. See MacArthur, *Second Front,* ch. 2, and William Schaap, "The Images of War," *Lies of Our Times,* July/August 1991.

20. See MacArthur, *Second Front,* ch. 4.

21. See Sklar, *Washington's War on Nicaragua,* 190ff.

22. See Victor Navasky, *Naming Names* (New York: Penguin, 1980).

23. See Marty Jezer, *The Dark Ages: Life in the United States, 1945–1960* (Boston: South End Press, 1982), chs. 13 and 14.

24. Quoted by Raphael Samuel, "British Marxist Historians," *New Left Review* 124 (March/April 1980), 28.

25. For example, see "Race and Rage," *U.S. News and World Report,* 11 May 1992.

7

Accumulation as Evisceration: Urban Rebellion and the New Growth Dynamics

Rhonda M. Williams

L.A. was a hybrid social revolt with three major dimensions. It was a revolutionary democratic protest characteristic of African-American history when demands for equal rights have been thwarted by the major institutions. It was also a major post-modern bread riot—an uprising of not just poor people but particularly of those strata of poor in southern California who've been most savagely affected by the recession. Third, it was an inter-ethnic conflict. . . .

—Mike Davis

After a sputtering start, George Bush's spin doctors gathered their wits about them and launched their post–Rodney King economic offensive: urban America is hurting because it has suffered from a lack of free enterprise and entrepreneurial zeal.[1] The president's strategic orchestration of a chorus of support is strong testimony to the power of a recurring theme of the Reagan-Bush years: we must rely upon unfettered capital accumulation to heal our individual and collective economic wounds. Twelve years later, many sores are still festering, and the ranks of the injured continue to swell. The administration's exhortations provide an occasion to evaluate critically the distributional consequences of economic growth during the past dozen years.

Economic growth in the 1980s was not the medicinal cure-all promised by early Reagan economic advisors. On the contrary, for many citizens, the side effects seemed as bad or worse than the original disease. Now, more so than in the mid-1980s, mainstream economists have reached a consensus on what happened, if not why: poverty and inequality rose in the 1980s, and labor-market opportunities worsened for younger workers with a high-school education or less. For African-American males with twelve or fewer years of education, the 1980s were catastrophic.

This essay provides an economic context within which to locate the post-verdict uprisings. I focus on a flurry of recent research which describes and analyzes the labor-market opportunities of young workers in particular, but not exclusively. In Los Angeles and elsewhere, urban rebellion was a multiracial and multinational uprising, the motives and identities of the participants diverse. Some were motivated by the outrage of the verdict, others by the opportunity to secure necessities for themselves and their families, still others by ongoing economic exploitation and racial oppression.

I emphasize the declining fortunes of younger urban blacks (and to a lesser extent, Latinos) for several reasons. Poor urban youth of color are very much the subjects of the social-policy discourse which casts urban blacks and Latinos as pathological deviates. The "underclass" literature explains their low wages, declining employment rates, and high unemployment rates as a consequence of cultural pathologies, family breakdown, and generally bad behavior.[2] Yet often these narratives obliterate discussion of a macroeconomy which is generating declining earnings and employment rates of a magnitude unprecedented in recent U.S. history. To the extent that members of this younger generation are well on their way to lower lifetime earnings than their elders, they usher in a new moment in a post–World War II national community accustomed to intergenerational upward mobility.

My focus on the changing economic landscape by no means signifies an attempt to reduce revolt to economics alone. On the contrary, my objectives are threefold. First, I provide a descriptive and analytic lens through which we can glimpse the economic realities confronting urban Central and African Americans distributing stolen food and diapers to their neighbors and friends;[3] second, I offer readers a sense of how most economists think and talk about the rise in inequality; and third, I argue that mainstream economic discussion represses discussion of socioeconomic agency and therefore contributes to the mystification of the processes which have palpably eviscerated so many communities of color.

THE CONTOURS OF GROWTH: WIDER GAPS, DEEPER WOUNDS

During the early and mid-1980s, economists argued vigorously among themselves about the fortunes of individual workers and their families in the United States. Some argued that poverty, wage inequality, and family-income inequality were on the rise, while others dismissed these findings as either a demographic or data-collecting fluke. For example, some suggested that the growth of female-headed households was the proximate cause of rising poverty rates (since they have higher poverty rates than other family types) and therefore not an indication of troublesome economic trends.

Within the North American mainstream (i.e., those economists operating within the neoclassical Keynesian synthesis presented in colleges and universities throughout the nation), the past few years have ushered in a new era of partial consensus: economic growth in the 1980s did not deliver the traditional portfolio of gains for many Americans, and growing wage inequality is the proximate cause. Economic growth has traditionally reduced poverty rates and increased the share of income received by the poorest families. Such was not the case in the 1980s: in 1989, after six years of sustained economic growth, the national poverty rate stood at 12.8% (1.8 to 3.5% higher than predicted from earlier expansions),[4] and family-income inequality increased.[5]

Rising poverty rates and income inequality could be caused by something other than slow income growth. For example, the exclusion of in-kind income (e.g., food stamps and Medicaid) could skew the data. Or, changes in the regional distribution of the poor could explain why aggregate data show that poverty rates in the 1980s were not as responsive to economic growth as they had been during previous boom periods. Yet such is not the case: inclusion of in-kind income and correcting for the regional distribution of the poor do not change the results. Similarly, neither changes in family composition nor the policy changes instituted during the earlier years of the Reagan administration can fully account for increased poverty rates.[6] According to Rebècca Blank,[7] the bottom line is remarkably straightforward: poverty rates in the 1980s were less responsive to macroeconomic growth in the 1980s because earnings among heads of families at the lower end of the income distribution did not grow substantially during the recovery. This, in turn, was a consequence of stagnant or declining real-wage growth among low-income workers.

Thus the consensus: family-income inequality is on the rise because wage inequality is on the rise. Wage inequality has increased across the board because wage growth has slowed or reversed for many segments of the population, particularly those who are young, without college educations, and/or are African Americans. Between 1979 and 1988, real earnings of 25 to 34-year-old men with twelve or fewer years of schooling declined dramatically. For white males without a high-school diploma, earnings (in 1988 dollars) declined from $19,848 to $16,108; for high-school graduates, the average earnings dropped from $24,889 to $21,776.[8]

For black males, the figures for nongraduates and graduates respectively are $14,596 to $14,594 and $19,449 to $16,638. Moreover, the earnings of young black men relative to their white counterparts declined at every educational level between 1973 and 1989.[9] For all young men, the earnings of college graduates increased some 30% relative to those with a high-school education or less.

White women without a high-school diploma also saw their real earnings fall, from $12,623 in 1979 to $10,853, during the same period. Earnings were constant for high-school graduates, and increased from $20,987 to $23,791 for college graduates. White women with college degrees enjoyed the largest earnings gain in the 1980s, followed by their black counterparts. Black women with high-school diplomas lost ground in the 1980s (their earnings dropped from $14,596 to $13,825), but not as rapidly as did those of their male peers.[10]

Changing our focus from earnings to employment hardly brightens the scenario. Although the employment-to-population ratio for white-male high-school dropouts and graduates held steady in the 1980s, their employment rates fell and unemployment rates rose relative to college graduates. For young black males, employment-to-population ratios fell considerably in the 1980s for high-school graduates (from 0.80 to 0.75) and dropouts (0.68 to 0.56). For women, employment-to-population ratios increased, with the noteworthy exception of black women with less than a high-school diploma.[11]

Comparable data on Latino populations is less extensive, in part because of the national, racial, and ethnic diversity of a population the U.S. Census Bureau aggregates as "Hispanics." The existing literature focuses on specific nationalities, is sometimes subsumed within discussions of immigration and length of time in the lower 48 states, and often appears in case-study form. Nonetheless, two important recent studies document respectively the growth in male, low-wage earnings[12] and changes in the wage distribution among blacks, Hispanics, and whites.[13]

Table 1 shows the percentage of employed black, white, and Hispanic men with low earnings (here defined as less that $12,000/year in 1987 constant dollars) by years of schooling completed in 1973, 1979, and 1987 (four years into the "Reagan recovery"). In each year and for every racial ethnic group, those with more education are noticeably less likely to have low earnings than those with more years of schooling. Table 1 is striking in that it vividly documents the increase in the percentage of men with low earnings within educational groups over the fourteen-year period. Black and Hispanic men with high-school diplomas were much more likely to be low earners in the late 1980s than in the early 1970s. In 1973, 27.7% of employed black men were low earners; by 1987, the percentage had skyrocketed to 44%. For Hispanics, the comparable figures are 22.2% and 38.2%. In each case, the percentage of low earners increased by more than half. For white men, the percentage of low earners increased from 15.6% to 22.9%.

For college graduates (here, those who have completed sixteen years of schooling), the racial gap increases substantially. In 1973, the black/white and Hispanic/white ratios are small (13.7/10.9 = 1.26 and 10.0/10.9 = 0.92). However, by 1987, the percentage of Hispanic college graduates with poverty-level earnings

Table 7.1   The Percentage of Men with Low Earnings by Education Years of Schooling
Completed

	0–8	9–11	12	13–15	16	17+	All
Whites							
1973	22.2	35.2	15.6	21.9	10.9	8.1	19.6
1979	29.1	43.6	18.1	21.5	10.2	7.8	21.3
1987	37.9	48.9	22.9	22.7	10.5	7.7	22.8
Blacks							
1973	45.5	44.4	27.7	29.1	13.7	11.6	35.8
1979	49.1	48.7	32.3	26.6	14.5	15.6	36.4
1987	56.9	56.0	44.0	32.6	19.7	14.0	41.7
Hispanics							
1973	33.9	42.5	22.2	17.1	10.5	17.9	29.4
1979	45.0	47.0	29.8	25.9	11.5	8.0	35.7
1987	56.4	55.6	38.2	33.2	21.0	13.9	43.4

Source: Gregory Acs and Sheldon Danizger, "Educational Attainment, Industrial Structure, and Male Earnings,
1973–1987," Discussion paper 94591, Institute for Research on Poverty, University of Wisconsin, May 1991.
Tabulations from the 1974, 1980, and 1988 Current Population Surveys. The figures reported are employed
men in each cell with earnings of less than $12,000 (in 1987 dollars). "Whites" and "Blacks" refer to persons
not of Hispanic origin.

doubled, and the Hispanic/white ratio climbed to 2.0. For African-American-male
college graduates, the percentage of low earners climbed to 19.7%, and the black/
white ratio increased to 1.88.

Table 2 documents changes in the wage distribution between 1979 and 1989
(two peak years in the labor market) for black, Hispanic, and white workers one
to ten years out of high school. Because they present calculated or actual hourly
wages rather than annual earnings (wages $\times$ hours $\times$ weeks worked), these
tables focus on the price of labor and abstract from labor-supply changes. If we
know a worker's hourly wage, we know if s/he can work out of poverty in a
full-time, year-round job. This table also traces the absolute decline in the fortunes
of recent high-school graduates, as opposed to their standing relative to the college
educated.

Table 2 shows the cumulative wage distribution (those earning below that
wage) of private-sector, high-school-educated workers one to ten years out of
high school. Wages are reported in constant 1991 dollars, and are shown in
relation to various poverty levels under the assumption that individuals work 40
hours a week for 52 weeks.[14] This presentation indicates the purchasing power
of the wage, not the reported poverty status of actual workers. The selected wage
intervals (again, in 1991 dollars) are as follows: the 1989 minimum wage was
$3.68 an hour, the 1991 first-quarter minimum wage was $3.80, the 1979 minimum was $5.34, the two-adult, two-child, poverty-level wage is $6.58, 1.25
times that wage is $8.23, and twice the hourly wage is $13.16.

Table 2 graphically summarizes the declining absolute wages of young high-

Table 7.2   Wage Distributions, Private-Sector, High-School Graduates, One to Ten Years
Out of School

	Black, Non-Hispanics Cumulative Percentages		Latino, Any Race Cumulative Percentages		White, Non-Hispanic Cumulative Percentages	
Full-time, Full-year Purchasing Power of Wage	1979	1989	1979	1989	1979	1989
Below 1989 Minimum Wage	2.0	6.8	1.8	6.8	2.1	5.0
Below 1991: I Minimum Wage	2.0	8.0	1.8	7.6	2.1	5.4
Below 1979 Minimum Wage	13.8	36.7	10.7	31.5	8.1	23.3
Below Two-Adult, Two-Child Poverty Level	38.1	57.2	36.0	52.5	29.0	40.3
Below 1.25 Poverty Level	57.9	77.2	54.2	69.3	48.2	61.8
Below 2.00 Poverty Level	88.1	95.7	87.7	93.6	84.3	91.0
Above 2.00 Poverty Level	100.0	100.0	100.0	100.0	100.0	100.0

Source: William E. Spriggs, Economic Policy Institute, 1992.

school graduates. One of the most striking results is that for each race and ethnic group (men and women), the percentage of workers earning a wage lower than the real value of the 1979 minimum wage increased sharply, and the share of workers earning an hourly wage that put them above twice the poverty level declined precipitously. For Latinos (of all races), the percentage of workers earning less than the 1979 minimum wage almost tripled between 1979 and 1989 (increasing from 10.7% to 31.5%). In 1979, 13.8% of African Americans earned hourly wages that, on a year-round, full-time basis, placed them at the poverty level. By 1989, that share increased to 36.7%. For whites, the increase was from 8.1% to 23.3%.

Turning to the other end of the wage distribution, we see that over 50% of young black and Latino high-school graduates earned less than the two-adult, two-child, poverty-level hourly wage in 1989, a dramatic increase from the late 1970s. Equally alarming is the decline in the percentage of wage earners bringing home a (gross) hourly wage which put them above twice that poverty level. For blacks, the percentage declined from 11.9% (calculated as 100–88.1) to 4.3%. For whites and Latinos respectively, the declines are from 15.7% to 9% and 12.3% to 6.4%.

Additional calculations (not shown here) reveal similar declines for more experienced workers.[15] Experienced, high-school-educated black- and white-male workers (those with eleven to twenty years of experience) also lost considerable ground in the 1980s. A comparison of similarly situated workers (two cohorts ten years apart but with the same years of education and experience) show substantive declines in the percentage of men that earned a wage above 1.25 times the poverty level. For white men, the percentage declined from 89.2% to 76.7%; for black men, the percentage dropped from 75.3% to 54.3%.

WHAT HAPPENED?

The previous discussion suggests a substantive shift in the contours of growth. Wages and earnings have dropped for younger workers without a college education, and men in particular face increasingly grim labor-market prospects. Although mainstream theorists have yet to converge upon a single, unified explanation of increasing inequality and declining absolute incomes, they have generated a set of explanations which privilege changes in labor demand, labor supply, and institutional practices.[16] This section summarizes the evidence to date, paying close attention to studies which speak directly to changes in the relative economic standing of young blacks and/or Hispanics.

Both popular and academic literatures explore the economic consequences of our changing industrial structure. Changes in the sectoral and occupational composition of labor demand can explain between one-quarter and one-third of the declining wages of young workers without college degrees. Studies to date suggest that the decline in the fraction of young men employed in manufacturing[17] explains one-quarter to one-third of their falling relative wages[18] and one-third to one-half the decline in the employment-to-population ratios of young blacks without a high-school diploma in the 1970s. Shifts in the share of total employment in manufacturing are significant because this sector traditionally has been a source of high-wage employment for high-school graduates. Employment growth in blue-collar jobs (e.g., machine operatives, laborers, etc.) has been particularly slow in manufacturing, but has also slackened in the service sectors as well.

Industry changes in labor demand and the decline in unionization also contributed to increases in the college/high-school wage gap. For white-male workers aged 25 to 34, the wage gap between college- and high-school-educated workers increased 17 percentage points between 1979 and 1987. Declining rates of unionization and the shift of employment to low-wage industries explain about half the change. Increases in the relative supply of high-school-educated white males explain less than a quarter of the increase in the wage differential.[19] Moreover, the growth in the trade deficit after 1979 further strengthened the overall demand shift against non-college-educated men and women.[20]

John Bound and Richard Freeman[21] explore the notion that skill-biased technological change accounts for the growing black/white employment/and/earnings gaps. In other words, they test the hypothesis that employers' demand for skilled workers is increasing and that black men have lost ground because they are, on average, less skilled than whites. However, Bound and Freeman do not find that racial gaps in educational attainment explain the deterioration of black men's labor-market position. On the contrary, it seems that black-male workers are losing ground because they lost some of the best high-wage manufacturing jobs and found employment in some of the lowest-paying, white-collar service jobs.

Black workers' disproportionately large losses from the decline in manufacturing continue to puzzle many analysts. The fact that black men in particular are losing ground within educational groups casts doubt on a skills-based explanation. Philip Moss and Chris Tilly[22] speculate that some combination of discrimination, race-specific job networks, lack of training, or a shortage of entrepreneurship among blacks may offer the missing link. I return to these explanatory factors in my next section's more focused discussion on discrimination.

Supply-side theorists also have examined the numbers of young persons at various educational and skill levels. Earlier expectations that the smaller "baby bust generation" (the cohort born in the 1960s and 1970s) would earn higher relative wages have proved wrong. For the cohort as a whole, college enrollments declined as the demand for graduates increased, and high-school-educated workers found themselves competing for fewer jobs. However, conventional measures indicate that competence has not plummeted among high-school graduates. Standardized test scores did not decline for less-educated white workers. For African Americans, the decline in demand for dropouts exceeded the decline in supply, and test scores have risen as relative and absolute earnings fell. And, the relative earnings of less-educated cohorts fell as they aged in the 1980s. This evidence strongly challenges the hypothesis that failing skills explain the declining earnings of these younger workers.

The decline in unionism and the shrinking real value of the minimum wage provide better statistical explanations of the worsened labor-market status of younger cohorts. Estimates by K. Blackburn, David Bloom, and Richard Freeman[23] suggest that declining union membership in the private sector (from 30% in 1970 to 12% in 1990) can statistically account for 20% of rising wage inequality, even after controlling for employment shifts across sectors. Declining union density explains about 5% of the decline in black earnings, and the effect is strongest for those in the Midwest with twelve or fewer years of schooling. As table 2 suggests, the real value of the federal minimum wage declined considerably between 1972 and 1990: the minimum wage increased by 109%, but inflation jumped 191%. Blackburn, Bloom, and Freeman's results are consistent with William Sprigg's findings that the falling real minimum wage reduced the earnings of young black men and women.

Mainstream discussions demonstrate ambivalence about the potential significance of increasing discrimination as an explanation of the worsening position of young black workers. On the one hand, most economists doubt the viability of long-term discrimination in a competitive capitalist economy. On the other hand, they confront evidence of the kind presented by the Urban Institute's matched-pairs study (blacks and whites with identical qualifications apply for the same jobs)[24] This and other similar case studies document the persistence of labor-market discrimination. Whites were more likely to advance in the application process and more likely to receive a job offer. The absence of comparable studies in the past makes researchers wary of making claims about changes in the level of discrimination over time. I return to this topic in the following section.

WHAT'S WRONG WITH THIS PICTURE?
A MACROSTRUCTURAL REPRISE

Mainstream discussions of growing wage inequality, declining real incomes, and growing racial employment and earnings gaps share a common strategy. Most authors statistically assess various hypotheses about inequality and poverty. Their empirical work answers questions such as, "What portion of the rising wage differential can be accounted for by changes in the changing industrial distribution and/or changes in the skills employers demand and/or changes in worker quality?" Researchers pursue proximate causes of changes in labor-market outcomes, but tend to eschew extending the causal chain.[25] In this section, I argue that the investigation of nonproximate causes, which abstracts from the particulars of supply, demand, and institutional change, is neither speculative nor superfluous. On the contrary, it is a necessary component of a more complete explanation and provide a context within which to assess the mass of statistical evidence.

The core of my argument is that the dominant narratives produced by academic economists generally lack an account of *agency* and, in particular, fail to situate business and worker behavior within the context of competitive capital accumulation. In this context, competition is a market structure, not an ongoing state of rivalry which inspires strategic responses. When mentioned at all, competition is subsumed within a list of factors precipitating change or implied in discussion of changing labor demand. It is not an ongoing and constitutive condition of accumulation, mediated by either the changing conditions of politics or those of the social and technical conditions of production.[26]

Consider discussions of the changing industrial and occupational distribution of employment as an explanation of increased wage inequality. Most accounts cite the decline of relatively high-paying, blue-collar jobs for high-school-educated workers as an important determinant of declining earnings for males in general and, in particular, of the declining employment rate for blacks with fewer than twelve years of schooling. Moreover, research to date also indicates that growing earnings inequality within manufacturing and service sectors explains much of the observed changes in the wage distribution.

Yet these analyses eschew a systematic discussion of the general phenomena of competitive capitalist accumulation, the class-specific behavior it generates, and how competition differentiates the conditions workers face.[27] At the most abstract levels, capitalist competition exists because capital as a whole has many owners who struggle with one another to realize profit. Within sectors (and abstracting from product differentiation, advertising, etc), capitalists compete by trying to cheapen their commodities (increase the productivity of labor) in order to capture market shares. Innovators in technical and organizational relations operate with higher profit margins and profit rates and provide workers greater opportunities to increase wages. Competition *between* sectors involves investor efforts to move their capital from low- to high-profit sectors. It is this movement which determines the changing industrial mix and distribution of labor demand (it also generates a tendency toward profit-rate equalization). Within this context, capital-intensive sectors (and productivity leaders within any sector) are more attractive to workers seeking wage increases.

When faced with declining profit rates in the late 1960s,[28] U.S. manufacturers decided to restore their competitive stature by assaulting the standard of living of the majority of working people. As a means to the end of restoring profits, management pursued strategic transformations of the technical and social relations of work. During the 1970s, manufacturers pursued cheaper foreign labor either by investing more overseas, importing cheaper foreign parts, or subcontracting to smaller firms here and abroad. In the 1980s, management responded by developing two-tiered wage systems, increasing the use of temporary and part-time labor, and pursuing active anti-union strategies.

This intensified scramble for market shares is consistent with increased intra-sector wage inequality for at least two reasons. Because competition forces down prices and profits, all producers are pressured to cut labor costs directly or via increased productivity. Unless a company increases its market, increased productivity within a firm reduced labor requirements. Within sectors, producers with the lowest costs dominate the competitive terrain. Employers' transformations of the composition of labor demand were strategic responses to competitive challenges. For high-school-educated workers displaced from manufacturing (or young people unable to enter as their parents had done), the competitive struggle between capitalists translated into a decline in labor demand in a historically unionized, high-wage sector and increased job competition in nonmanufacturing service sectors. Competition between capitals thus profoundly shapes the terms of job search and employment for workers.

The broadly defined service sector was the job-growth engine of the 1980s. "Services" include a range of industries, from distributive sectors (transportation, communications, utilities, wholesale trade) to retail trade, finance, insurance, real estate, government work, and education. The non-distributive service industries generally are characterized by lower levels of capitalization (and therefore narrower limits for wage increases) and unionization. Capitalist investment in the service sector has so far been synonymous with the growth of a polarized class structure. The upper tier consists of educated professionals and technically trained workers, the lower tiers include both those who clean, cook, and serve and those rendered completely superfluous to the new economy. Service workers' wages (including service workers in the manufacturing and service sectors) fell by 18.2% in the 1980s, and their benefits declined by 26.1%.[29]

Profit-seeking agency also looms large in discussions of productivity and wages. Many economists attribute the downward shift in the entire wage structure to lagging aggregate economic productivity, which has averaged less than 1% per year since 1973, a sharp drop from the 2–3% per year average for the earlier, post–World War II era. However, lower productivity growth does not explain the drop in real wages after 1979, since hourly productivity increased by 1.1% annually while real hourly wages fell. Impersonal market forces did not guarantee that wage gains followed productivity gains. The evidence from the 1980s suggests another more compelling story: antiunion corporate policy has weakened worker organization. The important criticisms one could make of organized labor in the past fifteen years notwithstanding, corporate policy has been effective. Even in those sectors where efficiency is on the rise (e.g., manufacturing), workers lack the political clout to wrest wage increases from capital.

A reclamation of agency would also fill the gaps in the literature seeking to explain the worsening labor-market conditions of young black males. Most academic economists remain puzzled as to why blacks might be the last hired and first fired during the past fifteen years. That is, the profession harbors a strong skepticism as to the long-term viability of discrimination under competitive market conditions.[30] The standard literature emphasizes the costs of racial discrimination (e.g., wage premiums to whites, longer search time to find qualified whites when blacks and Hispanics are shunted aside, etc.). Yet there exist nonmainstream explanations of rising racial inequality which foreground the benefits of discrimination to white workers and capitalists.

Radical economists argue that there are also costs to ending discrimination in a racialized capitalist social formation—that is, societies wherein race shapes individuals' understandings of themselves, their communities, and the workings of the social order. These costs arise from the social nature of work, and vary with labor-market conditions. For example, ending discrimination can disrupt traditional patterns of authority and force the adoption of new procedures for recruitment, screening, and training. Moreover, ending racial discrimination weakens cross-class white solidarity that can offset interclass conflict. Reductions in discrimination could also increase worker bargaining power and/or reduce team efficiency. In other words, employers' efforts to challenge white workers' privileges are costly. The cost calculus of discrimination is highly contingent and, for employers, involves the continuous reassessment of the relative costs and benefits.[31]

Rising unemployment reduces the costs of employment discrimination and increases the costs of ending discrimination. Unemployment began an upward trend in the early 1970s. The form and content of capitalist competition have intensified the stakes of job competition among working people. The decline of relatively high-wage employment opportunities for the high-school-educated majority increases the benefits to white workers of using their networks to secure jobs in general, and particularly high-paying jobs, for fellow whites. At the policy level, the Reagan and Bush presidencies sanctioned, legitimated, and orchestrated hostility to civil rights. Their assaults on antidiscrimination agendas and affirmative action further reduced the costs of discriminating. Faced with rising unemployment and declining wages, white workers seeking simply to hold their own, could gain relatively, if not absolutely, from exercising their agency to impose the costs of recessions and income stagnation on workers of color. For profit-conscious capitalists, discrimination facilitates workplace control and cost minimization. If we take seriously the notion that racial identification creates community between and within classes, discrimination need not disappear from existing capitalist economies, so long as incentives exist for its practice.

L.A. ONCE AGAIN

The above discussion locates declining wages, rising wage inequality, and increasing racial inequality within the context of dynamic and ruthlessly competitive capital accumulation. I have suggested that corporate restructuring—the growth of the low-wage service economy and the shrinking of manufacturing—has accompanied class recomposition—the transformation of wage and work relations to facilitate profitability. Back in 1982, Saskia Sassen-Koob described the relationship between restructuring and recompositions as the generation of a

> new growth dynamic—one not predicated on the existence of a thriving middle class and upper segment of the working class, as was the case throughout the 1950s.
>
> In the final analysis, this would mean that the growth of (what is still nominally) U.S. capital would fail to generate the benefits for a wide segment of the population in the U.S. historically associated with such capital growth.[32]

Sassen-Koob's words ring prophetic in their auguring of what the 1980s would yield.

At best, national statistics provide only a structural framework for thinking about the economic context for the L.A. uprising. Indeed, if on-site observer Mike Davis is correct, L.A. was a postmodern bread riot, but not one simply or mechanistically fueled by structural trends. Davis accorded primacy to specific economic conditions:

> [W]e are in the worst recession California has seen since the 30s. And the only account of it that you tend to get in the papers concerns unemployed aerospace engineers. It's been a vicious, disastrous recession for the newest strata of immigrants from Mexico and Central America, which is why the worst looting outside the Black areas occurred in the largely Mexican eastern half of South Central L.A., and in Central American immigrant areas like Hollywood and the MacArthur Park area.[33]

This essay clearly does not speak to the particulars of the L.A. recession—it provides the structural contours of which Davis speaks. However, the recession in southern California must be seen in light of the larger trends—otherwise we can't apprehend the depths to which working people have fallen. Growth 1980s style did not provide the promised renewal for a large proportion of United States workers. In the absence of a dramatic shift in political power and leadership, the 1990s will very likely provide more of the same.

Notes

The passage cited in epigraph to this essay comes from Mike Davis, "LA: The Fire This Time," *Covert Action Information Bulletin* 41 (Summer 1992): 12.

1. Although President Bush initially excluded it from top-level discussions, Secretary of Housing and Urban Development Jack Kemp's empowerment-through-ownership agenda achieved greater prominence within a week of the initial uprising. On the Sunday following the verdict in the Rodney King case, Kemp's editorial in the *Washington Post* (Sunday, 3 May 1992, C7) argued that "[e]liminating the tax on capital gains in urban enterprise zones would flood the inner cities with capital and help create ownership, entrepreneurship, and jobs." He also challenged Congress to discard the bureaucratic approach to ending poverty, calling for a strategy which will "empower individuals to control their lives through the power of property ownership and entrepreneurship." The cover of the Wednesday, 6 May 1992 *Post* featured a photograph of Bush with Kemp and two other Cabinet members.

2. For a recent critical assessment of the underclass, culture, race, poverty, and gender, see Adolph Reed, Jr., "The Underclass as Myth and Symbol," *Radical America* 24, no. 1 (1990): 21–40.

3. Mike Davis describes seeing Central Americans distributing stolen food and diapers to the tenements in neighborhoods west of downtown Los Angeles. See Davis, "The Fire This Time," 14.

4. I provide a range of estimates cited in the relevant literature. See David Cutler and Lawrence Katz, "Untouched by the Rising Tide," *The Brookings Review* (Winter 1992): 41–45, for the lower bound. Rebecca Blank provides a larger estimate of the gap between actual (12.8%) and

expected (9.3%) 1989 poverty rates in "Why Were Poverty Rates So High in the 1980s?" NBER Working Paper No. 3878, 1991.

5. See Cutler and Katz, "Untouched by the Rising Tide."

6. See Blank, "Poverty Rates."

7. See Ibid.

8. See Richard B. Freeman and Harry Holzer, "The Deterioration of Employment and Earnings Opportunities for Less Educated Young Americans: A Review of Evidence," unpublished manuscript, August 1991.

9. See Philip Moss and Chris Tilly, "Why Black Men Are Doing Worse in the Labor Market: A Review of Supply-Side and Demand-Side Explanations," prepared for the Social Sciences Research Council Subcommittee on Joblessness and the Underclass, July 1991.

10. See Freeman and Holzer, "The Deterioration of Employment."

11. See ibid.

12. Gregory Acs and Sheldon Danizger, "Educational Attainment, Industrial Structure, and Male Earnings, 1973–1987," Discussion Paper 94591, Institute for Research on Poverty, University of Wisconsin, May 1991.

13. William E. Spriggs, "Wage Distribution Changes for New Workers, 1979–91," Economic Policy Institute, 1992.

14. Spriggs used the wage-and-earnings file from the outgoing rotation of the monthly Current Population Survey. He included all workers who either reported an hourly wage or weekly wages plus hours. The CPI-U-X1 deflator was used both to convert nominal wages to 1991 dollars and to inflate 1979 poverty levels to 1991 poverty levels.

15. Courtesy of William Spriggs, Economic Policy Institute.

16. This essay deliberately set aside discussion of crime, drug use, and family composition as determinants of the rising inequality and increasing ranks of the working poor. This literature shades quickly into a race-specific discourse about the behavioral flaws of the black "underclass." The problems with these discussions are legion and will not be reiterated in this context.

17. Between 1973 and 1989, the proportion of men under 30 working in manufacturing fell from 28% to 19%.

18. K. Blackburn, David Bloom, and Richard Freeman, "The Declining Economic Position of Less Skilled American Men," A Future of Lousy Jobs, ed. Gary Burtless (Washington, DC: Brookings Institution, 1990).

19. Lawrence Mishel and David Frankel, Economic Policy Institute, The State of Working America, 1990–91 (Armonk, NY: M. E. Sharpe, 1991), 223.

20. Ibid, 103.

21. John Bound and Richard Freeman, "What Went Wrong?: The Erosion of Relative Earnings and Employment of Young Black Males in the 1980's," mimeo, National Bureau of Economic Research, 1990.

22. Moss and Tilly, "Why Black Men Are Doing Worse."

23. Blackburn, Bloom, and Freeman, "The Declining Economic Position."

24. R. J. Struyk, M. A. Turner, and M. Fix, Opportunities Denied, Opportunities Diminished: Discrimination in Hiring (Washington, DC: The Urban Institute, 1991). For another important and undercited case study of discrimination amid industrial change, see Bruce Williams's Black Workers in an Industrial Suburb: The Struggle against Discrimination (New Brunswick: Rutgers University Press, 1987).

25. Moss and Tilly make this explicit in their discussion of the explanations for and evidence on the declining labor-market fortunes of young black men. See "Why Black Men Are Doing Worse," 24.

26. Different tendencies characterize the policy literature and business press, which are much more likely to acknowledge employers' efforts to cut wages as a means to cut costs and preserve profits. For examples, see "What Happened to the American Dream?" *Business Week,* 19 August 1991, 80–85, and Mishel and Frankel, *The State of Working America.*

27. For an extended discussion of competition and the differentiation of both the working class and capital, see Rhonda M. Williams, "Competition, Discrimination, and Differential Wage Rates: On the Continued Relevance of Marxian Theory to the Analysis of Earnings and Employment Inequality," *New Approaches to Economic and Social Analyses of Discrimination,* ed. Richard Cornwall and Phanindra Wunnava (New York: Praeger, 1991).

28. Radicals disagree on the fate of post–World War II profits. Some argue that profits have trended downward since the war and that the late 1950s and early 1960s were a boom period. Another side argues that the immediate post-war era was a boom time for capital. For a discussion, see Robert Cherry, "Race and Gender Aspects of Marxian Macroeconomic Models," *Science and Society* 55, no. 1 (Spring 1991): 60–78.

29. Mishel and Frankel, *The State of Working America,* 75.

30. See William A. Darity, Jr., and Rhonda A. Williams, "Peddlers Forever?: Culture, Competition, and Discrimination," *American Economic Review: Papers and Proceedings* 75, no. 2 (May 1985): 256–61.

31. For a fuller elaboration of these models, see Steven Shulman, "Racial Inequality and White Employment: An Interpretation of the Bargaining Power Hypothesis," *Review of Black Political Economy* 18, no. 3 (Winter 1990): 5–20, and Rhonda M. Williams, "Capital, Competition, and Discrimination: A Reconsideration of Racial Earnings Inequality," *Review of Radical Political Economics* 19, no. 2 (1987): 1–15.

32. See Saskia Sassen-Koob, "Recomposition and Peripheralization at the Core," *Contemporary Marxism* 5 (Summer 1982).

33. See Davis, "The Fire This Time."

8

The Los Angeles "Race Riot" and Contemporary U.S. Politics

Michael Omi
and
Howard Winant

On thinking about Hell, I gather
My brother Shelley found it was a place
Much like the city of London. I
Who live in Los Angeles and not in London
Find, on thinking about Hell, that it must be
Still more like Los Angeles.

—Bertolt Brecht

INTRODUCTION

The charred buildings were still smoking when George Bush arrived in L.A. for a whirlwind tour of the South Central area. Speaking on 8 May 1992 at the Challenger Boys' and Girls' Club in the heart of the riot zone, the president sought to explain the previous week's events: "Things aren't right in too many cities across our country, and we must not return to the status quo. Not here, not in any city where the system perpetuates failure and hatred and poverty and despair." (Bush, 1992).

At first, such remarks may seem startling. Had the devastation Bush witnessed suddenly transformed him into a critic of institutional racism and corporate capitalism? When he referred to "the system," was the president thinking of the relegation of millions of racially stigmatized poor to the torpor and despair of ghettos? Was he alluding to the widespread acceptance of this warehousing as an apparent condition for the prosperity of the elite, and for the survival of a suburban, and largely white, middle class? Did he have new plans to reverse the withdrawal of already-meager public benefits and services from the inner cities?

Was he contemplating ending the brutal police occupation and surveillance of the ghettos out of a newfound respect for human and civil rights?

Hardly. Bush had something quite different in mind. He argued that the federal government had spent as much as $3 trillion over 25 years in an attempt to address the problems of poverty and racism, all with little success. We must now, he said, face some "unpleasant realities." First and foremost among these was the realization that "liberal" social-welfare programs had not resolved the problem of poverty. In fact, he argued, such programs fostered dependence on the state, nurtured irresponsible personal behavior, and led to the overall deterioration of inner-city communities.

How then to address the needs of the urban ghettos and barrios? What new policy alternative would the administration launch to confront the deterioration, the destruction, the despair? Bush concluded his address with an outline of the broad features of his approach: "[My] belief [is] that we must start with a set of principles and policies that foster personal responsibility, that refocus entitlement programs to serve those who are most needy, and increase the effectiveness of government services through competition and through choice." (Bush, 1992).

Thus the administration echoed neoconservative analysts who argue that poverty results from moral failure, lack of personal responsibility, and dependence on the welfare state.[1] While he revived the 1960s denunciations of "rioting for fun and profit," the president offered a rehash of "trickle-down" policy recommendations like subsidized enterprise zones and privatization of public housing.

Not to be outdone by Republican criticisms of the poor, Democratic presidential candidate Bill Clinton has adopted a more pragmatic version of the same rhetoric. While perfectly willing to criticize the Reagan and Bush administrations for neglecting the inner cities and manipulating racial fears, Clinton, too, argues that many 1960s programs have not worked, and suggests that, in the future, government programs must "demand greater responsibility" from the poor. (Brownstein 1992, A8)

Within the Clinton camp, a host of political sages linked to the Democratic leadership Council and the *New Republic* expatiate on the duties of family and community, preaching like television evangelists to nonwhite women about proper child rearing and the values of the work ethic. As E. J. Dionne informs us, "Values such as taking responsibility for one's family, struggling to be self-reliant, remembering that the communities of which we are a part have a right to expect something of us are neither left nor right." (1991).

Other Democratic "wise men," like Mickey Kaus and Laurence Mead, join neoconservative analyst Charles Murray in urging the elimination of welfare *tout court*. In place of AFDC they would substitute various combinations of market discipline and authoritarian workfare. As Kaus has put it, "There are good reasons why people hate welfare, because welfare provides an economic substitute for work. It's a bad thing with bad social consequences. People have always hated welfare and people have always been right." ("Roundtable" 1992, 75).

Nor has this "tough love" approach been confined to Democratic policy papers and party platforms. In New Jersey, for example, liberal Governor Jim Florio recently lent his support to a new law which will deny increased benefits to mothers who bear additional children while on welfare.

Thus have we come, so it seems, full circle. Poverty and discrimination, seen in the past as problems requiring state action, are now seen as the *results* of state activity. What was once the solution (activist social policies) has now become the problem (dependence), and what was once the problem (the lash of poverty) has now become the solution (market forces).

Surely this dramatic analytical inversion is indicative of broader changes in racial ideology and politics in the post–civil rights era. Slowly during the 1970s, and more rapidly during the Reagan-Bush years, the tables turned—in matters of race—from benign to malign neglect. In the aftermath of the great racial transformations of the 1960s, the state—and the major political parties—professed a sincere interest in racial equality and in genuine pluralism. More recently we have seen the triumph of race baiting, racially coded appeals for votes, and victim blaming.

Out of this situation, out of this cesspool of combined brutality and neglect in racial matters, came the 30 April–2 May 1992 explosion in Los Angeles. The massive disturbance occurred on the eve of the most important presidential campaign in decades, threatening to recast the election into a debate about race, social inequality, and urban decay (Apple 1992, Y9). The riot took an unprecedented form. Unconfined to a concentrated ghetto territory, unrestricted to a racially homogeneous group, the riot reasserted what may be the sole significant power that remains in the hands of the marginalized and oppressed—the power to disrupt.

It is our belief that, by riveting attention on the failed Reagan-Bush strategy to use race as the lever to displace the U.S. political spectrum to the right, the Los Angeles riot marks an end to the rightward drift in U.S. racial politics in general. However, there remains a significant gap between the lessons the riot has to teach and the ability of the U.S. political system to learn them. The political process has indeed shifted right over the past decades. As a result, Americans are poorer, less politically engaged and effectual, and culturally more benighted. All of these transformations have been wrought, to a significant extent, by the adroit deployment of racial politics. Their reversal, their transcendence, cannot occur overnight.

What does the Los Angeles riot tell us about racial politics in the U.S.? Above all else, it serves as an immanent critique of the mainstream political process, of the political convergence which dominates national politics today. It demonstrates the continuing significance, and the continuing complexity, of race in American life. And it shows the ineffectiveness of any authoritarian strategy, whether neo-conservatism or pragmatic liberalism, in addressing the problems of inequality in America.

In what follows we address three problems. First, we consider *the new convergence in mainstream racial politics.* As we have noted, President Bush's timorous call to repudiate the legacy of the 1960s bears more than a passing resemblance to a new Democratic drive to deemphasize race and play better in the suburbs. This new convergence in mainstream racial politics continues the 1980s legacy of the marginalization of racially defined minority constituencies. Furthermore, the intersection of mainstream Right and mainstream Left takes place in a symbolic manner. As political rhetorics joust over the merits of their moralisms, they fail to address the complexities of race in the ways they are experienced, represented culturally, and structured into politics. The L.A. riot challenged these manipulative approaches to race. It drew attention to the continuing presence of race in the social structures and meaning systems which organize the U.S. social order and identify its members.

Given this context, we next consider *the nature and varieties of racial identity today.* A quarter century after the civil rights movement's peak, the meaning of race and the nature of racial identity have become far more problematic, far more ambivalent, than they were in earlier periods of U.S. history.[2] The L.A. riot testifies to the complexity of contemporary racial dynamics. Despite various depictions to the contrary, the riot was not a black, but, rather, a multiracial affair. It involved significant antagonisms among racially defined minority groups, most notably between blacks and Koreans. It also involved substantial class conflicts within particular racially defined groups. What do these splits and conflicts signify?

Third, we discuss the riot as a phenomenon of *resistance to state coercion.* The riot was sparked, as so often in the past, by police violence and impunity; but at a deeper level, it was a response to impoverishment and neglect. The suffering of a society subjected to a drawn-out process of regressive economic restructuring, increasing authoritarianism, and an increasingly vapid discourse about "values" is concentrated among the racially defined minorities of the ghettos and barrios. The riot represented an act of defiance, a somewhat desperate effort to respond to the impoverishment, not only of the ghetto poor, but of U.S. society as a whole. As such, we believe it sets certain limits on the state's ability to enforce and extend the human suffering concentrated at the "lower depths" of our society.

CONVERGENT RACIAL POLITICS

In the U.S., understanding of the meaning of race is forged in large measure through the political system. Debates over state policy and political-party affiliation and media coverage of important racial events such as the Rodney King incident and the Los Angeles riot inculcate in the general public a "common-sense" or hegemonic conception of the significance of race. Historically, racial "common sense" has fluctuated wildly. Beliefs about equality, about the nature of racial difference, and indeed about what constitutes a race have shifted dramatically over time. In the post–World War II period, and even more so in the post–civil rights period, conflict over the significance of race has been continuous and vituperative.

Today's "common sense" about race is more a product of past controversies than an accurate rendering of present circumstances or actual experience. Just as the riots were multiracial events despite the political and media efforts to paint them in terms of black insurrection and white law and order, so, too, is experience "racialized" in an ever more complex fashion. Class differences fissure racially defined groups, creating far different stakes for middle-class Latinos in Silver Lake, for example, than for those in Pico Union, a poor neighborhood which includes many Central American refugees and undocumented workers. Blacks in Baldwin Hills are not powerless and desperate; their situation is quite distinct from that of blacks in Compton.

Yet part of the continuing reality of racism revealed in the riot lies precisely in the incomprehension, and indeed the willful ignorance, that the political process demonstrates when racial issues are at stake. The system is intellectually limited; it can "think" only one thought at a time. Either the riot is the product of the failed 1960s policies, and the dependence and sloth they induced in their unfortunate victims, as President Bush would have it, or it is a result of the greedy and regressive domestic policies pursued by the Reagan and Bush administrations, as Mr. Bush's critics would suggest. Faced with a choice between these two positions, we would obviously select the latter; but this limited choice, between what Winant (forthcoming) has elsewhere labeled the racial projects of neoconservatism and pragmatic liberalism, leaves a lot to be desired.

Here is the present situation: on the right wing of the mainstream, and firmly linked to the Republican party, is the neoconservative project; on the left wing of the mainstream, and equally firmly rooted in the Democratic party, is the pragmatic-liberal project. Neither view is uniformly held; certainly there are outriders in both parties. But, within the mainstream, the battle over what is to be the hegemonic view of race is joined—perhaps more intensely than at any other moment in decades—between the neoconservative and pragmatic-liberal projects. Due to the persistent racialization of politics in the U.S., the stakes are high. In 1992, the prize is the presidency and the future direction of domestic policy. Yet, also because of the persistent racialization of politics in the U.S., neither neoconservatives nor pragmatic liberals are able to address the problems of race and poverty in a sufficiently comprehensive way. Racial "common sense," whether of the mainstream Right or the mainstream Left, therefore persists in its failure.

The impoverished racial "common sense" of 1992, and the present convergence between the neoconservative and pragmatic-liberal racial projects, is dictated by a political logic in which the major parties compete for the suburban—largely white—vote. The current situation is dramatically delineated by Thomas and Mary Edsall in their book *Chain Reaction* (1991). The Edsalls describe how race became a powerful "wedge issue" which fractured the traditional liberal coalition. Since 1965, they assert, whites have found less and less reason to carry the burden of redressing social grievances. Working-class and middle-class whites have been directly affected, the Edsalls claim, by school integration, preferential hiring, and higher taxes to fund group-specific programs. The result of all this has been massive defections from the Democratic party and the consolidation of a conservative Republican majority.

Dramatic new patterns of segregation have emerged as whites have moved to the suburbs surrounding the declining cities, many of which have majority black and Latino populations. The nation, the Edsalls claim, is moving steadily toward a national politics that will be dominated by the suburban vote. The suburbs allow white, middle-class voters to meet their own communities' needs by taxing themselves for direct services (e.g., schools, libraries, police), while denying resources to the increasingly poor and nonwhite cities. Appeals to the middle class's "fiscal conservatism" and "communitarian" impulses thus have a hidden racial agenda: to prevent white tax dollars from going into programs to benefit racial minorities and the poor. The Edsalls argue:

> What all this suggests is that a politics of suburban hegemony will come to characterize presidential elections. With a majority of the electorate equipped to address its own needs through local government, not only will urban blacks become increasingly isolated by city-county boundaries, but support from the federal government, a primary driving force behind black advancement, is likely to diminish. (231)

Here is the reasoning that underlies President Bush's neoconservative appeal to "personal responsibility." Beneath all the color-blind rhetoric, not only of Bush but of his academic intelligence agents, Irving Kristol, Nathan Glazer, Charles Murray, and Thomas Sowell, lies a strong belief that racial inequality is an effect of other, nonracial factors. Because its origins lie in differentiated human capacities, racial inequality can never be achieved through politics.[3] The distance between this view and victim blaming is short.

Confronting this neoconservative racial project is a pragmatic-liberal project advanced by the newly "centrist" Democratic party under Bill Clinton. This project takes a leaf from the neoconservative book in its attempt to deemphasize race and accept some of the "personal responsibility" logic. It seeks, however, to reinvigorate the coalition which, from the 1930s to the 1960s, united minority and white workers under the New Deal and Great Society banners. The pragmatic liberals draw heavily on the work of sociologist William Julius Wilson, who has acted as an advisor to Clinton.[4]

Wilson believes that Clinton has assembled a "remarkable biracial coalition" by promoting programs which unite, as opposed to divide, racial minorities (particularly blacks) and whites. In doing so, Wilson says, Clinton has destroyed the myths that blacks respond only to race-specific issues, and that whites, particularly the poor and working class, will not support a candidate heavily favored by blacks: "[I]f the message emphasizes issues and programs that concern the families of all racial and ethnic groups, whites will see their mutual interests and join in a coalition with minorities to elect a progressive candidate." (1992, A15)

This belief flows from Wilson's analysis in *The Truly Disadvantaged* (1987). There he argues that the impersonal forces of the market economy explain more about the current impoverishment of the inner-city, African-American poor than any analysis relying on notions of racial discrimination. While Wilson does not dismiss the effects of historical racial discrimination his conclusion is that capital is "color-blind," and that the large-scale, demographic, economic, and political changes which have negatively affected the ghetto have little to do with race. Therefore, "group-specific" policies, emanating from the reforms of the civil rights era, can do little or nothing for the African-American underclass or ghetto poor. Wilson thus calls for "universal programs," rather than group-targeted ones, to halt the deterioration of inner-city communities: "The hidden agenda is to improve the life chances of groups such as the ghetto underclass by emphasizing programs in which the more advantaged groups of all races can positively relate." (120)

This "hidden agenda," of course, justifies a pragmatic attempt to woo white middle-class voters. Their needs—for more and better jobs, access to education and health care, and reductions in drug trafficking and crime—can be linked to those of the minority poor if the "wedge issue" of race can be blunted. Hence the "convergence" between neoconservative and pragmatic-liberal approaches to racial policy. The overlap is not total: there is a good deal more room for race baiting, and for sheer neglect of the cities, on the neoconservative side, while pragmatic liberals are willing to consider certain "group-specific measures" which neoconservatives reject out of hand.[5] Yet both the neoconservatives and the pragmatic liberals share the conviction that racial matters, and racial-minority constituencies, should receive less attention in the political process. The "dirty little secret" of continued racial hostility, segregation, and discrimination of all sorts is not to be addressed politically. Not now, and not in the foreseeable future.

AMBIVALENT RACIAL IDENTITIES

Even during "normal" times, when no racially significant riots or other crises loom, the contours and significance of racial identity are complex and delicate matters. The idea that we know what it means to be, say, black, Latino, or white is quite untenable. There are multiple problems involved in racial identification. Among these are, first, the sociocultural variability and conflict involved in defining racial categories; second, the significance, for a given individual or group, of membership in a particular racial category; and, third, the ability of individuals and groups to make judgments about the racial identities of others. Beyond these experiential factors lie structural ones. Some examples of these include the deployment of shifting and often hidden racial criteria in stratification and discrimination, spatial patterns of inequality, etc., and the mobilization of racial signifiers in politics, both explicitly and covertly.

Long-standing disputes exist in each of these general areas. For instance, consider the continuous discussion which takes place among blacks (and in scholarship about blacks) on the subject we can call "what's in a name?" Who are "blacks"? Are they "Africans"? "Negroes"? What is the significance of color in identifying them, as well as others? The vicissitudes of naming this racialized group have a history as long as the presence of Africans in the Western Hemisphere; this debate is coterminous with North American black writing itself (Gates 1985; Hanchard 1990; Davis 1991). Similar conundra have preoccupied Latino/Hispanic, Native-American, and Asian-American groups, as well as those who study them.[6] More recently, the white category has become problematic as well, as an increased remoteness from the "ethnicizing" experience of immigration has created more and more "unhyphenated" whites, whose group identity more and more coincides with their race (Liberson and Waters 1988; Alba 1990).

A monumental event like the L.A. riot not only reasserts collective racial interests, it also recasts racial-group identities. We have already noted that the riot was a "multicultural" one: blacks, Latinos, and whites were all seriously engaged in looting and burning. There were few reports of Asian-American participation; rather, Asians—and particularly Koreans—appeared to be the rioters' chief victims. Black hostility was especially directed at Korean merchants (Rutten 1992; Kim and Yang 1992).

The riot acted as a "pressure cooker," intensifying and revealing the ambivalences, fault lines, and polarizations which characterize U.S. racial identities today. The complex patterns it disclosed cannot possibly be examined in depth here; intensive primary and archival research will be needed to understand them fully. Here we wish only to point out a few intriguing instances of these variations.

Geography. The riot was not spatially confined, as had been its most obvious precedent, the Watts uprising of 1965. Although it began in a black ghetto neighborhood near Watts, it quickly spread out, particularly toward the north. Intense looting and arson took place in Koreatown, whose very location—between the black South Central area and Hollywood—signifies the "middleman minority" and "buffer" roles played by Korean merchants.[7] Without question, the Korean-American community was the most severely damaged by the riots. More dispersed incidents took place, however, as far north as Santa Monica Boulevard. Although police response was conspicuously limited or even nonexistent in the early phases of the riot, the downtown area was afforded significant protection. This, plus an informal truce between black and Chicano gangs (and more broadly, between the two communities), kept the riot from spreading significantly to the east, while to the west and south, targets were limited.[8]

Class. These geographical patterns, the concentrated attack on Korean merchants whose economic role placed them in a very exposed position, and extensive nonblack participation in the looting and burning all suggest that class factors, as well as racial ones, were significantly in play during the riot. It will not come as news that the riot was a response to poverty: looting is not generally a middle-class pastime. The novelty lies in the way the riot made visible the partial fissures and fault lines which now exist within minority racial communities and even within individual racial identities. At the same time, the riot demonstrated the unity—partial but real—which links the urban poor, regardless of race. Its effect was to *attenuate racial identities in favor of class identities* for those low-income people who were involved in the rioting or closely linked to it.

The riot also had a profound effect on those minorities who were not poor and who, by and large, did not participate. Hatred and distrust for the police were extremely strong in the black and Latino communities, as many better-off residents—some of them celebrities such as Wesley Snipes—recalled police mistreatment they had received. Since the immediate cause of the riot was the Rodney King verdict (which we discuss in greater depth below), and since the behavior of the police during the riot itself was a mysterious and undoubtedly exacerbating factor, the tendency of middle-class blacks and Latinos to identify with the rioters was increased. Thus the effect of the riot was to *attenuate class identities in favor of racial ones* for those middle-class minorities who were, by and large, not involved in the actual disturbances. Many members of the latter group actually made their way to the riot zone in the later stages or immediate aftermath of the disturbances, to express their solidarity, perhaps, to check on the safety of relatives or friends, or simply to experience and thereby clarify their ambivalence and uncertainty at having "made it" out of the ghetto or barrio.

Intragroup Cleavages. The riot demonstrated the cleavages that underlie such panethnic racialized identities as "Latino/Hispanic" or "Asian American." Among the former group, a key division between documented and undocumented people, long visible on other cultural and political terrains, was intensified during the riots. This fault line intersected another division, that between Mexican American/Chicanos and Central Americans, to produce a complex pattern of antagonisms in the Latino community. The LAPD arrested 2700+ Latinos during the riot, the majority for looting, but many for curfew violations as well. This number represented about half of all the arrests made, incidentally; more Latinos were arrested than blacks. Of this number, more than 1200 "were found to be 'without papers,' and were turned over—in violation of city policy—to the Immigration and Naturalization Service for deportation" (Rutten 1992, 53). More than 300 Central American refugees were in their number, and more than 600 were deported;[9] with typical ignorance and bigotry, Police Chief Daryl Gates singled out Central Americans as "participating in this riot in a very, very significant way" ("Voices" 1992, A7).

The wholesale assault on Korean merchants dramatically intensified existing political splits among Asian Americans. Generally aligned with the Democratic party and officially supportive of civil rights and antidiscrimination initiatives, Asian-American communities have long harbored inner racial antagonisms. Class divides many groups both from other Asians and internally. Solidly middle-class Japanese Americans, largely working-class Filipinos, generally low-income Southeast Asians, and Chinese Americans and Korean Americans whose class positions vary significantly all come into conflict where economic and political issues are concerned. In addition, there are significant parallels with Latino/Hispanic divisions over issues of assimilation and integration: long-established residents may disdain those who are "fresh off the boat." By and large, Asian Americans abhorred the rioting, even where they were not its direct victims. Yet there was also substantial sympathy with the plight of the impoverished inner city. At a rally held on 2 May 1992 in Koreatown, there were numerous calls for peace between blacks and Koreans, while "[s]everal elderly Korean men left the parade route to shake the hands of Latinos and African-Americans who were watching" (Chang and Krikorian 1992, A3). Signs demanded "Justice for Rodney King," quite a remarkable slogan given the past week's experience (Rutten 1992, 53).

Intergroup Cleavages. Black/Korean tensions have been widespread for years, reflecting patterns of antagonism between low-income communities and the "middleman minority" entrepreneurs who provide services to them. Such arrangements have a worldwide similarity, extending to Chinese in Malaysia, East Indians in Africa, etc. For Koreans operating businesses in the ghetto, as for Jews before them, high personal risks (for example, of robbery and arson) are offset by low rents and reduced competition. For black ghetto residents, these businesses appear to offer inferior products at high prices; their owners and employees (often family members) act fearful and hostile to customers; indeed their mere presence seems to "crowd out" potential black-owned competitors. Black-led boycotts of Korean grocers have occurred from coast to coast, and gunplay has been widespread on these premises. Robberies, as well as shootings of suspected shoplifters, are common. One such case, that of the killing of 15-year-old Latasha Harlins by an L.A. Korean-American grocer in early 1991, and the subsequent handing down of a suspended sentence, served as an immediate prelude to the rioters' assaults on Korean merchants.

In contrast to other Asian Americans (and to other racial minorities generally), the Korean community had maintained a low profile in Los Angeles politics, running almost no candidates for local office, mounting few public protests about its underrepresentation. Nor had Mayor Tom Bradley acted to mediate black/Korean disputes as had, for example, David Dinkins in New York. A big factor in Bradley's base has traditionally been what Mike Davis calls "the inner circle of Southside ministers and cronies" (1990, 309)[10] which included a number of figures actively promoting grocery boycotts. Thus, when the riots came, the mayor and Chief Gates did little to defend Koreatown itself, not to mention Korean businesses in South Central. Armed Korean men soon mounted the rooftops of many establishments and organized neighborhood patrols.

THE NATURE AND LIMITS OF STATE COERCION

The proximate cause of the riot, of course, was the acquittal of the LAPD officers who had brutally beaten motorist Rodney King. We can add little to the journalistic accounts which have saturated the nation (and the world) about the beating and the trial. The beating itself—this must be recognized—was a routine event which would have attracted no attention had not witness George Holliday captured it on videotape. The farcical acquittal was based on many factors: political toadying and miscalculation in the Los Angeles County D.A.'s office,[11] a botched courtroom strategy which wound up identifying the jury with the defendants,[12] and, probably most important, a change of venue to all-white Simi Valley. "Of the 8300 officers on the LAPD," according to reporters Marc Cooper and Greg Goldin (1992, 39), "a staggering 2000 of them live in Simi."

But the riot was more than an emphatic rejection of a single verdict; it was a protest against the systematic aggressions to which poor and nonwhite residents of Los Angeles are routinely subjected, especially if they are black.[13] The police are simply the most visible reminder of subordinate status. Certainly the LAPD enforces that status (or more properly, the complex combination of statuses that constitute racial identity) quite crudely and brutally. But, however it acts on the street, the LAPD's combination of neglect and violence pales in comparison to the state's overall repertoire. If we measure brutality in terms of human costs— in lives destroyed, communities savaged, pain inflicted—then surely the denial of jobs, education, health care, drug treatment, and housing is far more serious brutality than any number of police beatings. So, rather than stew about a mis- carriage of justice, it is more valuable to reframe the riot as an eruption of resistance against the coercive powers of the state.

It is fairly widely accepted that, over the past two decades, a massive restruc- turing of U.S. society has taken place. The changes involved have been manifold. They have included a regressive redistribution of income and a decline in real wages, a significant shift to the ideological right in terms of public discourse, and an increase in the use of coercion on the part of the state. It is not necessary to consider these shifts only in racial terms to recognize their profound nature. For example, we could document the increasingly repressive atmosphere experienced by unions (especially those daring to exercise their rights to strike or organize), or the increased state commitment—beginning under Carter but greatly aug- mented under Reagan and Bush—to the denial of women's rights, notably repro- ductive rights.

Coercive state power has been extensively involved in this restructuring. Obvi- ously not everyone has been subjected to the same coercive powers. For most of the U.S. citizenry, it has not been necessary to apply authoritarian measures in order to effect the desired changes. The socioeconomic condition and political power of the majority of the labor force—the middle class, the skilled work force—could, in general, be allowed to erode rather than be assaulted directly. There were exceptions: the PATCO strike, for example. But these were relatively unusual.

Where racial minorities were concerned, however, this pattern was reversed. Here the exceptions were the "coping strata," in Martin Kilson's term, those exemplary groups which had, against all odds, achieved (a sometimes precarious) middle-class status. For the restructuring of the U.S. political economy, for the majority of blacks and Latino/Hispanics, for Native Americans and many Asian Americans, this restructuring has largely been a disaster. It has been carried out in many respects at their economic expense, it has been rationalized by discussions of their supposed defects, and it has been enforced by an intensity of repression not seen in the U.S. since the 1960s.

Thus the underfunding of schools and the restriction of educational opportunities, the flight of less-skilled employment from the cities to the *maquilas* and their equivalents around the world, the growth of underground and illegal economies dealing in drugs and illegally sweated labor, all of this has become a way of life in the ghettos and barrios of the U.S. The creation of a "Third World within" has been a corollary of the reactionary restructuring we are describing.

Most central to this new authoritarianism has been a sustained attack on the welfare state. Although the primary victims of this attack are minority women and children,[14] these are but the cannon fodder for a larger assault on the bargaining power of working and middle-class people in the economy, and on the political power of the majority of the population in the electoral process (Piven and Cloward 1982; Phillips 1991). Economic restructuring, political repression, ideological rationalization—in respect to unfair taxes, lax morals, and a propensity toward violence—all these elements come together in the assault on the welfare state.

And while this stew has been prepared largely in the Republican—which is to say neoconservative—kitchen, it is being eagerly lapped up by many "moderate" Democrats as well. One has only to examine the *New Republic* or consider the latest moralizing by Jim Sleeper (1990) or Mickey Kaus (1992) to find its pragmatic-liberal incarnation.

What, then, generates a riot, even of a "new kind" like that of Los Angeles? Without question, there must be a spark, there must be an outrage. But there also must be a rage, and rage is not born in a moment. The kind of rage that created the L.A. riot was a political sentiment: nobody cares about me, about us; nobody offers us a chance; there is no hope for us in this system; it's built on our despair. Such sentiments are hardly ineffectual, for they indicate that the price of American decline is the creation of a stratum of society with "nothing left to lose." Having no other, more acceptable, political means at their disposal, the urban poor resort to what Orlando Patterson (1979) has called their "counter-leviathan power." This power—to disrupt, to frighten, to resist, to limit the coercive powers of the state even at great cost and risk—retains its effectiveness.

CONCLUSION

The L.A. riot signaled the limits of the reactionary racial politics practiced during the Reagan-Bush years. More eloquently than any blue-ribbon report or policy tract, the riot made the case for a new social policy. The uprising demonstrated the need to reverse the decay of U.S. cities and the declining economy linked to the urban crisis. Both the Republican and Democratic parties rushed to apply their policy prescriptions to the nation's urban wounds. Some version of the immediate needs highlighted by the uprising—jobs, education, and investment in the urban environment—was compatible with the political agenda being framed by *both* the Republican and Democratic candidates in their 1992 electoral campaigns.

For the neoconservatives clustered around Republican campaign headquarters, these were the natural issues of a "traditional values" campaign, one which would emphasize privatization of welfare-state programs, incentives for inner-city investment, and school choice. To the neoconservatives, the riot's message was the failure of the welfare state; this was, they thought, a tune which would play very well among suburban, middle-class, white voters. It was a political formula which could build on white resentments, on the coded racial appeals of the Reagan-Bush years, while still claiming to believe in racial equality. As in years past, neoconservative racial politics could work by denying the significance of race.

The riot's message for the pragmatic liberals grouped in the Democratic camp was only somewhat different. To them, the fires of L.A. helped justify a more activist social policy, greater state investment in job creation, education, infrastructure, etc., precisely because these were not "group-specific" measures. Jobs, education, and increased social investment were justifiable demands now because whites who were not poor, and who did not live in the central cities, wanted them as well. For the pragmatic liberals, then, a promise to return to the more activist policies of the welfare state would be successful if it principally addressed the needs of suburban, middle-class, white voters. Of course, it would not hurt to mouth some platitudes about the scourge of racism, but the crucial thing was to reach the suburbs with the message that the middle class, and not the low-income minorities who supposedly sucked up all the taxes, were to be the chief beneficiaries of liberal largesse. To this end, appropriate moralizing about "personal responsibility" and "family values" had to be inserted into Democratic Party discourse. Thus for the first time, liberals would adopt the "code word" strategy previously associated with the Republican right; in order to win back the white suburbanites, they, too, claimed the right to blame the victim, to disparage the "dependence" of welfare mothers. For their own reasons, but with some of the same authoritarian rhetoric employed by the neoconservatives, the pragmatic liberals, too, denied the significance of race.

There were two ironic elements to this situation. The first irony was that, as the riot had demonstrated, racial matters had attained a complexity and variety which both these political formulae were incapable of addressing. Coded racial appeals to whites made less sense in the context of a multiracial riot. Despite the best efforts of politicians and media mouthpieces, the L.A. riot was not simply a black affair. Unlike Watts in 1965, the flashpoint of this riot—the Rodney King beating and its sequel, the Simi Valley trial and acquittal—had been witnessed by millions. Few doubted that an injustice had been committed. This riot occurred in a post–civil rights era America, one substantially leavened by the presence of middle-class blacks and Latino/Hispanics, few of whom leaped to the defense of the LAPD or the state in general, particularly when the issue was repression directed at racial minorities. A situation in which blacks, Latinos, and whites were the rioters and blacks, Latinos, whites, and Asians the *victims* of the violence generated a certain amount of explanatory difficulty, except perhaps where compassion for Korean merchants was concerned. When even these—surely the most unambiguous class of "riot victims" visible on the nightly news—revealed themselves as having some sympathy for the impoverished inner-city dwellers, how could the official story cope?

The second irony was that it was the very destruction of the welfare state which had jeopardized not only the interests and egalitarian aspirations of racially defined minorities, but those of the middle class as well. Whatever short-term benefits they had gained by moving to the suburbs and voting against the "tax and spend" social programs excoriated by the Republicans, the white middle class now stood to lose because an eviscerated welfare state meant lousy schools, inferior and costly health care, eroding infrastructure, and, worst of all, declining wages, capital flight, and unemployment! The Republican formula for electoral victory—driving a wedge between suburb and city, between white and racial minority voters—had worked well enough as long as the burdens of economic decline and political powerlessness could be shifted onto the shoulders of racial minorities. When general economic decline spread from the ghettos and barrios to the suburbs, and when the flames of L.A. demonstrated the limits of any further assaults on the inner cities, "universal programs for reform" (Wilson) suddenly regained their attractiveness. Finally, it took the riot to drive home the point that all their anxieties about crime and drugs and taxes were pretty minimal in comparison to the fears a full-blown urban uprising could unleash. The middle class heard a clear message in the riot, one that was as old as the nation: if we do not hang together, we shall surely hang separately.

Notes

1. Bush did not hesitate to use racial "code words" in this and other comments on the riot. See Rosenbaum, 1992, p. A14.

2. In other writings we have charted in some detail the vicissitudes of the racial-formation process in the postwar and post–civil rights periods. See Omi and Howard Winant, 1991, and Michael Omi and Howard Winant, 1986.

3. The voluminous neoconservative literature is firm on this point. Thomas Sowell, for example, has argued that one's "human capital" is to a large extent culturally determined. Therefore the state cannot create a false equality which runs counter to the reality of the magnitude and persistence of cultural differences. Such attempts at social engineering are likely to produce negative and unintended results: "If social processes are transmitting real differences—in pro-

ductivity, reliability, cleanliness, sobriety, peacefulness[!]—then attempts to impose politically a very different set of beliefs will necessarily backfire, for the truth remains the same, regardless of what is transmitted through social processes." (Sowell, 1983, p. 252)

4. It should also be noted that one of Clinton's chief advisers, pollster Stanley B. Greenberg, is the author of an important early study on "democratic defection," which pointed to "group-specific" Democratic racial policies as a key factor in the production of suburban-white "Reagan Democrats" in the 1980s. See Stanley B. Greenberg, 1985.

5. "My proposal for dealing with the racial issue in social welfare is to repeal every bit of legislation and reverse every court decision that in any way requires, recommends, or awards differential treatment according to race, and thereby put us back onto the track that we left in 1965. We may argue about the appropriate limits of government intervention in trying to enforce the ideal, but at least it should be possible to identify the ideal: Race is not a morally admissible reason for treating one person differently from another. Period." Murray, 1984, p. 223.

6. These debates are too voluminous and complex to be treated adequately, or even referenced, here. Some worthwhile beginning points might be, for Native Americans: Cornell, 1988; for Latinos/Hispanics: Rodriguez, 1989, for Asian Americans: Lopez and Espiritu, 1990.

7. Light and Bonacich, 1988, remains the best account of the development of Koreatown.

8. In making these comments we have relied on published accounts, whose inaccuracies (to judge by 1960s reference points) are likely to be high. Advance apologies for errors may thus be in order.

9. We have benefited from material provided by the Central American Refugee Center (CARE-CEN), which has worked to defend this community from discrimination for many years. They can be reached at 668 S. Bonnie Brae, Los Angeles, CA 90057.

10. Davis's otherwise marvelous book is conspicuously lacking when it comes to Los Angeles Asian groups.

11. "[L.A. District Attorney Ira] Reiner, whose tenure in office has been marked by a series of failures, had himself selected Terry L. White, a black prosecutor with an undistinguished record, to try the King case. . . . Reiner faces stiff competition in the June primary from two of his deputies. When he chose White, he seemed to have his eye on potential black voters; in any case, he had chosen him before a change of venue was granted, not anticipating that a black prosecutor would face a jury without any blacks." Rutten, 1992, 52.

12. Paul de Pasquale, one of the defense attorneys, put it this way in his closing argument: "This unpleasant incident [the beating] is what we have police for. The circumstances here were consistent with the job the man was hired to do. He was part of the line between society and chaos. . . . This is not some orgy of violence. This is careful police work." Mydans, 1992, p. A1.

13. In the wake of the riot and the attention directed toward the LAPD, many reports of systematic racism and brutality have surfaced. A recent lurid expose is Rothmiller and Goldman, 1992. Here an insider describes being trained in systematic racism, misprision and subornation, harassment and torture. An excellent analysis—published before the Rodney King incident—can be found in Davis, 1990, pp. 267–317.

14. For this reason Ronald Reagan's attack on "welfare queens" has always struck us as particularly vicious. Who else did Reagan (and Bush after him) think was going to care for low-income children? To assault the one group which—against all odds—was still attempting to nurture and protect the most vulnerable members of society, and to do this while rendering that job more difficult by slashing and burning what meager resources were yet available to these low-

income and minority women, will always seem to us an act so obscene and cruel that it makes ordinary child abuse look benign by comparison.

Works Cited

————, "Roundtable: Domestic Social Policy After the L.A. Uprising," *Tikkun* Vol. 7, no. 4 (July–August, 1992).

Alba, Richard D., *Ethnic Identity: The Transformation of White Identity* (New Haven: Yale University Press, 1990).

Apple, R. W. Jr., "Riots and Ballots," *The New York Times,* May 2, 1992.

Brecht, Bertolt, "On Thinking About Hell," *Poems, 1913–1956,* John Willett and Ralph Manheim, eds. (New York: Methuen, 1979).

Brownstein, Ronald, "Clinton: Parties Fail to Attack Race Divisions," *Los Angeles Times,* May 3, 1992.

Bush, George, "Excerpts From Speech by Bush in Los Angeles," *The New York Times,* May 9, 1992.

Chang, Irene, and Greg Krikorian, "30,000 Show Support in Koreatown March," *Los Angeles Times,* May 3, 1992.

Cooper, Marc, and Greg Goldin, "Some People Don't Count," *Village Voice,* May 12, 1992.

Cornell, Stephen, *The Return of the Native: American Indian Political Resurgence* (New York: Oxford University Press, 1988).

Davis, F. James, *Who Is Black? One Nation's Definition* (University Park, PA: Pennsylvania State University Press, 1991).

Davis, Mike, *City of Quartz: Excavating the Future in Los Angeles* (London: Verso, 1990).

Dionne, E. J., *Why Americans Hate Politics* (New York: Simon and Schuster, 1991).

Edsall, Thomas Byrne with Mary Edsall, *Chain Reaction: The Impact of Race, Rights, and Taxes on American Politics* (New York: Norton, 1991).

Gates, Henry Louis Jr., "Editor's Introduction: Writing 'Race' and the Difference It Makes," in idem, ed., *"Race," Writing, and Difference* (Chicago: University of Chicago Press, 1985).

Greenberg, Stanley B., *Report on Democratic Defection,* Report Prepared for the Michigan House Democratic Campaign Committee (Washington, D.C.: The Analysis Group, 1985).

Hanchard, Michael, "Identity, Meaning, and the African-American," *Social Text* 24 (1990).

Kaus, Mickey, *The End of Equality* (New York: Basic, 1992).

Kim, David D., and Jeff Yang, "Koreatown Abandoned," *Village Voice,* May 12, 1992.

Lieberson, Stanley, and Mary C. Waters, *From Many Strands: Ethnic and Racial Groups in Contemporary America* (New York: Russell Sage Foundation, 1988).

Light, Ivan H., and Edna Bonacich, *Immigrant Entrepreneurs: Koreans in Los Angeles, 1965–1982* (Berkeley: University of California Press, 1988).

Lopez, David, and Yen Espiritu, "Panethnicity in the United States: A Theoretical Framework." *Ethnic and Racial Studies* 13 (1990).

Murray, Charles, *Losing Ground: American Social Policy, 1950–1980* (New York: Basic Books, 1984).

Mydans, Seth, "Los Angeles Police Officers Acquitted in Taped Beatings," *The New York Times,* April 30, 1992.

Omi, Michael, and Howard Winant, "Contesting the Meaning of Race in the Post-Civil Rights Period," paper presented at the Annual Meetings of the American Sociological Association, Cincinnati, August, 1991.

Omi, Michael, and Howard Winant, *Racial Formation in the United States: From the 1960s to the 1980s* (New York: Routledge, 1986).

Patterson, Orlando, "The Black Community: Is There a Future?" in Seymour Martin Lipset, *The Third Century: America as a Post-Industrial Society* (Stanford: Hoover Institution Press, 1979).

Phillips, Kevin, *The Politics of Rich and Poor: Wealth and the American Electorate in the Reagan Aftermath* (New York: HarperCollins, 1991).

Piven, Frances Fox, and Richard A. Cloward, *The New Class War: Reagan's Attack on Welfare and Its Consequences* (New York: Pantheon, 1982).

Rodriguez, Clara, *Puerto Ricans: Born in the USA* (Boston: Unwin Hyman, 1989).

Rosenbaum, David E., "White House Speaking In Code on Riot's Cause," *The New York Times,* May 6, 1992.

Rothmiller, Mike, and Ivan G. Goldman, *L.A. Secret Police: Inside the LAPD Elite Spy Network* (New York: Pocket Books, 1992).

Rutten, Tim, "A New Kind of Riot," *The New York Review,* June 11, 1992.

Sleeper, Jim, *The Closest of Strangers: Liberalism and the Politics of Race in New York* (New York: Norton, 1990).

Sowell, Thomas, *The Economics and Politics of Race: An International Perspective* (New York: Quill, 1983).

"Voices," *Los Angeles Times,* May 3, 1992.

Wilson, William Julius, "The Right Message," *The New York Times,* March 17, 1992.

Wilson, William Julius, *The Truly Disadvantaged: The Inner City, the Underclass, and Public Policy* (Chicago: University of Chicago Press, 1987).

Winant, Howard, "Race: Theory, Culture, and Politics in the United States Today," in Marcy Darnovsky, Barbara Epstein, and Richard Flacks, eds., *Social Movements and Cultural Politics* (New York: Oxford University Press, forthcoming.)

Part Four

On the Streets of Los Angeles

———————————

9

Anatomy of a Rebellion:
A Political-Economic Analysis

Melvin L. Oliver,
James H. Johnson, Jr.,
and
Walter C. Farrell, Jr.

It is quite impossible to understand the events surrounding the acquittal of the
four police officers accused of brutally beating Rodney King without placing them
within the local and national circumstances and forces that have deepened class
and racial inequalities over the past two decades. Both at the local and national
level, the trajectory of economic, political, and social trends has exacerbated the
ever-so-fragile social fabric of our nation's cities, making ripe the conditions that
kindled the social explosion that occurred in Los Angeles on 29 April 1992.

In this essay, we reflect on the Los Angeles civil disorder of 1992 from an
urban political economy perspective. It is our contention that the course and
magnitude of changes in the urban political economy of American cities in general,
and Los Angeles in particular, were crucial in bringing to the forefront the contradictions underlying the Los Angeles urban rebellion. Thus, this essay is an
anatomy of the civil unrest that seeks to unravel its relationship to rebellions of
the past, highlighting both the ever-changing and unchanging nature of the relationship of black Americans to the economic and political order, and the consequences of the introduction of new actors into the sociopolitical mix of large
American cities. In order to accomplish this, we situate the civil unrest within

This chapter is based on a previous analysis of the civil disorder in Los Angeles entitled ''The
Los Angeles Rebellion: A Retrospective View,'' which appeared in *Economic Development Quarterly*
6 (1992) 356–372 and was co-authored by James H. Johnson, Jr., Cloyzelle K. Jones, Walter C.
Farrell, Jr. and Melvin L. Oliver.

the broader context of the recent demographic, social, and economic changes occurring in the Los Angeles milieu. The object of this analysis is to ground the rebellion in the context of a political system that is frayed at the edges in its attempt to integrate new voices into the body politic and, at the same time, is incapable of bringing into the economic mainstream significant portions of the African-American community (traditionally one of the most economically marginal segments of American society). Can the efforts that have been spawned as a consequence of the urban rebellion achieve a modicum of success in confronting these difficult challenges? We address this issue in a brief but critical review of existing policies and proposals that have been advanced to "rebuild" Los Angeles. Finally, we outline our own strategy for redeveloping South Central Los Angeles, one which is designed to address the real "seeds" of the civil unrest.

ANATOMY OF THE REBELLION

The recent civil unrest in Los Angeles was the worst such event in recent U.S. history. None of the major civil disorders of the 1960s, including the Watts rebellion of 1965, required a level of emergency response or exacted a toll—in terms of loss of life, injuries, and property damage and loss—comparable to the Los Angeles rebellion of 1992 (table 1). The burning, looting, and violence that ensued following the rendering of a not-guilty verdict in the police-brutality trial required the deployment of not only the full forces of the Los Angeles Police Department (LAPD) and the Los Angeles County Sheriff's Department, but also 10,000 National Guardsmen and 3,500 military personnel (table 2). The Fire Department received 5,537 structure fire calls and responded to an estimated 500 fires. An estimated 4,000 businesses were destroyed. Fifty-two people died and 2,383 people were injured, including 20 law-enforcement and fire personnel. Property damage and loss have been estimated at between $785 million and $1 billion (table 1).

In contrast to the civil disorders of the 1960s, this was a multiethnic rebellion. The diversity is reflected in table 3, which depicts, for the period 30 April through 4 May, arrests by race/ethnicity. It has been estimated that 1,200 of the 16,000 plus arrested were illegal aliens, roughly 40% of whom were handed over to INS officials for immediate deportation (table 4). Also in contrast to the civil disorders of the 1960s, the burning and looting were neither random nor limited to a single neighborhood; rather, the response was targeted, systematic, and widespread, encompassing much of the legal city. This fact has lead us to purposefully and consistently refer to the civil unrest as a rebellion as opposed to a riot.

Table 9.1   Toll from Selected Rebellions

City/State	Date	Number Arrested	Number Injured	Number Dead	Property Damage	Other Characteristics
Newark, NY	12–17 July 1967	n.a.	1,500	26	$58,796,605	300 fires set
Detroit, MI	23–28 July 1967	7,000	2,000	43	$162,396,707	—
Los Angeles, CA	11–17 August 1965	n.a.	1,032	34	$182,565,079	—
Washington, DC	4–9 April 1968	6,036	1,202	9	$45,292,079	—
Los Angeles, CA	29–30 April 1992	16,291	2,383	52	$785 million– 1 billion	500 fires set

Source: "Toll from Other Riots," *USA Today,* 5 May 1992, 4A, and Timothy Noah and David Wessel, "Urban Solutions: Inner City Remedies Offer Novel Plans—and Hope, Experts Say," *Wall Street Journal,* 4 May 1992, A1, A16.
NOTE: n.a. = not available.

THE VERDICT AND THE REBELLION IN RETROSPECT

We think it is safe to say that both the verdict rendered in the police-brutality trial, and the widespread burning, looting, and violence which ensued after the jury issued its decision, shocked most Americans. In retrospect, however, we would like to suggest that both the verdict and the subsequent rebellion were quite predictable. The treatment of black suspects by the police and black defendants by the courts represents a continuity in the experience of blacks in relationship to the criminal-justice system.

The outcome of the trial, in our view, was predictable for two reasons. The first pertains to the defense attorneys' successful bid for a change of venue for the trial. Simi Valley, the site of the trial, and Ventura County more generally, is a predominantly white community known for its strong stance on law and order, as evidenced by the fact that a significant number of LAPD officers live there.[1] Thus, the four white police officers were truly judged by a jury of their peers.[2] Viewed in this context, the verdict should not have been unanticipated.

The second development that made the outcome of the trial predictable, in retrospect, was the defense attorneys' ability to put Mr. King, instead of the four white police officers, on trial. (We should note here, parenthetically, that the media is also guilty in this regard, as evidenced by its consistent characterization of the case as "the Rodney King trial.") The defense attorneys, in effect, played the so-called "race card"; they painted Mr. King as unpredictable, dangerous, and uncontrollable, much as Mr. Bush, in the 1988 presidential campaign, used Willie Horton, the convicted rapist released on a temporary work furlough only to commit another heinous crime, to paint Mr. Dukakis as being soft on crime.[3]

In today's society, the Willie Horton stereotype, recent surveys tell us, is often applied categorically to black males, irrespective of their social and economic status, but especially if they reside in the inner city.[4] It is our contention that the

Table 9.2   Law Enforcement Personnel on Duty

Los Angeles Police and County Sheriff's Department	3,720
California Highway Patrol	2,300
Fire	2,700
National Guard	10,000
Army	2,500
Marines	1,500

Source: "L.A. Aftermath at a Glance," *USA Today,* 6 May 1992, 3A.

jury agreed with the defense attorneys' portrayal of Mr. King as dangerous and uncontrollable, and thus rendered a verdict in favor of the four white police officers, notwithstanding the seemingly irrefutable videotaped evidence.

Why do we think, in hindsight, that the civil unrest following the verdict in the police-brutality trial was predictable? We believe that the response was not about the verdict in the police-brutality trial per se; rather, the civil unrest reflected the high degree of frustration and alienation that had built up among the citizens of South Central Los Angeles over the last 20 years. The rebellion, as we view it in retrospect, was a response not to a single but rather to repeated acts of what is widely perceived in the community to be blatant abuse of power by the police and the criminal-justice system more generally.[5]

The civil unrest was also a response to a number of broader, external forces which have increasingly isolated the South Central Los Angeles community, geographically and economically, from the mainstream of the Los Angeles society.[6] These forces include: recent structural changes in the local (and national) economy; wholesale disinvestment in the South Central Los Angeles community by banks and other institutions, including the local city government; and nearly two decades of conservative federal policies which have simultaneously affected adversely the quality of life of the residents of South Central Los Angeles and accelerated the decline and deterioration of their neighborhoods.

Moreover, these developments were occurring at a time when the community was experiencing a radical demographic transformation, an unprecedented change in population accompanied by considerable tensions and conflict between long-term residents and the more recent arrivals.[7] Viewed from this perspective, the verdict in the police-brutality trial was merely the proverbial straw that broke the camel's back.[8]

SEEDS OF THE REBELLION

The videotaped beating of Mr. Rodney King was only the most recent case in which there were serious questions about whether LAPD officers used excessive force to subdue or arrest a black citizen. For several years, the City of Los Angeles

Table 9.3   Los Angeles Rebellion, 1992: Arrest by Race/Ethnicity (30 April through 4 May 1992)

	LAPD	Sheriff's Department	Total	Percent
Latino	2,764	728	3,492	36.9
Black	2,022	810	2,832	29.9
White	568	72	640	6.8
Other/Unknown	84	2,408	2,492	26.4
Total	5,438	4,018	9,456	100

Source: Virginia I. Postrel, "The Real Story Goes beyond Black and White," *Los Angeles Times,* 8 May 1992, A11.

has had to pay out millions of taxpayers' dollars to settle the complaints and lawsuits of citizens who were victims of LAPD abuse. Moreover, the black citizens of the city of Los Angeles have been disproportionately victimized by the LAPD's use of the choke hold, a tactic employed to subdue individuals who are perceived to be uncooperative. During the 1980s, 18 citizens of Los Angeles died as a result of LAPD officers' use of the choke hold; 16 of them reportedly were black.[9]

Accordingly, the not-guilty verdict rendered in the police-brutality trial was also only the most recent in a series of cases in which the decisions emanating from the criminal-justice system were widely perceived in the black community to be grossly unjust. This decision came closely on the heels of another controversial verdict in the Latasha Harlins case. A video-tape revealed that Ms. Harlins—an honor student at a local high school—was fatally shot in the back of the head by a Korean shopkeeper following an altercation over a carton of orange juice. The shopkeeper received a six month suspended sentence and was ordered to do six months of community service.[10]

These and related events have occurred in the midst of drastic demographic change in South Central Los Angeles. Over the last two decades, the community has been transformed from a predominantly black to a mixed black and Latino area (figure 1). Today, nearly one-half of the South Central Los Angeles population is Latino. In addition, there also has been an ethnic succession in the local business environment, characterized by the exodus of many of the Jewish shopkeepers and a substantial influx of small, family-run Korean businesses. This ethnic succession in both the residential environment and the business community has not been particularly smooth. The three ethnic groups—blacks, Latinos, and Koreans—have found themselves in conflict and competition with one another over jobs, housing, and scarce public resources.[11]

Part of this conflict stems from the fact that the Los Angeles economy has undergone a fairly drastic restructuring over the last two decades.[12] This restructuring includes, on the one hand, the decline of traditional, highly unionized, high-wage manufacturing employment; and on the other, the growth of employment in the high-technology-manufacturing, the craft-specialty, and the advanced-

Table 9.4.   Los Angeles Rebellion, 1992: Illegal Aliens Arrested and Deported by Country of Origin

Mexico	360
El Salvador	62
Guatemala	35
Honduras	14
Jamaica	2
Other Countries	4
Total	477

Source: George Ramos and Tracy Wilkinson, "Unrest Widens Rifts in Latino Populations," *Los Angeles Times,* Washington edition, 8 May 1992, 1.

service sectors of the economy. As figure 2 shows, South Central Los Angeles—the traditional industrial core of the city—bore the brunt of the decline in manufacturing employment, losing 70,000 high-wage, stable jobs between 1978 and 1982.[13]

At the same time these well-paying and stable jobs were disappearing from South Central Los Angeles, local employers were seeking alternative sites for their manufacturing activities. As a consequence of these seemingly routine decisions, new employment growth nodes or "technopoles" emerged in the San Fernando Valley, in the San Gabriel Valley, and in El Segundo near the airport in Los Angeles County, as well as in nearby Orange County (figure 3).[14] In addition, a number of Los Angeles–based employers established production facilities in the Mexican border towns of Tijuana, Ensenada, and Tecate. Between 1978 and 1982, over 200 Los Angeles–based firms, including Hughes Aircraft, Northrop, and Rockwell, as well as a host of smaller firms, participated in this deconcentration process.[15] Such capital flight, in conjunction with the plant closings, has essentially closed off to the residents of South Central Los Angeles access to what were formerly well-paying, unionized jobs.[16]

It is important to note that, while new industrial spaces were being established elsewhere in Los Angeles County (and in nearby Orange County as well as along the U.S.-Mexico border), new employment opportunities were emerging within or near the traditional industrial core in South Central Los Angeles (figure 3). But, unlike the manufacturing jobs that disappeared from this area, the new jobs are in competitive sector industries, which rely primarily on undocumented labor and pay, at best, minimum wage.

In part as a consequence of these developments, and partly as a function of employers' openly negative attitudes toward black workers, the black-male jobless rate in some residential areas of South Central Los Angeles hovers around 50%. Whereas joblessness is the central problem for black males in South Central Los Angeles, concentration in low-paying, bad jobs in competitive sector industries is the main problem for the Latino residents of the area. Both groups share a

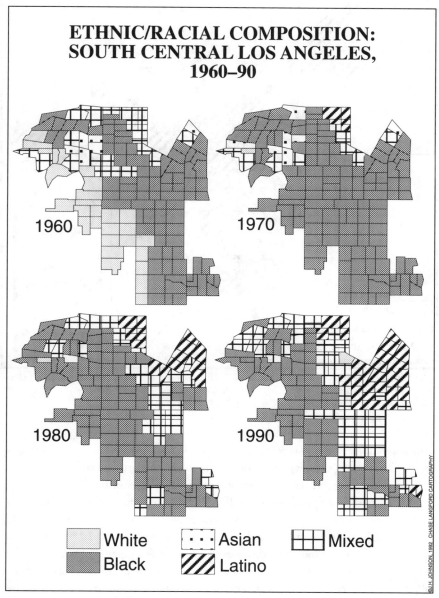

ETHNIC/RACIAL COMPOSITION:
SOUTH CENTRAL LOS ANGELES,
1960–90

1960

1970

1980

1990

White   Asian   Mixed
Black   Latino

©J.H. JOHNSON, 1992 CHASE LANGFORD CARTOGRAPHY

SOURCE: Los Angeles Community Development Department, *Ethnic Clusters of Los Angeles* (Los Angeles, Community Development Department 1977, 1982), and Korean Chamber of Commerce of Los Angeles, *Directory of Korean Businesses* (Los Angeles, Korean Chamber of Commerce of Los Angeles, 1987).

Figure 9.1   Ethnic Change in South Central Los Angeles, 1960–80, and Locations of Korean Businesses, 1987

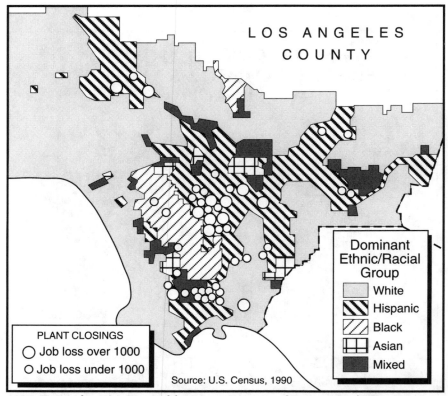

SOURCE: Data from U.S. Bureau of the Census, *1990 Census of Population* (Washington, DC: U.S. Department of Commerce, 1991), and the Data Center, *Plant Shutdown Directory* (Oakland, CA: The Data Center, 1978–1982).

Figure 9.2   Plant Closings in L.A. County, 1978–82

common fate: incomes below the poverty level (figure 4). Whereas one group is the working poor (Latinos), the other is the jobless poor (blacks).[17]

In addition to the adverse impact of structural changes in the local economy, South Central Los Angeles also has suffered from the failure of local institutions to devise and implement a plan to redevelop and revitalize the community. In fact, over the lat two decades, the local city government has consciously pursued a policy of downtown and westside redevelopment at the expense of South Central Los Angeles. One needs only to look at the skyline of downtown and the so-called Wilshire corridor—that twenty-mile stretch extending along Wilshire Boulevard from downtown to the Pacific Ocean—to see the impact of this policy.[18]

Finally, the seeds of the rebellion are rooted in nearly two decades of conservative policy making and implementation at the federal level. Many policy analysts talk about the adverse impact on minorities and their communities of Democratic president Lyndon Johnson's "War on Poverty" programs of the 1960s, but we

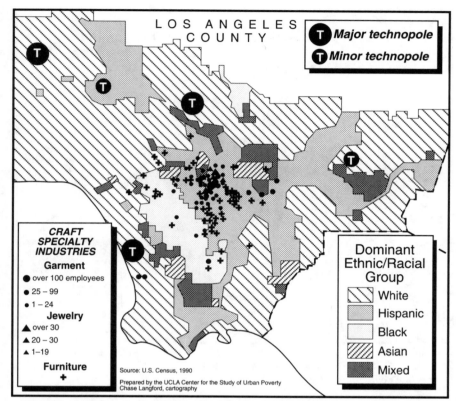

SOURCE: Maya Blum, Kathryn Carlson, Estela J. Morales, Ross Nussbaum, and Patricia J. Wilson, "Black Male Joblessness, Spatial Mismatch, and Employer Preferences: A Case Study of Los Angeles," unpublished paper, Center for the Study of Urban Poverty, University of California, Los Angeles, May 1992.

Figure 9.3   Locations of Craft Specialty Industries and Job Growth Technopoles in L.A. County, 1990

must not lose sight of the fact that the Republicans have been in control of the White House for all but four (the Carter years) of the past 20 years.[19] A number of public policies implemented during this period, and especially during the years when Mr. Reagan was president, we contend, served as sparks for the recent civil unrest. Three of these policy domains are worthy of note here.

The first pertains to the federal government's establishment of a laissez-faire business climate in order to facilitate the competitiveness of U.S. firms. Such a policy, in retrospect, appears to have facilitated the large number of plant closings in South Central Los Angeles and capital flight to the U.S./Mexico border and various Third World countries. Between 1982 and 1989 there were 131 plant closings in Los Angeles, idling 124,000 workers. Fifteen of these plants moved to Mexico or overseas.[20]

The second involved the federal government's dismantling of the social safety

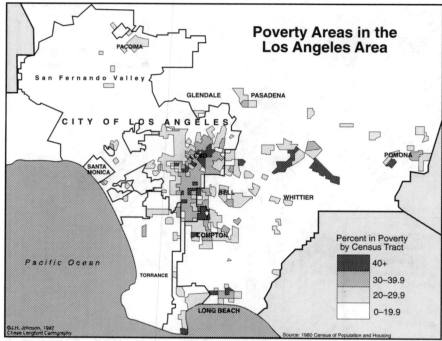

SOURCE: Data from U.S. Bureau of the Census, *1980 Census of Population and Housing, Census Tracts* (Washington, DC: U.S. Department of Commerce, 1981).

Figure 9.4 Poverty Areas in Los Angeles Area

net in minority communities. Perhaps most devastating for the South Central Los Angeles area has been the defunding of community-based organizations (CBOs). Historically, CBOs were part of that collectivity of social resources in the urban environment which encouraged the inner-city disadvantaged, especially disadvantaged youth, to pursue mainstream avenues of social and economic mobility and discouraged dysfunctional or antisocial behavior. In academic lingo, CBOs were effective "mediating" institutions in the inner city.[21]

During the last decade or so, however, CBOs have become less effective as mediating institutions. The reason for this is that the federal support they received was substantially reduced. In 1980, when Mr. Reagan took office, CBOs received an estimated 48% of their funding from the federal government.[22] As part of the Reagan Administration's dismantling of the social safety net, many CBOs were forced to reduce substantially programs that benefited the most disadvantaged in the community. Inner-city youth have been most adversely affected by this defunding of community-based initiatives and other safety-net programs.

It should be noted, moreover, that the dismantled social safety net has been replaced with a criminal dragnet. That is, rather than allocate support for social programs that discourage or prevent disadvantaged youth from engaging in dysfunctional behavior, over the past decade or so, the federal government has pursued a policy of resolving the problems of the inner city through the criminal-justice system.

Given this shift in policy orientation, it should not be surprising that, nationally, 25% of prime-working-age young black males (ages 18–35) are either in prison, in jail, on probation, or otherwise connected to the criminal-justice system.[23] Although reliable statistics are hard to come by, the anecdotal evidence suggests that at least 25% of the young black males in South Central Los Angeles have had a brush with the law. What are the prospects of landing a job if you have a criminal record? Incarceration breeds despair and in the employment arena, it is the scarlet letter of unemployability.[24]

Educational initiatives enacted during the late 1970s and early 1980s, which were designed to address the so-called "crisis" in American education, constitute the third policy domain. There is actually a very large body of social-science evidence which shows that such policies as tracking by ability group, grade retention, and the increasing reliance on standardized tests as the ultimate arbiter of educational success have, in fact, disenfranchised large numbers of black and brown youth. In urban school systems, they are disproportionately placed in special-education classes and are more likely than their white counterparts to be subjected to extreme disciplinary sanctions.[25]

The effects of these policies in the Los Angeles Unified School District (LAUSD) are evident in the data on school-leaving behavior. For the Los Angeles Unified School district as a whole, 39.2% of all of the students in the class of 1988 dropped out at some point during their high-school years. However, for high schools in South Central Los Angeles, the drop-out rates were substantially higher, between 63% and 79% (figure 5). It is important to note that the drop-out problem is not limited to the high-school population. According to data compiled by LAUSD, approximately 25% of the students in the junior high schools in South Central Los Angeles dropped out during the 1987–88 academic year (figure 6).

Twenty years ago it was possible to drop out of school before graduation and find a well-paying job in heavy manufacturing in South Central Los Angeles. Today, however, those types of jobs are no longer available in the community, as we noted previously. Juxtaposing the adverse effects of a restructured economy and the discriminatory aspects of education reforms, what emerges is a rather substantial pool of inner-city males of color who are neither at work nor in school. These individuals are, in effect, idle; and previous research shows us that it is this population which is most likely to be in gangs, to engage in drug trafficking, and to participate in a range of other criminal behavior.[26] Moreover, we know that it is this population of idle, minority males that experiences the most difficulty

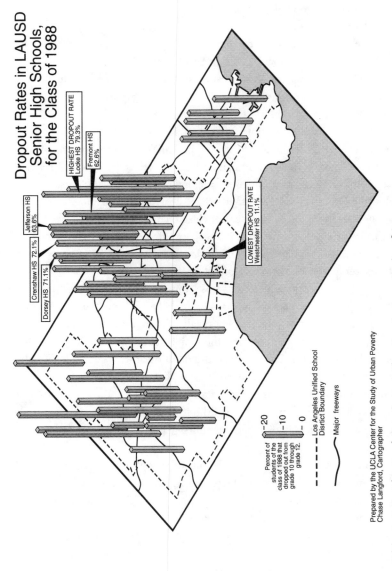

Figure 9.5   Drop-out Rates in LAUSD Senior High Schools, for the Class of 1988

SOURCE: California Basic Educational Data System, *Three Year Summary: Number of Dropouts in California Public High School Instruction* (Sacramento, CA: CBEDS, 1989).

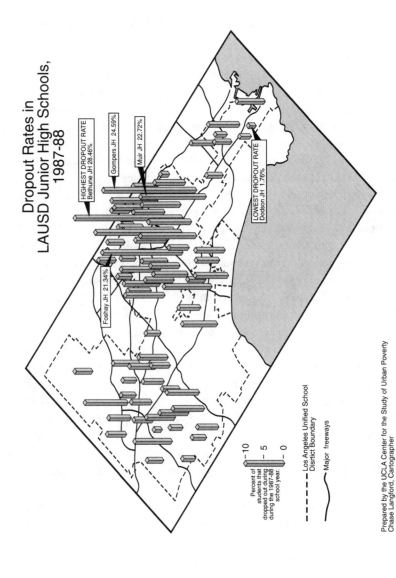

Dropout Rates in
LAUSD Junior High Schools,
1987-88

HIGHEST DROPOUT RATE
Bethune JH 28.46%

Gompers JH 24.59%

Muir JH 22.72%

LOWEST DROPOUT RATE
Dodson JH 1.76%

Foshay JH 21.34%

Percent of
students that
dropped out during
during the 1987-88
school year.

– – – Los Angeles Unified School
District Boundary

—— Major freeways

Prepared by the UCLA Center for the Study of Urban Poverty
Chase Langford, Cartographer

Figure 9.6 Drop-out Rates in LAUSD Junior High Schools, 1987–88

SOURCE: California Basic Educational Data System, *Three Year Summary: Number of Dropouts in California Public High School Instruction* (Sacramento, CA: CBEDS, 1989).

forming and maintaining stable families, which accounts, at least in part, for the high percentage of female-headed families with incomes below the poverty level in South Central Los Angeles.

EXPLAINING THE SOURCES OF A MULTIETHNIC REBELLION

The most distinctive aspect of the Los Angeles rebellion was its multiethnic character. While blacks were the source of the disturbances as they broke out on the first night of the rebellion, by the second evening it was clear that the discontent that emerged initially was shared by many of the city's largest racial group, the Latino community. As we have just pointed out, the economically depressed Latinos in Los Angeles are comprised of a working-poor population, characterized by a large and significant core of Mexican and Central American immigrants. But what is interesting is that the rebellion did not encompass the traditional Mexican-American community of East Los Angeles. Indeed, the fires and protest were silent in these communities as political leaders and local residents ardently cautioned residents against "burning your own community."[27] Nevertheless, Latinos in South Central Los Angeles did not hesitate to participate in looting, particularly against Korean merchants. How do we explain this pattern?[28]

One important element necessary to explain the uneven participation of Latinos in the rebellion is to place the Latino experience into the context of struggles to incorporate that community politically into the electoral system in Los Angeles city and county. With the largest Latino population outside of Mexico City, Latinos have been severely underrepresented in city and county governments. In a struggle emanating from the 1960s, Latinos, particularly Mexican Americans, have been involved in protesting this situation, in ways ranging from street-level, grass-roots activity to highly coordinated court challenges to racially biased redistricting schemes that have unfairly diluted Latino voting strength.[29] That struggle has just recently begun to bear fruit. In the important court case *Garza et al. v. County of Los Angeles,* Los Angeles County was found guilty of racial bias in the redistricting process and ordered to accept an alternative redistricting plan that led to the election of Gloria Molina as the first Latino(a) to serve on the powerful five-person Los Angeles County Board of Supervisors.[30] Recent maneuvering at the city level will ensure significant representation of Latinos on the Los Angeles City Council, but not without considerable conflict between entrenched black and Latino City Council leaders over communities that are racially mixed.[31] Los Angeles is a city in flux politically.

While it is clear that an emerging Latino majority will assume greater political power over time, the political-empowerment process has left several portions of the Latino population behind. In particular, Mexican Americans in Los Angeles, who have a longer history there and are more likely to constitute greater portions of the voting-age-citizen population, are the key recipients of the political spoils that have come in the Latino struggle for electoral power. All the elected officials to come into power as a consequence of these struggles are Mexican, and while they articulate a "Latino" perspective on the issues, they also tend to represent a narrow "Mexican" nationalism.[32] The growing Central American population, which is residentially based in South Central Los Angeles and not in the traditional core of East Los Angeles, has not benefited for the most part from the political empowerment of Mexicans in Los Angeles. They are recent immigrants, not able to vote, and thus have become the pawns in negotiations with the county and city over the composition of political districts. Black and white politicians now represent districts with up to 50% of the population being Latino. But because they are unable to vote, a declining black or white population of 25% to 35% can maintain control over these districts without addressing the unique need of a majority of the community. The upshot has been the political neglect of a growing community whose problems of poverty have been just as overlooked as those of the black poor.

This contrast was easily observed during the rebellion as traditional Mexican-American community leaders were either silent or negative toward the mass participation of Latinos in the rebellion. Those Latinos in South Central had little stake in the existing political and economic order while East Los Angeles was riding the crest of a successful struggle to incorporate their political demands into the electoral system. Just as the black community is divided into a middle and a working class that are connected to the system by way of their political and economic ties, the Latino community in Los Angeles is increasingly divided by income, ethnicity, and citizenship.

The second element necessary to understand the involvement of Latinos, particularly Central American and Mexican immigrants, in the rebellions is the existence of interethnic hostilities between these groups and Korean Americans. While much is made of African-American and Korean-American conflict, little is said about an equally and potentially more volatile conflict between Latinos and Koreans.[33] While the crux of African-American and Korean-American conflict is based on the uneasy relationship between merchant and customer, the Latino-Korean conflict has the added dimensions of residential and workplace conflict. Latino involvement in the rebellion was most intense in Koreatown. Koreatown is an ethnic enclave demarcated by both the Korean control of businesses and a dwindling Korean residential presence. The community, in fact, is residentially mixed, with large portions of Latinos and Koreans. Latinos in this community come into contact with Koreans on multiple levels and, from all we know from current research, experience considerable hostility in each level.[34] First, in terms of residence, Latinos complain of discrimination on the part of Korean landlords as buildings and apartments are rented according to racial background. Second, as customers in Korean establishments, Latinos complain of forms of disrespectful treatment similar to that about which black customers complain. Third, as employees in Korean small businesses, Latinos point to high levels of exploitation by their employers. Thus, in this context, it was not surprising to see the vehemence and anger that the Latino community in South Central Los Angeles expressed, especially toward the Korean community.

THE FEDERAL BLUEPRINT

How do we simultaneously deal with the seeds of the rebellion, as we have characterized them above, and rebuild the physical infrastructure of South Central Los Angeles? In attempting to answer this question, we shall limit the discussion here to the federal government's blueprint, as the local "Rebuild L.A." initiative remains somewhat vague in both scope and content.[35]

Table 5 highlights the Bush administration's plan to revitalize the South Central Los Angeles community. In actuality, the main elements of the plan constitute what Secretary of Housing and Urban Development Jack Kemp termed, prior to the Los Angeles rebellion, his blueprint for a "Conservative War on Poverty."[36]

Mr. Kemp promotes enterprise zones, as table 5 shows, as being the key to job creation and retention in the inner cities. He proposes to eliminate capital-gains taxes and reduce levies for business that will locate in specified inner-city areas. However, there is no history of success of such strategies in poor communities like South Central Los Angeles.

Moreover, recent research has indicated, as we noted earlier, that those white businesses in the inner city are especially reluctant to hire black males. Employer responses to a field survey in Chicago showed that they generally embrace the prevailing racial stereotypes about this group—that they are lazy, lack a good work ethic, are ineducable, and perhaps most important, dangerous.[37]

Couple this social reality with the fact that the major priorities for businesses when making locational decisions are access to markets, access to a quality labor force (code words for no blacks), infrastructure, and crime rates. These business factors are considered to be much more important in site selection than tax rates. And where enterprise zones have been successful, employers have brought their work force with them rather than employing community residents, or they have used these enterprise locations as warehouse points where there is a need for few workers.[38]

Secretary Kemp has had a long-term commitment to empowering the poor by making them homeowners—the theory being that individuals will have a stronger

Table 9.5   The Federal Blueprint

Program	Description	$ Allocation
Emergency Aid	To address immediate needs of citizens impacted by the crisis.	$600 million
"Weed and Seed"	Beef up law enforcement and social services (Headstart, Job Corps, WIC, Safe Haven Program) in the inner city.	$500 million
"Project HOPE"	Encourage home ownership among residents of public-housing projects.	$1 billion
"Move to Opportunity"	Five-city plan to subsidize welfare families that move from depressed inner-city areas, using housing vouchers and providing advice.	$20 million
Welfare reform	Raise to $10,000 from $1,000 the amount of assets that welfare recipients may accumulate without losing benefits. Builds on Wisconsin Plan to discourage welfare mothers from having more babies.	
Urban Enterprise Zones	Establishment of specifically designated areas where investment and job creation would be encouraged through incentives such as tax breaks and regulation relief.	

Source: Jessica Lee, "Bush Presents His Urban Policy," USA Today, 6 May 1992, 8A.

commitment to maintaining that which they own and to joining in other efforts to enhance their general neighborhood environment. Project HOPE, as it is called, would make home ownership affordable (table 5). This idea had languished in the Bush administration for the last four years, until the Los Angeles rebellion pushed it to center stage.[39]

However, this program would lock poor people into communities that are isolated, socially and economically, from mainstream employment and educational opportunities. And it would do nothing to expand the housing stock. Project HOPE is analogous to the reservation status provided to Native Americans in the government's effort to empower them. As a result, in part, of their isolation over time, Native Americans currently have some of the highest rates of unemployment, alcoholism, and domestic abuse of any American ethnic or racial group.

The federal blueprint, as table 5 shows, also includes monies to give the poor, inner-city residents of South Central Los Angeles greater choice in deciding what school their children will attend. The encouragement of educational choice among public and private schools—using public dollars—needs to be carefully monitored. Although promoted as the solution to the crisis in public education, poor parents are at risk of being losers in a system where choice is "unchecked." The much-heralded Wisconsin Parental Choice Plan has achieved a modicum of success because this public/private initiative was carefully designed to meet the educational needs of poor children.

The Wisconsin legislature structured this plan to mandate that private educational providers develop their recruitment strategies and curricular offerings specifically to accommodate poor students. Since nonpoor youngsters already had a wide range of educational choice, it was appropriate that poor children—who are the least well served in our educational system—have their interests served. Educational choice should be driven by the needs of the poor if we are to revitalize education in inner cities.[40]

Finally, the Bush administration proposes to spend $500 million on a "Weed and Seed Program," which is designed to rid the community of the violent criminal element and to provide support for programs like Headstart and the Job Corps which are known to benefit the urban disadvantaged and their communities (table 5). As it is currently envisioned, however, the program places too much emphasis on the "weed" component and not enough on the "seed" component. Of the $500 million proposed for the program, only $109 million is targeted for "seed" programs like Headstart. With nearly 80% of the proposed funding targeted for the "weed" component, the primary goal of the program is, clearly, to continue the warehousing of large numbers of poor inner-city youth in the penal system.[41]

This, in our view, is a misplaced programmatic focus, as it is ever so clear that harsher jail and prison terms are not deterrents to crime in inner-city areas like South Central Los Angeles. What is needed in South Central Los Angeles, instead, is more "seed" money; to the extent that increased police power is deployed in South Central Los Angeles, it should be via a community policing construct where officers are on the street, interfacing with community residents prior to the commission of a crime.

We are, quite frankly, dubious of the so-called conservative war on poverty and, in particular, of its likely impact in South Central Los Angeles. The federal blueprint, and apparently the local "Rebuild L.A." initiative headed by Mr. Peter Ueberroth as well, is built on the central premise that, if the proper incentives are offered, the private sector will, in fact, play the leading role in the revitalization and redevelopment of South Central Los Angeles. We do not think this is going to happen for the reasons stated earlier: the types of governmental incentives currently under consideration in Washington are not high on private businesses' locational priority lists.

In view of these facts, and the social-science evidence is clear on the ineffectiveness of enterprise-zone legislation both in Britain and in 36 states in this country,[42] we firmly believe that what is needed to rebuild South Central Los Angeles is a comprehensive public-works service-employment program, modeled on President Roosevelt's Works Progress Administration program of the 1930s. Jobs to rebuild the infrastructure of South Central Los Angeles can provide meaningful employment for the jobless in the community, including the hard-core disadvantaged, and can be linked to the skilled trades' apprenticeship-training programs.

To incorporate the hard-core disadvantaged into such a program would require a restructuring of the Private Industry Council's Job Training Partnership Act Program (JTPA). The program must dispense with its performance-based approach in training where funding is tied to job placement. This approach does not work for the hard-core disadvantaged because training agencies, under the current structure, have consistently engaged in creaming—recruiting the most "job-ready" segment of the inner-city population—to ensure their continued success and funding. Meanwhile, the hard-core unemployed have received scant attention and educational upgrading.[43]

We are now convinced that a WPA-type initiative, combined with a restructured JTPA program, will go a long way toward resolving the chronic jobless problem, especially among young males of color in the community, and toward rebuilding the infrastructure of South Central Los Angeles.

Such a program would have several goals that would enhance the social and economic viability of South Central Los Angeles. First, it would create meaningful jobs that could provide the jobless with skills transferable to the private sector. Second, it would rebuild a neglected infrastructure, making South Central Los Angeles an attractive place to locate for business and commerce. Finally, and most important, by reconnecting this isolated part of the city to the major arteries of transportation, by building a physical infrastructure that could support the social and cultural life of this richly multicultural area (e.g., museums, public buildings, housing), and by enhancing the ability of community and educational institutions to educate and socialize the young, this plan would go far in providing a sustainable "public space" in the community. For it is our contention, that only when South Central Los Angeles is perceived as a public space that is economically vibrant and socially attractive will the promise of this multicultural community be fulfilled. Thus far, private-sector actions and federal-government programs and proposals have done nothing to bring us nearer to reaching this goal.

CONCLUSIONS

The fires have been extinguished in South Central Los Angeles and other cities, but the anger and rage continue to escalate, and they are likely to reemerge over time to the extent that the underlying political and economic causes are left to fester. While political, business, and civic leaders have rushed to advance old and new strategies and solutions to this latest urban explosion, much of what is being proposed is simply disjointed and/or déjà vu.

Clearly there is a need for additional money to resolve the underlying causes of this urban despair and devastation, but money alone is not enough. Government is constitutionally mandated to ensure "domestic tranquillity," but government alone cannot empower poor communities. And although blacks and other people of color have a special role and obligation to rebuild their neighborhoods because they are the majority of the victims and the vandals, they cannot solely assume this burden of responsibility.

What is needed, in our view, is a reconceptualization of problem solving where we meld together, and invest with full potential, those strategies offered from liberals and conservatives, from Democrats and Republicans, and from whites and people of color. Three cities (Milwaukee, Los Angeles, and Detroit, respectively) have served, individually and collectively, as urban laboratories where we have engaged in action research and proffered solutions to the urban problems which have generated violent outbursts.

The contentious state of police/minority-community relations has served as the linchpin of urban unrest in each instance. While relations have improved in several large cities in recent years, the Los Angeles Police Department has been frozen in time. Black and Hispanic males have been particularly brutalized in their encounters with police, the majority of whom are white males. But more disconcerting is the fact that poor, central-city minority communities have become more crime-ridden of late. Thus, minorities find themselves in the ambiguous situation of needing greater police service on the one hand and protection from the excesses of those same services on the other. This contradictory situation had kept relations between these groups at a race/class boiling point.

More police officers are desperately needed in high-crime communities that are disproportionately populated by the poor. Local, state, and federal dollars (federal funds for this initiative are in the crime bill before Congress) need to be allocated quickly toward this end. At present, violent felons are beginning to outnumber police officers in many of our urban centers.[44] As we noted previously, this increase in police power should be deployed via a community policing program. Such an effort can serve to control minor offenses and to build trust between police and community residents. Community policing has evidenced positive results in Detroit and Philadelphia and is showing encouraging signs in Milwaukee and numerous other large and small cities. In addition, the intensive recruitment of minority officers and specific, ongoing (and evaluated) diversity training will further reduce police/minority community tensions. But most important in this effort is enlightened, decisive leadership from the office of the chief, a position of abysmal failure in Los Angeles.

The national administration's initial response to the rebellion was to blame it on deficiencies among the urban poor, particularly on the supposed lack of "family values" and the predominance of female-headed households.[45] This jaundiced view ignores the real sources of the conflict and concentrates instead on the symptomatology of growing up in concentrated-poverty communities where the social resources and assistance necessary to negotiate mainstream society success-fully are either totally lacking or insufficient.[46] Thus, the policy implication that needs to be drawn from the rebellion is that, in order to bring the poor and disenfranchised into mainstream society, in order to enhance their acceptance of personal responsibility, and in order to promote personal values consistent with those of the wider society, we must find a way to provide a comprehensive program of meaningful assistance to this population. But clearly, a change in personal values along, as suggested by some right-wing analysts, will not substitute for job training, job creation, and the removal of racial stereotypes and discrim-ination.[47] The spatial concentration of contemporary poverty presents significant challenges to policy makers and human-service providers alike. Although numer-ous programs and initiatives have been instituted to combat these problems, they suffer from three important weaknesses.

First, there is a lack of coordination among programs aimed at improving the life chances of citizens in poor communities. Second, no systematic steps have been taken to evaluate existing efforts, to ensure that the programs are effectively targeting the "hardest to serve," adults with low skills and limited work history, and youth who are teen parents or school dropouts. Third, there is no compre-hensive strategy for planning future resource allocations as needs change and as these communities expand in size.

A recent national study of training and employment programs, under the Job Training Partnership Act, revealed that little has been done to address the reme-dial educational needs of high-school drop-outs and that those with the greatest need for training and employment services are not targeted. However, overcom-ing these and other program weaknesses is not sufficient to solve these complex problems. A strategic plan is needed to alleviate the social ills associated with concentrated poverty.

There is a need to conduct a comprehensive inventory of agencies and insti-tutions that provide services to populations in poverty areas. We also need to assess and evaluate the service providers' performance in an attempt to identify strengths, weaknesses, and missing links in their service-delivery systems. On the basis of these findings, a strategy should be devised for a more effective and coordinated use of existing resources and for generating new resources to address unmet needs. Finally, we need to propose a plan of action that would encourage development in the 1990s that links together the various program initiatives.

And, most important, representatives of the affected ethnic and racial groups must be in key decision-making roles if these efforts are to achieve success.[48] Citizens of color, individually and through their community, civic and religious institutions, bear a responsibility to promote positive values and lifestyles in their communities and to socialize their youth into the mainstream. But they cannot do this alone.

They cannot be held accountable for the massive plant closings, disinvestments, and exportation of jobs from our urban centers to Third World countries. There must be an equality in status, responsibility, and authority across race and class lines if we are to resolve our urban crises. Government, in a bipartisan fashion, must direct its resources to those programs determined to be successful with the poor, the poor must be permitted to participate in the design of programs for their benefit, and society at all levels must embrace personal responsibility and a commitment to race and gender equity.

How likely are these reforms to be implemented? If one were to analyze the prospects of these changes from the perspective offered in this paper, the answer would not be an optimistic one. However, an important consequence of the rebellion was to shake the very foundation of the taken-for-granted quality of our discourse and practice about race and class in American society. It opens up the opportunity for reassessing positions, organizing constituencies, and collectively engaging issues that have been buried from sight until now. Given these new openings, the Los Angeles urban rebellion of 1992 gives us all the opportunity to work on building a society in which "we can all get along."

Notes

1. See Jane Gross, "In Simi Valley, Defense of a Shared Way of Life," *New York Times,* 4 May 1992, A9.

2. See David Margolick, "As Venues Are Changed, Many Ask How Important a Role Race Should Play," *New York Times,* 23 May 1992, A1.

3. See Walter C. Farrell, Jr., James H. Johnson, Jr., and Cloyzell K. Jones, "Field Notes from the Rodney King Trial and the Los Rebellion," 28 and 29 April and 2, 3, and 4 May 1992.

4. See, for example, Jolene Kirschenman and Kathryn Neckerman, "We'd Love to Hire Them But . . . : The Meaning of Race For Employers," *The Urban Underclass,* ed. Christopher Jencks and Paul Peterson (Washington, DC: The Brookings Institution, 1990), 203–24; R. J. Struyk, M. A. Turner, and M. Fix, *Opportunities Denied, Opportunities Diminished: Discrimination in Hiring,* (Washington, DC: The Urban Institute, 1991).

5. See Jason De Parle, "Year-old Study on Police Abuse Is Issued by U.S.," *New York Times,* 20 May 1992, A1 and A10; Joseph D. MacNamara, "When the Police Create Disorder," *Los Angeles Times,* May 1992, M1 and M6; Melvin L. Oliver, Walter C. Farrell, Jr., and James H. Johnson, Jr., "A Quarter-Century of Slipping Backward," *Los Angeles Times,* 10 August 1990, B7; Dennis Schatzman, "50–60 Percent of Riot Arrestees Had No Prior Contact with the Law," *Los Angeles Times,* 28 May 1992, A1 and A16; David K. Shipler, "Khaki, Blue, and Blacks," *New York Times,* 26 May 1992, 15.

6. See Ed Soja, Rebecca Morales, and Goetz Wolff, "Urban Restructuring: An Analysis of Social and Spatial Change in Los Angeles," *Economic Geography* 58 (1983): 221–35; Melvin L. Oliver

and James H. Johnson, Jr., "Interethnic Conflict in an Urban Ghetto: The Case of Blacks and Latinos in Los Angeles," *Research in Social Movements, Conflicts, and Change* 6 (1984): 57–94; James H. Johnson, Jr., and Melvin L. Oliver, "Interethnic Minority Conflict in Urban America: The Effects of Economic and Social Dislocations," *Urban Geography* 10 (1989): 449–46; James H. Johnson, Jr., and Melvin L. Oliver, "Economic Restructuring and Black Male Joblessness: A Reassessment," *Urban Labor Market and Job Opportunity,* ed. George Peterson and Wayne Vrohman (Washington, DC: The Urban Institute, 1992), 113–147.

7. See Oliver and Johnson, "Interethnic Conflict in an Urban Ghetto," and Johnson and Oliver, "Interethnic Minority Conflict in Urban America."

8. See Melvin L. Oliver, "It's the Fire Every Time, and We Do Nothing," *Los Angeles Times,* 1 May 1992, B7.

9. See Farrell, Johnson, and Jones, "Field Notes."

10. See Elaine Kim, "They Armed in Self-Defense," *Newsweek,* 18 May 1992, 10, and Seth Mydans, "Jury Acquits Los Angeles Policemen in Taped Beating," *New York Times,* 29 April 1992, A1 and A8.

11. See Oliver and Johnson, "Interethnic Conflict in an Urban Ghetto"; Johnson and Oliver, "Interethnic Minority Conflict in Urban America"; and James H. Johnson, Jr., and Curtis C. Roseman, "Increasing Black Outmigration from Los Angeles: The Role of Household Dynamics and Kinship Systems," *Annals of the Association of American Geographers* 80 (1990): 205–22.

12. See Soja, Morales, and Wolff, "Urban Restructuring"; Johnson and Oliver, "Economic Restructuring and Black Male Joblessness" *Urban Geography* 12, no. 6, pp. 542–562.; and Johnson and Oliver, "Economic Restructuring and Black Male Joblessness: A Reassessment."

13. See Soja, Morales, and Wolff, "Urban Restructuring."

14. See A. J. Scott, "Flexible Production Systems and Regional Development: The Rise of New Industrial Spaces in North America and Western Europe," *International Journal of Urban and Regional Research* 12 (1988): 61–113, and A. J. Scott, *Metropolis: From Division of Labor to Urban Form* (Berkeley: University of California Press, 1986).

15. See Soja, Morales, and Wolff, "Urban Restructuring."

16. See Johnson and Oliver, "Economic Restructuring and Black Male Joblessness."

17. See Johnson and Oliver, "Economic Restructuring and Black Male Joblessness"; Soja, Morales and Wolff, "Urban Restructuring"; and Ed Luttwak, "The Riots: Underclass vs. Immigrants," *New York Times,* 15 May 1992, A15.

18. See Robert Beauregard and H. Braviel Holcomb, *Revitalizing Cities, Resource Publication in Geography* (Washington, DC: Association of American Geographers, 1981).

19. See Gary Orfield and Carole Ashkinzae, *The Closing Door: Conservative Policy and Black Opportunity* (Chicago: University of Chicago Press, 1991).

20. These statistics for the years 1982–1989 were extracted from *The Data Center's Plant Shutdowns Monitor Directory* (Oakland, CA: The Data Center, 1978–1982).

21. See P. L. Berger and R. J. Newhaus, *To Empower People: The Role of Mediating Structures in Public Policy* (Washington, DC: American Enterprise Institute, 1977), and Melvin L. Oliver, "The Urban Black Community as Network: Toward a Social Network Perspective," *Sociological Quarterly* 29 (1988): 623–45.

22. See L. M. Salamon, "Non-Profit Organizations: The Lost Opportunity," *The Reagan Record,* ed. John L. Palmer and Isabel V. Sawhill (Cambridge, MA: Ballinger Publishing Co., 1984), 261–85.

23. See Marc Mauer, "Americans Behind Bars," *Criminal Justice* (Winter 1992): 12–18 and 38.

24. See Johnson and Oliver, "Economic Restructuring and Black Male Joblessness."

25. See Gary Orfield, "Exclusion of the Majority: Shrinking College Access and Public Policy in Metropolitan Los Angeles," *The Urban Review* 20 (1988): 147–163.

26. See W. K. Viscusi, "Market Incentives for Criminal Behavior," *The Black Youth Employment Crisis,* ed. R. B. Freeman and H. J. Holzer (Chicago: University of Chicago Press, 1986).

27. George Ramos and Tracy Wilkinson, "Unrest Widens Rifts in Latino Population," *Los Angeles Times,* 5 June 1992, 1.

28. See Peter Kwong, "The First Multicultural Riots," *Inside the L.A. Riots,* ed. Don Hazen (Los Angeles: Institute for Alternative Journalism, 1992), 88–93.

29. See James Regalado, "Conflicts over Redistricting in Los Angeles County: Who Wins? Who Loses?" *Racial and Ethnic Politics in California,* ed. Byran O. Jackson and Michael B. Preston (Berkeley: I.G.S. Press, 1991), 373–93.

30. See J. Morgan Krousser, "How to Determine Intent: Lesson from L.A.," *Social Science Working Paper* 741 (1992), California Institute of Technology.

31. See James A. Regalado, ed., *Political Battles over L.A. County Board Seats: A Minority Perspective* (Los Angeles: Edmund G. "Pat" Brown Institute, 1989).

32. See Ramos and Wilkinson, "Unrest Widens Rifts in Latino Population."

33. See Kwong, "The First Multicultural Riots."

34. In focus groups conducted immediately following the rebellion, Spanish-speaking, mostly immigrant respondents spoke eloquently of their interactions with Koreans in terms of housing, business, and work. While none of the participants condoned the violence, and only one respondent admitted participating in the looting, many expressed in graphic terms incidents of being harassed by Korean-American shopkeepers because of the assumption they would steal, or of being turned down for housing because the Korean-American landlord wanted to keep the apartment complex all Korean-American, or of being forced to work overtime for a Korean-American employer. This form of interethnic conflict has rarely surfaced, but we believe it is central to understanding the multi-ethnic character of the L.A. rebellion.

35. See Richard Stevenson, "With Few Tools, Ueberroth Begins Mission in Riot Areas," *New York Times,* 5 May 1991, A23.

36. Marshall Ingwerson, "Radical Intent: HUD Chief Wants Poverty to Top Conservative Agenda," *Christian Science Monitor,* 11 October 1991, 9.

37. See Kirschenman and Neckerman, "We'd Love to Hire Them But . . . "

38. See David Osborne, "The Kemp Cure-All," *New Republic,* 3 April 1989, 21–25, and Neal R. Peirce, "Kemp's Enterprise Zones: Breakthrough or Chimera?" *Nation's Cities Weekly,* 5 June 1989, 4.

39. See Kathleen Decker, "Kemp Champions Blacks and Poor: Secretary Preaches Theme of Hope in Squalor of Ghettos," *Los Angeles Times,* 19 April 1989, A1.

40. See Walter C. Farrell, Jr., and Jacquelyn E. Mathews, "School Choice and the Educational Opportunities of African American Children," *Journal of Negro Education* 59 (1990): 526–37, and Gary George and Walter C. Farrell, Jr., "School Choice and African American Students: A Legislative View," *Journal of Negro Education* 59 (1990): 521–25.

41. See Terry Eastland, " 'Weed and Seed': Root Out Crime, Nurture Poor," *Wall Street Journal,* 14 May 1992, A1.

42. See Osborne, "The Kemp Cure-All."

43. See Susan B. Garland, "90 Days to Learn to Scrub? Sure, If Uncle Sam's Paying," *Business Week*, 20 January 1992, 70.

44. See "Put Police before Prisons," editorial, *New York Times*, 23 May 1992, A10.

45. See "Excerpts from Vice President's Speech on Cities and Poverty," *New York Times*, 19 May 1992, A12; Lawrence M. Mead, "Job Programs and Other Bromides," *New York Times*, 19 May 1992, A15; and James Q. Wilson, "How to Teach Better Values in Inner Cities," *Wall Street journal*, 18 May 1992, A14.

46. See William Julius Wilson, *The Truly Disadvantaged* (Chicago: University of Chicago Press, 1987), 198, and James H. Johnson, Jr., and Melvin L. Oliver, "Modeling Urban Underclass Behavior," *Center for the Study of Urban Poverty, Occasional Paper 3*, UCLA Institute for Social Science Research, 1990–1991.

47. See John D. Kasarda, "Why Asians Can Prosper Where Blacks Fail," *Wall Street Journal*, 28 May 1992, A20; Mead, "Job Programs and Other Bromides"; and James Q. Wilson, "How to Teach Better Values in Inner Cities."

48. See Robert Woodson, "Transform Inner Cities from the Grassroots Up," *Wall Street Journal*, 1 June 1992, A12.

10

Uprising and Repression in L.A.

An Interview with Mike Davis
by the *CovertAction* Information Bulletin

What happens to a dream deferred?

Does it dry up
like a raisin in the sun
Or fester like a sore—
And then run?
Does it stink like rotten meat?
Or crust and sugar over—

Maybe it just sags
like a heavy load.

Or does it explode?
                                        —Langston Hughes

CovertAction: What happened in Los Angeles? Was it a riot, an uprising, a rebellion, an insurrection, and why would you term it one or the other?

Mike Davis: I think the majority of the participants, particularly the youths who started it, see the events that began on April 29th as a rebellion. When I was at a meeting of the Crips and Bloods in Inglewood in mid-May, it was referred to as a slave rebellion. Although the term "riot" doesn't have negative connotations for me as a labor historian, I think the wishes of the people who were the motive force should be honored.

In any case, you can't reduce the events to a single essence—one major characteristic or identity. L.A. was a hybrid social revolt with three major dimensions. It was a revolutionary democratic protest characteristic of African-American history when demands for equal rights have been thwarted by the major institutions. It was also a major postmodern bread riot—an uprising of not just poor people

---

CovertAction Information Bulletin first published its interview with Mike Davis, here "Uprising and Repression in L.A.," in their Summer 1992 edition, no. 41. It is reprinted here with the kind permission of *CovertAction*'s editors.

but particularly of those strata of poor in southern California who've been most savagely affected by the recession. Thirdly, it was an interethnic conflict—particularly the systematic destroying and uprooting of Korean stores in the Black community.

So it was all of those things at once and issues of rage, class, and race cannot be separated out. Sometimes they coalesced, sometimes they were parallel in time and space.

CAIB: Is it ironic that a revolt against racism manifested itself in one of its aspects as interracial violence?

MD: No, it has, of course, happened before in the riots of the '60s. When Martin Luther King came to L.A. in August 1965, right at the end of the first Watts rebellion, he was initially confused about the causes. But after talking to people on the street and having some pretty straightforward confrontations, he decided that it was a class rebellion, ''a rebellion of the underprivileged against the privileged.'' Those were exactly his words. And he acknowledged that the two targets of it were, first of all, the police and White institutions and, secondly, White-owned stores. So in August 1965, by and large, White people themselves were scarcely attacked.

In those days the grievances that really fueled the attack on the White-owned stores were a little different than now. For instance, many of the White-owned stores then were owned by Jewish Americans—some of whom had good relations with the community.

The real target of people's wrath in the '60s was the credit stores, the kind of place where you'd buy a bed on time and end up paying the price of a new car. Because they lacked access to major retail centers, ghetto residents were forced into a form of debt peonage.

This time the contradictions are different. The issue centers not just on high prices (although you'll hear that), but above all on abusive treatment of Black customers. Of course, the grievance which I think lay heavier than Rodney King's beating on the hearts of many Black youths was the murder of Latasha Harlins by a Korean shopkeeper in L.A. I say murder because I can see no other word for the act of shooting her in the back of the head.

CAIB: In addition to the differences in targets, what other differences and similarities are there between '65 and '92? What about the racial composition, the issues, and the numbers of people involved?

MD: What the district attorney's office, and probably the city attorney as well, have been doing is trying to paint this as the action of a criminal fringe. They are both law-and-order Democrats who have their eyes on the attorney general's office in Sacramento. But they, along with all the Republican candidates in this state, as well as other born-again law-and-order Democrats like Mel Levine, are echoing the 1965 McCone Commission on Watts in claiming that there are no valid reasons for taking to the streets.

Yet, after the McCone Commission came out, UCLA researchers spent a long time doing detailed surveys in the community, and what they discovered is that far from it being the action of a criminal fringe, the 1965 rebellion was extremely popular. At least 22,000 people, they found, took an active part in looting, burning, fighting the police. Another 50,000 to 60,000 people were passive bystanders in the streets cheering them on. So you had maybe 75,000 people involved. I would say that at least twice that number took part in the recent rebellion—probably with the same ratio of active participants to passive supporters.

Of the first 5,000 people arrested, 52 percent were Latino and only 39 percent Black. So it's clear, at least to the extent of the looting and some of the arson, that this was as much a Latino as a Black rebellion. And in order to understand that, you have to comprehend the severity of the current economic crisis in Los Angeles. It is an obvious linkage that the media have almost never made. Although they talk about gaps between haves and have-nots, what actually fueled this outbreak is not a general structural trend, but a specific economic condition: we are in the worst recession southern California has seen since the '30s. And the only account of it that you tend to get in the papers concerns unemployed aerospace engineers.

It's been a vicious, disastrous recession for the newest strata of immigrants from Mexico and Central America, which is why the worst looting outside the Black areas occurred in the largely Mexican eastern half of South Central L.A., and in Central American immigrant areas like Hollywood and the MacArthur Park area.

Of course, another thing that's different from '65 is that, geographically, the affected region is at least twice the area of the 1965 riot and curfew area, even extending tentacles into White middle-class areas. Undoubtedly, although you did have some opportunistic looting—yuppies in BMWs and a whole variety of people—the main force driving it was a need for consumer goods and necessities. A lot of people couldn't buy things like milk, diapers, or bread for three or four days. There was a huge power shortage and everybody's food spoiled. People who didn't want to were absolutely forced to loot.

CAIB: Many Central Americans who've lived with war know that when there's a chance to get food in a situation that chaotic, you need to grab it, because there's no telling how long the breakdown will continue, and in the meantime you and your family could starve.

MD: Absolutely. I observed the looting in several areas very carefully, and I spent hours among the looters. There was tremendous enthusiasm for athletic shoes, obviously, but particularly in the MacArthur Park area, people went for basic necessities. I saw people who looted and then watched them take a carload of food and diapers and distribute it among their neighbors in the tenement apartments of the Central American area west of downtown L.A.

CAIB: What have been the repercussions of the uprising for Central Americans? Have there been large INS [Immigration and Naturalization Service] incursions into the neighborhoods, deportations, or any other evidence that the INS has taken advantage of the situation?

MD: Definitely. What's happened is absolutely terrifying. First of all, from a very early point, the repression itself was federalized and federally driven.

Mike Hernandez, the progressive Chicano councilperson representing MacArthur Park, asked very early on for police protection for Latino store owners. The response: his area was the last to get any kind of police protection. Instead, by Friday (the rebellion started on Wednesday) 1,000 INS and Border Patrol (the latter drafted from as far away as Texas) poured into the area and set up command posts at 3rd and Vermont and MacArthur Park. They've already deported nearly 700 people.

In my *Nation* piece [1 June 1992, pp. 734–46], I mistakenly said that these people were accused of looting, but it now turns out that large numbers of the deportees were never charged at all. (Those against whom charges were lodged are still in custody at the INS detention center on Terminal Island and County Jail.) The roundup has broken up families and sent terror through the Central American community. Many of those arrested were simply day laborers standing on the same corners they always stand on, people just caught on the street, even a 14-year-old mentally retarded girl who was deported to Mexico. In direct violation of Los Angeles city policy, the LAPD assisted the INS and the Border Patrol. INS agents were being taken around by the LAPD in police cars, supposedly as translators.

Very clearly, the INS and Border Patrol have used the uprising to vacuum up people in the community. More than just taking the opportunity to deport large numbers of people, they have used the situation to instill fear. It's been a reign of terror followed by political attacks not only on the Black community, but to a surprising degree on Central Americans.

If it's true that the Bush administration is divided between ''softs'' and ''hards'' on urban issues, the ''hards'' are really hitting on the immigration question. In L.A., a number of right-wing Republicans campaigning for office have singled out the immigrants. Very early on, the Justice Department claimed that a third of those arrested were illegal immigrants. Although the figure is simply not true, it was bandied around by every right-wing political figure. Even some of the supposedly liberal Chicano leaders tried to distance themselves from the Latino loot-

ing. Despite the fact that thousands and thousands of Mexican immigrants participated, some of these leaders blamed it on Salvadorans who are ''refugees'' and
not ''real immigrants'' like Mexicans.

But now, as a direct result of the backlash, the struggle of the Guatemalans
(the second largest Central American group in the community) to gain temporary
protected status [TPS] is totally defeated. The Salvadorans, the largest group, have
been given an informal one-year extension of their temporary protected status by
the Bush administration. Bush sent a letter to Salvadoran president Cristiani saying: Congratulations, they can stay here for another year and then we'll see what
happens. Because the agreement is not legally binding, the 75,000 Salvadorans in
the neighborhood across the street from me are now totally hostage to how the
backlash develops.

Because they sense that they've become the most vulnerable scapegoats, the
Central American community is rushing to register voters, to encourage people
to become active in local politics and to make alliances. That is the silver lining
in this huge shock to the Central American community.

CAIB: That leads us to ask who benefits and who loses in an uprising like L.A.?
In '65, the Black Panther Party was formed in the wake of Watts, but it in turn
was crushed by the massive government repression of COINTELPRO and other
operations. Do you see patterns like that emerging?

MD: Of course. In a period when the majority of the Democratic Party is no
longer available as a reformist instrument and New Deal liberalism is virtually
dead, nonviolent social disorder is about the only way that you can put the survival
issues of the community on the agenda to address the continuing daily economic
and literal violence.

This rebellion is going to produce very mixed results: On the good side, it has
further politicized the gangs. Political consciousness always existed in the sense
that members, many of whom were sympathetic to Black-nationalist ideology,
understood the relentless logic of how destructive gang warfare was becoming.
But until the rebellion, there was never an opportunity for the first person to
take the step toward stopping the cycle.

The rebellion offered that possibility, and what we've seen since has just been
astonishing. We're talking about meetings and gatherings of hundreds of Crips
and Bloods, five, six, seven hundred at a time. Recently, these have been violently
broken up by the police. But, even if the truce breaks down, for most of them,
being a gangbanger is no longer the thing to be. Now the thing to be is, in some
sense, a liberation fighter.

Various internal groups have influenced this process of politicization. There are
original veteran gang members who were politicized in prison and elsewhere and
who represent a kind of post-Panther revolutionary Black politics. The Nation of
Islam has also been very important (Louis Farrakhan is probably the only national

figure most youths pay any attention to). It played a very constructive role in promoting gang peace. But they all know they're under attack, and they all know that provocations are being made.

CAIB: Have there been instances of infiltration of the gangs or of agents provocateurs fomenting trouble?

MD: One of the major establishment critiques of police conduct has been the failure of LAPD intelligence to foresee the magnitude of the rebellion or the coalescence of the gangs. Both Willie Williams, the new police chief, and ex–FBI, ex–CIA director William Webster, head of the commission investigating LAPD conduct during the rebellion, have emphasized beefing up police intelligence. In practical terms, this strategy is not so much a matter of a romanticized policy of deep-cover infiltration of the gangs, as simply a ruthless escalation of police pressure on pathetic drug users who are friends or kin of gang members.

One of the most cost-effective tactics for mass-producing snitches is the so-called "reverse buy," where police act as drug dealers in order to entrap customers, who are then offered the choice of serving hard time or becoming informants. Indeed, the "reverse buy" is a cornerstone of the attorney general's "Weed and Seed" program now being implemented in 16 different metropolitan areas, including Los Angeles, Atlanta, Chicago, and Washington, D.C. It is also, of course, morally obnoxious and indicative of a full-blown police state.

In the meantime, the LAPD and the sheriffs are doing everything possible to disrupt the gang unity process. Under various pretexts, they have attacked every mass gathering, arresting scores of youths, usually for trivial offenses. The gangs, however, have refused to be suckered into violent confrontations with the police. They are acting smart, keeping their focus on unification and peacemaking. This response, of course, only further infuriates the police, who seem to fear gang unity above all else.

An incredible amount of obvious police disinformation—much of it reminiscent of COINTELPRO—is currently in circulation. The sheriffs, in particular, have leaked an "intelligence report" that claims, on the authority of anonymous informants, that the Crips and Bloods are planning an assault on a police station as well as ambushes of individual cops on their way home from work. Appended to the report is a crudely drawn leaflet proclaiming: "Eye for an Eye—Let's Kill Two Cops."

The sheriffs' document also categorically states that the Crips and Bloods are acting under "the direction and leadership of Muslims" (presumably Louis Farrakhan's Nation of Islam). This conclusion suggests that local, and perhaps federal, law enforcement agencies are exploring an all-embracing conspiracy scenario that links gangs, urban unrest, Farrakhan, and perhaps even certain Colombians and Iraqis.

CAIB: In L.A., we saw the police and government use a high level of technology in intelligence gathering and repression techniques. What was the role of this increased sophistication, and what can we expect in the future?

MD: The mass arrests following the rebellion have depended upon the combined information-processing capacities of the FBI and local law enforcement. In particular, the comprehensive data bases on Black and Latino youth which the LAPD and sheriffs have been constructing over the past decade have been augmented by the FBI's expertise in analyzing video and photographic evidence.

It is now clear that one of the main functions of the "antigang" dragnets such as the LAPD's Operation Hammer has been to create a rap sheet on virtually every young Black male in the city. Data are not simply being kept on people arrested, but rather people are being detained solely in order to generate new data.

Thanks to massive street sweeps, the gang roster maintained by the LAPD and sheriffs has grown from 14,000 to 150,000 files over the last five years. This accumulation has allowed the district attorney, Ira Reiner, to make the hyperbolic claim that 47 percent of all young Black males in L.A. County are active gang members. Needless to say, these files are not only employed in identifying suspects, but have also become a virtual blacklist. Under California's recent "Street Terrorism Enforcement and Prevention Act" (STEP), for instance, membership in a gang presumably as proven by inclusion in one of these data bases, can become a separate felony charge.

The large-scale nocturnal operations mounted after midnight by the police and National Guard have been based on two sources: the "We Tip" public hot lines which have supposedly generated a thousand fruitful tips on looters and arsonists, and, of course, the police information banks on gang members. In the guise of searching for stolen property, the feds have been looking for the thousands of stolen guns. They haven't been very successful in that or in finding the 400 stolen police uniforms.

In my area, at the edge of the MacArthur Park Central American community, they were sweeping through the neighborhood, knocking on doors and walking right in. They have arrested people for sitting in their living rooms and not being able to produce a sales slip for their TV or couch.

In addition, the FBI has joined with the police in making unprecedented demands that the media and private individuals surrender every single negative and every inch of video tape taken during the rebellion.

The cops, of course, have tried to impress everyone with their speedy identification of the youths supposedly responsible for the beating of the White truck driver. But the real threat of these massive new data bases and information technologies is not their role in a few sensationalized instances, but their application on a macro scale in the management of criminalized populations.

In Los Angeles I think we are beginning to see a repressive context that is literally comparable to Belfast or the West Bank, where policing has been transformed into full-scale counterinsurgency (or "low-intensity warfare," as the military likes to call it), against an entire social stratum or ethnic group. This means that virtually every member of the "terrorist" population is "managed" by the police in some fashion, whether through literal imprisonment or through new restrictions on freedom of movement and association. The effect is as if a permanent state of martial law were imposed on specific neighborhoods or sections of the city.

The implications reach further than L.A.—emerging technologies may be used to surveil and control entire quarters of urban areas. As someone involved in land-use issues, I've been going to meetings about Geographical Information Systems or GIS. Now geographers and urban planners, as well as traffic engineers and developers, are enthralled by the imminent prospect of basing the management of complex urban systems—traffic flows, zoning, and so on—on LANDSAT satellites linked to GIS software. Since the image-resolution capabilities of commercial satellite systems are now approaching the threshold of distinguishing individual automobiles, and perhaps even people and their pets, it will be possible to monitor the movements of entire populations. As one GIS expert at UCLA pointed out to me, this will quickly revolutionize the policing of inner-city areas.

CAIB: Not long ago, the National Security Agency conducted a secret test using one of its signals intelligence satellites to track one automobile traveling all the way across the country from the East to the West Coast, day and night, through storms and all kinds of conditions.

MD: That's phenomenal. Of course satellite surveillance and GIS mapping will be augmented by the increasingly common use of automatic vehicle-location systems like *Lojak* or its more sophisticated cousin *Teletrac.* In Los Angeles, and I suspect in most large cities, especially those participating in the federal "Weed and Seed" program, the courts have been utterly promiscuous in allowing the police to clandestinely tag suspects' cars with these devices. It is not farfetched to imagine a situation in a few years where everyone on probation, or entered in one of the criminal data bases, will have to submit to some form of 24-hour electronic surveillance. We shall soon see police departments with the technology to put the equivalent of an electronic bracelet on entire social groups.

As Charles Murray and other reactionary ideologues have predicted, this will abet the trend toward certain neighborhoods becoming virtual outdoor prisons.

CAIB: How have the local and federal levels worked together and what have been the roles of the FBI and the Justice Department?

MD: This is the biggest domestic repression since the Nixon era and it was federalized within 48 hours of the first explosion of anger. Although the feds were called in by Mayor Tom Bradley and Governor Pete Wilson, over the head of Chief Daryl Gates, President Bush was delighted to oblige for obvious electioneering reasons. Moreover, the White House and the Justice Department have taken the initiative in making Los Angeles the exemplar of their militarized New Urban Order. Some features of the repression in L.A. recall the worst "assembly-line justice" that accompanied the uprisings of the 1960s, but other aspects, particularly the enlarged federal role, represent a new model of urban counter-insurgency.

Let me deal with the more familiar features first. This response of local law enforcement has been more draconian than in 1965, both in the magnitude of arrests and in the consistency of overcharging. L.A.—1992, in fact, more closely resembles the aftermath of the great Detroit uprising of 1969, when local authorities threw the book, and more, at alleged rioters. As in Detroit, the city attorney and D.A. in L.A. have suspended plea bargaining and gone for the maximum possible indictments, bail amounts, and sentences.

Normally, most looters, for instance, would have been charged with petty theft or misdemeanor burglary. Since the riot, however, they have been indicted for felony burglary. They now face two- or three-year prison sentences rather than a simple fine. (The D.A. has indicated they won't accept anything less than one year for guilty pleas.) At the same time, curfew violators, many of whom are homeless people or Spanish-speaking immigrants ignorant of the curfew, have all been held on $8,000 bail—an astronomical amount for such a petty charge. What makes this even more hypocritical is that the nominally citywide curfew seems only to have been enforced in communities of color. I've verified that a group of city attorneys threw a wild party on the fourth night that lasted far beyond curfew. Then on Monday morning, they came into court and sanctimoniously asked the judge for 30-day sentences for hapless curfew arrestees.

However repulsive, these practices are not unfamiliar. But the federal role has added at least three new and ominous elements. First of all, we have seen the unveiling of the domestic version of the Rapid Deployment Force. We can assume, henceforth, that elite elements of the Army and Marines will be quickly moved into any large-scale urban disorder at an early stage, and not as a reluctant last-ditch measure, as when paratroopers were finally sent into Detroit in 1967.

Secondly, military deployment was accompanied by an unprecedentedly massive introduction of a thousand personnel from every branch of federal law enforcement, including marshals, FBI, DEA [Drug Enforcement Administration], Border Patrol, and the Bureau of Alcohol, Tobacco, and Firearms. On the one hand, INS and Border Patrol agents, assisted by the LAPD, swept through the streets of MacArthur Park and other immigrant Latino neighborhoods like a giant vacuum cleaner, deporting every undocumented person they could lay their hands on. Most of the six hundred to seven hundred people deported in this way were not involved and were never charged with any riot-related offense. They were simply walking the streets or waiting at street-corner day-labor markets. On the other hand, a 100-person task force of FBI and DEA agents, together with local police and sheriffs, have taken the lead in tracking down the alleged gang "ring-leaders" of the uprising.

Thirdly, prosecutors from the U.S. Attorney's office, working in a special task force with the D.A., are superimposing layers of additional federal offenses on key defendants. The legal lynching of the four youths accused of attacking the truck driver and other motorists is the most vivid example so far of how the Bush administration's "weeding" of the cities will work. In this case, "interference with interstate commerce," a felony that carries a possible 20-year sentence, has been charged on the surreal grounds that the truck driver's cargo (local gravel) was being hauled to a destination where it might be mixed with out-of-state ingredients.

Moreover, at the time of this interview, we do not yet know how many RICO [Racketeering Influence and Corrupt Organizations Act] indictments may yet be returned against leading gang members. (The D.A. and U.S. Attorney's offices have indicated that there will be "many.") RICO, of course, is a contemporary version of the Criminal Syndicalism Laws of the First World War or the Alien and Sedition Acts of the early Republic: an all-embracing conspiracy statute that circumvents traditional canons of evidence and due process. As I indicated earlier, this RICO net may ultimately be cast very far and wide, as the feds try to implicate Farrakhan and others in the supposed "conspiracy."

CAIB: Will the recent appointment of Willie Williams to succeed Gates make a difference to L.A.?

MD: The kinder and gentler LAPD, led by Williams, will be a real rebuilding with increased emphasis on intelligence and the development of a coordinated riot-and-disturbance-control strategy that probably will continue to be closely coordinated with the feds. Unlike in the '60s, when the National Guard marched back home, this time a staff element remains in the city. The Marines at Camp Pendleton will also remain on alert. I think that we are going to see an institutionalization of that kind of federal presence.

While the major internal contradictions about race in the LAPD will remain, I believe that Williams will be fairly effective in cleaning up the surface. The LAPD is, in a sense, in transition to being a multiracial police department. It's ironic, but you can have a kinder, gentler LAPD that includes more people of color, with fairly effective systems for dealing with the more egregious abuses, and at the same time have a rapidly rising level of repression.

CAIB: As FBI director from 1978 to 1985, William Webster was involved in the COINTELPRO operations. As Director of Central Intelligence from 1985 to 1991, he ran covert operations for the CIA. What are the implications of his appointment to the investigating committee?

MD: In a nutshell, I would say that Webster's been brought in to focus only on why the police weren't more effective in putting down the disturbance, not on any misconduct on their part. Furthermore, he will develop far-ranging suggestions about crowd control and political intelligence, and probably set in place some system of coordination on a countywide and statewide level that can be copied across the country.

Webster's brief seems to center almost entirely on all the mistakes in the so-called initial-deployment planning and intelligence for the riot. There are liberals in this city who were appalled by the Rodney King decision, but equally appalled that the police didn't wade in immediately and, I don't know what, shoot looters or crush demonstrations? It's become a totally hypocritical kind of discourse.

CAIB: Will Officer Steven Powell and his overtly racist ilk survive the new order?

MD: Williams has signaled his intention to purge the department. In 1991, the Christopher Commission produced its analysis of what was wrong with the LAPD. It precisely parallels the apologies of the McCone Commission and concludes that if you get rid of a "criminal fringe" of 60 or 70 out-of-control, ultraviolent officers, everything will be hunky-dory. Williams, who has indicated that he's going to find ways to purge the "Powells," will get an extraordinary mandate and honeymoon period, during which time it will be much more difficult to mount any criticisms of the police.

Even now, the only criticism you hear from the White liberals in L.A. is that the LAPD wasn't more "competent" and overwhelming in its immediate response. It's come into their neighborhoods and middle-class people are really scared for the first time. They don't make any distinction between poor Latinos in Hollywood looting a market and the top leadership of the Crips or Bloods.

Their exaggerated fears will ultimately override principles and considerations of justice in West Los Angeles, as it has in Simi Valley. The actuality of and potential for repression are hardly mentioned. People just don't realize the number of homes that have been illegally entered by the police at 2:00 A.M. in South Central L.A. Nor do they realize that the Webster Commission and the increasing intelligence-gathering powers and repressive strategy of the police are no more likely to know boundaries in the 1990s than they were back in the 1920s or 1960s.

CAIB: The LAPD has a certain amount of autonomy that's fairly unusual for cities. What about the Sheriff's Department? Under whom do they operate?

MD: They have more autonomy. Perversely, it's partially because the sheriff is elected. Sherman Block is a liberal Jewish Republican; he's extremely smooth and politically invulnerable. Those people who live in unincorporated areas don't have access to anything like a city councilperson or alder. There are big sections such as East L.A., Firestone, and the Willowbrook areas which look just like ordinary parts of the inner city except they're unincorporated. They're controlled by the sheriffs who have untrammeled authority over their lives.

So, the real question of police abuse and community control in L.A. County has been a question of the sheriffs as well as the LAPD, particularly if you're Latino. More of the Latino working class is actually affected by the sheriffs than they are by the LAPD.

So, it's important to remember that it is not only the police who are a problem, but the Sheriff's Department which has been even worse. It's truly more out of control and has even higher levels of brutality against people of color. Over the last two years, the sheriffs have been responsible for more than a dozen unlawful killings, several of which were virtually cold-blooded assassinations.

And although the Sheriff's Department is probably more racially integrated than the LAPD, this has had absolutely no effect in preventing avowedly White-supremacist groups from operating inside the department. Last year, for example, a judge corroborated long-standing rumors that a White racist "gang" known as the Vikings had been organized inside the Lynwood Station in a majority Black and Latino suburb. This notorious station is under lawsuit for literally scores of major abuses, ranging from murder and torture to unlawful detention and beatings.

But somehow all this blood just seems to wash off Sheriff Sherman Block's manicured hands. Unlike Chief Gates, he keeps his foot out of his mouth and cultivates a cordial relationship with the press.

Recently, Block announced his interest in next year's mayoral election. It would be the ultimate irony for Los Angeles to finally get rid of Gates as police chief only to have Sheriff Block as the next mayor.

CAIB: Given the potential for backlash and the current level of fear, will the events in L.A. have an important impact on the upcoming presidential election?

MD: Absolutely. George Bush is going to run as the president who put the troops in L.A. and sent the federal prosecutors in behind them. He's going to tell the country that only a Republican president is capable of protecting the suburbs and maintaining law and order.

"Operation Weed and Seed" (one of the scariest, most invidious slogans and programs I've ever heard of) is the new Bush urban program for the '90s. On the "seed" side, this upward distribution of wealth is just another way to implement the capital-gains tax break Bush has been unsuccessful in getting through Congress and to universalize enterprise zones in the inner city.

But actually, he's quietly gone further already. He's told the cities: "If you're short of money, if you want aid, sell your airport, privatize your public sector." So he's advocating for U.S. cities the same kinds of "structural adjustment" that the World Bank and the IMF are imposing in the Third World.

The "weed" part, on the other hand, includes this whole conjugation of repressive tactics that we had a taste of in the L.A. uprising: cultivating the use of RICO and other superdraconian federal penalties, ostensibly to remove the so-called gang leadership.

CAIB: Thank you.

Part Five

Ideology, Race, and Community

11

"Look, a Negro!"

Robert Gooding-Williams

My body was given back to me sprawled out,
distorted, recolored, clad in mourning in that
white winter day. The Negro is an animal,
the Negro is bad, the Negro is mean. . . .
—Frantz Fanon

Your country? How came it yours?
—W. E. B. DuBois

INTRODUCTION

In this essay, I will investigate the impact of racial ideology (by which I mean, roughly, the interpretation of racial identities in the representation of racially classified individuals or groups) on the trial of the policemen who beat Rodney King and on media coverage of the L.A. uprising. My principal aim will be to analyze critically the ways in which racial ideology, during the policemen's trial and the media's coverage of the uprising, functioned to characterize black bodies and, implicitly, to interpret the sociopolitical status of blacks in the United States.

In pursuing this aim, my critique of racial ideology will differ from a more familiar approach to ideology critique that, owing most of its influence to the writings of Marx and Freud, attempts to demystify social phenomena by identifying their social origins. Marx, for example, criticizes the fetishism of commodities by showing that exchange values are not simply properties of things, but also effects of capitalist social relations. Similarly, psychoanalysis reveals the significance of otherwise unintelligible neurotic symptoms by relating them to prior contexts of childhood trauma.[1] Black bodies, however, unlike Marx's exchange

I wish to thank Andrea Ayvazian, Tom Dumm, Sara Gooding-Williams, Tom McCarthy, Dale Peterson, Paul Rockwell, Karen Sanchez-Eppler, Lorenzo Simpson, and Judy Wittenberg for their comments on an earlier draft of this paper.

values and Freud's neurotic symptoms, do not ordinarily strike us as resembling mysterious fetishes or "hieroglyphics" that have been waiting to have meaning attributed to them.[2]

Black bodies, in fact, have been supersaturated with meaning, as they have been relentlessly subjected to characterization by newspapers, newscasters, popular film, television programming, public officials, policy pundits and other agents of representation. Characterizations of black bodies often represent their actions and/or attributes as consequences of discrimination, social pathology, state policy, unemployment, jungle chaos, physical prowess, genial good-heartedness, or some other cause or causes. Many of these characterizations are false, and so need to be vigorously contested. But, over and beyond contesting such false characterizations, a critique of racial ideology should also explore the ways in which explanations and other representations of black bodies function as forms of sociopolitical imagination. To be more precise, it should investigate the ways in which these representations present themselves as allegories of social organization and political community. The point of such an investigation would not be to *demystify* black bodies (that is, the point would not be to identify the social causes of their actions and attributes), but to *demythify* them, that is, to subject to critical scrutiny the allegories of American social and political life intimated in characterizing them.[3]

In what follows, I will elaborate further my concept of racial ideology, drawing on Toni Morrison's discussion of Africanism in American literature and on a recent popular film (popular film being one of the most influential sources of racial ideology in our time) for my examples. I will then use my concept of racial ideology to analyze, first, the defense lawyers' representation of Rodney King to the jurors who exonerated his assailants, and second, the media's representation of black participation in the uprising prompted by the jurors' verdicts. I present this analysis as a possible starting point for further inquiry. It is not intended to be exhaustive of the issues it addresses.

THE CONCEPT OF RACIAL IDEOLOGY

I understand the concept of racial ideology to have as its extension (i.e., the scope of its reference) all *racial representations,* that is, all representations of racially classified individuals or groups (of individuals). Thus, in contemporary American society, where all individuals and groups are subject to racial classification, the concept of racial ideology applies in fact to all representations of social activity. Though the notion of racial ideology I am proposing may seem at first glance to be *too* inclusive, since it identifies *all* representations of racially classified individuals or groups as ideological, its inclusiveness is in fact one of its strengths. By advocating a relatively broad and encompassing concept of racial ideology, I mean to resist the temptation to restrict in advance the proper domain of a critique of racial ideology.

Michael Omi and Howard Winant have argued that ''In US society . . . a kind of 'racial etiquette' exists, a set of interpretive codes and racial meanings which operate in the interactions of daily life. . . . Everybody learns some combination, some version, of the rules of racial classification, and of their own racial identity, often without conscious teaching or conscious inculcation. Race becomes 'common sense'—a way of comprehending, explaining, and acting in the world.''[4] Here, Omi and Winant remind us that racial classification is pervasive in American society. In the most familiar cases, e.g., the classification of individuals as ''black'' or ''white,'' it proceeds on the basis of visible physical characteristics that almost everyone learns to read on sight as signifiers of racial identity.[5] Most Americans take it for granted that they are competent and even adept participants in the practice of racial classification; they tend to acknowledge explicitly their participation in this practice only when they encounter individuals whom they cannot immediately racially categorize. First of all and most of the time, racial classification operates as an unthematized but constitutive dimension of social interaction in American society.

Because racial classification is pervasive; because, in fact, there are no occasions in American society in which racial classification is not present as a dimension of social interaction, it is possible and even reasonable to read all representations of the individuals or groups present in American society—by which I mean all visual, verbal, and written depictions of these individuals or groups, fictional depictions included—as interpretations of the racial identities which all racial classifications posit.[6] In a society in which racial classification is a constitutive feature of social life, all representations of social life make implicit reference to racial identities. Thus, all representations of social life can be read as interpretations of racial identities. The critique of racial ideology, as I conceive it, proceeds from the heuristic assumption that all such representations *should be* read as interpretations of racial identities.[7]

To be sure, readings of the sort I envision are not always informative or illuminating. And readings of this sort, far from being exhaustive, constitute just *one* of many viable and politically significant perspectives on the representation of American social life.[8] Still, an essential part of a critique of racial ideology is to produce such readings, without presupposing that some racial representations should be excluded a priori from the set of potentially fruitful objects of ideology critique.

THE CONCEPT OF IDEOLOGY CRITIQUE: GENEALOGY, SOCIOPOLITICAL ALLEGORY, AND DEMYTHIFICATION

The conception of ideology critique I wish to elaborate has three components: (1) the genealogical exposure of racial representations; (2) the reading of genealogically exposed racial representations as sociopolitical allegories; and (3) the demythification of the allegorical content of genealogically exposed racial representations.

My conception of genealogical exposure draws its inspiration from Nietzsche.[9] As I conceive it, a genealogical exposure of racial representations discloses the interpretive origins of those representations. Its point, more exactly, is to identify the acts of interpretation which constitute racial representations. Following Nietzsche, I regard an act of interpretation as a characterization of a physical object, individual, practice, or other subject matter that ascribes to it some purpose(s) or function(s) or other significance (e.g., the characterization of the practice of punishment as having the purpose of preventing further harm).[10] To disclose the interpretive origin of a racial representation is, for my purposes, to show that that representation has been constituted through the ascription of some purpose(s) or function(s) or other significance to a racially classified individual or group of individuals, and to the racial identity(ies) which he, she, or it has been classified as embodying.

The best examples I know of the genealogical exposure of racial representations can be found in Toni Morrison's study of American Africanism, *Playing in the Dark: Whiteness and the Literary Imagination.* As Morrison defines it, "American Africanism" refers to "the ways in which a nonwhite, Africanlike (or Africanist) presence or persona was constructed in the United States, and the imaginative uses this fabricated presence served."[11] In her analysis of American Africanism, Morrison attempts to show that in American literature "black matters," that it makes a difference.[12] Her aim, as I read her, is to disclose and explore the many ways in which works of American literature adapt themselves to and characterize individuals who have been racially classified as black. The questions she asks— "How does literary utterance arrange itself when it tries to imagine the Africanist other? What are the signs, the codes, the literary strategies designed to accommodate this encounter? What does the inclusion of Africans or African-Americans do to and for the work?"—clearly implicate the genealogical dimensions of her project, as they pertain explicitly to the functions which literary works assign to racially classified individuals (what the inclusion of such individuals does to and for a work), and to the ways in which literary works "arrange" themselves so as to "accommodate" these functions.[13]

Morrison's genealogical exposures of Africanist racial representations in American literature show that these representations were constituted through the ascription of multiple purposes and functions to individuals racially classified as black (the black characters appearing in the fictions Morrison discusses). Some of the purposes and functions she identifies are: ''surrogate and enabler of self-reflexion''; figure for what is ''hip, sophisticated, (and) ultra-urbane''; means to defining the goals and enhancing the qualities of white characters; and ''means of meditation—both safe and risky on one's own humanity.''[14] What Morrison calls ''the serviceability of the African presence'' is a constitutive force in American literature, whose pervasiveness she wishes to highlight.[15] By bringing into view the many roles and purposes which American writers have ascribed to black characters and figures of blackness, she lets us see a large part of the quite complicated network of meanings which American culture has attributed to what it construes as a black racial identity.[16]

Let me now turn to an example of American Africanism, in order to begin to explain the possibility of reading genealogically exposed racial representations as sociopolitical allegories. The example I have in mind is that of the male-nurse figures who appear in Hemingway's fiction. These male nurses, Morrison points out, are almost always black. ''Cooperative or sullen,'' she writes, ''they are Tontos all, whose role is to do everything possible to serve the Lone Ranger without disturbing his indulgent delusion that he is indeed alone.''[17] Morrison goes on to discuss at length the functions of these figures, noting both their enabling and disenabling qualities vis-à-vis their white male patrons.[18] Her remarks along these lines are striking, in part because of the insight they bring to Hemingway's writings, but likewise because they remind us that fictive individuals of the sort she analyzes pervade American culture. In popular film, for example, figures of black nurses and sidekicks abound, gendered sometimes as male, sometimes as female, bound often to Lone Rangers, but sometimes to romantic lovers. A by-now classic example is the figure of Sam (Dooley Wilson), who in *Casablanca* appears as nurse, as sidekick, and as a desexualized cupid figure whose raison d'être is to keep alive the myth of (white) heterosexual romance. A more recent example is the figure of Oda Mae Brown (Whoopi Goldberg), who in *Ghost* reprises the role of the cupid figure by appearing literally as the medium through whom two white heterosexual lovers, estranged by death, can touch each other one last time.[19]

The nurse, sidekick, and cupid figures appearing in *Casablanca* and *Ghost,* no less than those cropping up in Hemingway's fiction, serve various functions within the narratives in which they occur. Once the representations of these black characters have been genealogically exposed, the assignment to these characters of particular roles can be read allegorically as commenting on the social and political status of blacks in America. In the cases of *Casablanca* and *Ghost,* for example, allegorical readings let us see how the assignment of particular narrative functions to black characters can intimate the view that the African presence in American social and political life, though serviceable, is expendable. More familiar to contemporary audiences than Hemingway's fiction, and, for that matter, than classical Hollywood films like *Casablanca,* the example of *Ghost* is especially significant, because it highlights the fact that American Africanism, besides being an essential feature of an established American literary tradition, continues to be perpetuated in contemporary American culture.

Based loosely on Shakespeare's *Macbeth* (the dead protagonist's ghost is meant to recall Banquo's ghost), *Ghost* is about the effort of a dead but "legitimate" white American patriarch and capitalist to defend his realm against the designs of an "illegitimate" usurper. The film persuades its audiences to endorse this effort, by conflating it with the expression of an intensely passionate heterosexual love. Personifying a (socially posited) black racial identity, Oda Mae functions in the film to facilitate both the communication of this love and the protagonist's destruction of the "tyrant" who has displaced him. Once she fulfills her function, she is dispensable (as is Sam in *Casablanca*). Read as an allegorical commentary on contemporary American society, Oda Mae represents the claim that though the black presence in America is *not essential* to America's identity as a political community, it constitutes a useful, convenient, and sometimes welcome means for propping up and stabilizing the patriarchal and capitalist social order which is the foundation of that community.[20] *Ghost*'s dominant fantasy, reminiscent of the "indulgent delusion" Morrison attributes to the Lone Ranger, is that America can use blacks for its purposes, and yet retain an identity to which a black presence is not essential.[21]

By discussing *Ghost,* I have hoped to show how a genealogically exposed racial representation can be read as a sociopolitical allegory.[22] I have hoped, too, to begin to explain my concept of demythification. "Demythification," as I use that term, refers to the critical use of evidence and argument to gauge the truth value of the sociopolitical allegories implicit in racial representations.[23] Demythifying *Ghost,* for example, could involve an appeal to evidence and argument contradicting the view that the black presence in America, though convenient, is not an essential part of America's identity as a nation.[24] Such evidence is readily available and has been for a long time. W. E. B. DuBois used it, when almost a century ago he attacked the myth which *Ghost* embraces.

> Your country? How came it yours? Before the Pilgrims landed we were here. Here we have brought our three gifts and mingled them with yours: a gift of story and song . . . ; the gift of sweat and brawn to beat back the wilderness . . . ; the third a gift of Spirit. Around us the history of the land has centered for thrice a hundred years; out of the nation's heart we have called all that is best to throttle and subdue all that was worst, . . . Actively we have woven ourselves with the warp and woof of the nation,—we fought their

battles, shared their sorrow, mingled our blood with theirs, and generation after generation have pleaded with a headstrong careless people to despise not Justice, Mercy, and Truth, lest the nation be smitten with a curse. Our song, our toil, our cheer, and warning have been given to the nation in blood-brotherhood. Are not these gifts worth the giving? Is not this work and striving? *Would America be America without her Negro people?*[25] (emphasis mine)

DuBois argues that the Negro has given America its song, built its foundations, and, weaving him/herself with the warp and woof of the nation, born the brunt of its struggle for justice, mercy, and truth. His point is that the Negro has played so important a role in creating America, and in fostering its highest aspirations, that America's identity as a distinct political community is not conceivable absent the centuries-long presence of blacks in America. DuBois demythifies the claim set forth allegorically in *Ghost,* that this presence has been a peripheral and inessential one, by insisting that America would not be America without its Negro people.[26]

DuBois's eloquence is unusually compelling. But *Ghost,* it is important to see, is just one of many film and television events that can be usefully subjected to ideological criticism. Less important, therefore, than the details of my analysis of this film is the recognition that what *Ghost* exemplifies, namely, the use of racial representations to interpret racial identities, pervades American culture. Although the interpretation of racial identities varies from one racial representation to another, and though the complexity of some racial representations far and away exceeds that of others, the fact remains that American culture lives and breathes by racial representations, using them relentlessly to make sense of American history, society, and politics.

Thus, when we consider the role of racial ideology in the trial of the policemen who beat Rodney King and in the media's depiction of the L.A. uprising, we should acknowledge from the beginning that courtroom and media representations of black bodies grow out of a long and ongoing tradition of American Africanism. The racial representations present in *Ghost, Casablanca,* and the works of fiction Toni Morrison discusses are but a small sample of the great storehouse of interpreted images of black people that American jurors, lawyers, and media pundits have available to them as elements of the culture they have in common. That particular jurors, lawyers, and pundits should have made use of some of these images in the contexts of the Simi Valley trial and the television coverage of the L.A. uprising simply marks them as Americans.

LOOKING AT NEGROES IN SIMI VALLEY; OR, WHY NO ONE SHOULD HAVE BEEN SURPRISED BY THE RODNEY KING VERDICTS

This sentence, "Look, a Negro!" appears repeatedly in chapter 5 of Frantz Fanon's *Black Skin, White Masks,* where it seems quickly to acquire a significance reminiscent of Wagner's musical *leitmotiven.* Fanon's aim in this chapter is to describe the lived experience of being black in pervasively negrophobic societies.[27] "Look, a Negro!" he suggests, is a typical example of the racializing identifications which persistently punctuate day-to-day life in such societies. Fanon interprets such identifications as performative utterances that assail the Negro, destroying his or her "corporeal schema" and imposing on him or her a "racial epidermal schema."[28]

By "corporeal schema" Fanon means the image each of us has of him- or herself as a body located somewhere in physical space. It is an image that each of us ordinarily constructs and needs repeatedly to reconstruct as he or she moves about the world. Reminiscent of Jean Lhermitte, who situates the corporeal schema or "body image" on the "fringe" of consciousness, Fanon himself describes it as the source of an "implicit knowledge" that each of us possesses of the position of his or her body in relation to other physical objects.[29]

Living in the white world, "the man of color encounters difficulties in the elaboration of his corporeal schema."[30] The racial epidermal schema which is the source of these difficulties is itself an image of Negro bodies, but not an image whose constituent elements are the "sensations and perceptions" one uses to form one's body image.[31] It is, rather, an image "woven . . . out of a thousand details, anecdotes, [and] stories" that negrophobes foist upon blacks and encourage them to claim as their own.[32] Fanon describes the experience of being subjected to the racial epidermal schema as that of being physically fastened or affixed to an image of oneself; one feels as if one had acquired a second epidermis (hence the concept of a racial *epidermal* schema) that had been superimposed on one's body and then come to haunt it like a shadow. The verbal performances which effect this sense of being enslaved to an image, since they also shatter one's body image, leave one feeling literally and utterly dislocated in physical space.[33]

> "Look, a Negro!" It was an eternal stimulus that flicked over me as I passed by. I made a tight smile.
>
> "Look, a Negro!" It was true. It amused me.
>
> "Look, a Negro!" The circle was drawing a bit tighter. . . .
>
> "Mama, see the Negro! I'm frightened!" Frightened! Frightened! Now they were beginning to be afraid of me. I made up my mind to laugh myself to tears, but laughter had become impossible.

> I could no longer laugh, because I already knew that there were legends, stories, history, and above all *historicity*. . . . [34]

The verbal bombardment described here reaches its peak when the little boy expresses his fear. For Fanon, the boy's view of the Negro (of Fanon himself in this case) as an object of fear is significant, as it suggests (1) that the image (racial epidermal schema) of the Negro posited by the boy's verbal performance has a narrative significance and (2) that such images are available to the boy as elements of a socially shared stock of images that qualify the historicity (the historical situatedness) both of the boy and of the Negro he sees.

The boy's expression of fear posits a typified image of the Negro as behaving in threatening ways. This image has a narrative significance, Fanon implies, as it portrays the Negro as acting precisely as historically received legends and stories about Negroes generally portray them as acting. Speaking in terms I introduced earlier in this essay, one could say that the image of the Negro the boy posits is an *interpreted image,* that is, a racial representation that was constituted by assigning a particular function (e.g., the function or role of causing fear in white people) to Negroes when they appeared in the legends and the stories we have inherited from the past. This interpreted image, like many that Toni Morrison discusses, belongs to a cultural legacy that has set the social stage for verbal and other assaults on black bodies.

Fanon helps us understand why no one should have been surprised by the Rodney King verdicts, as he points to what most of us who were surprised—myself included—permitted ourselves to forget. Having seen the videotape of King being beaten, we allowed ourselves to indulge the (in some cases closeted) positivist fantasy—think of it as the ''Dragnet'' fantasy—that the facts (''Please, just the facts, Ma'am'') were enough, because *brute* (and brutal) facts, plain and unembellished, speak for themselves. [35] If ever there were brute facts, we thought, then surely this fact—that Rodney King had been unjustly beaten and unforgivably abused—was one of them. Yet the attorneys who defended King's assailants knew better. They knew better, because they knew what Fanon knew and went to such great lengths to explain: namely, that in modern Eurocentric societies no black bodies can be kept safe from the assault of negrophobic images and representations. [36]

''Look, a Negro!'' Fanon's leitmotif pithily expresses the rhetorical strategy of the attorneys defending King's abusers. Rather than assume that filmed facts speak for themselves, these lawyers turned to a received stock of already-interpreted images of black bodies, and used some of these to assault the black body appearing in the video. Time and again they sought to affix these images to that body, as if to say repeatedly: ''Look, a Negro!'' By the end of the trial, these images had become for the jury indistinguishable from King's body, the jury having learned to see in the "brute facts" a narrative recycling of interpreted images familiar to them from other stories—what one critic calls "a retake."[37] By the end of the trial, the jury indeed had seen the Negro it was looking to see.

Put a bit differently, my argument here is that the defense attorneys in the King trial successfully mobilized a battery of commonplace prejudices—in the sense of prejudgments—by convincing the jurors to read the King tape as confirming those prejudices.[38] Fanon is helpful, I am claiming, because he saw that such prejudices are linked to interpreted images, and that these images have a narrative significance.

Let me be more specific about the defense attorneys' rhetorical strategy. After inviting the jurors to see events from the point of view of the police officers, the defense attorneys elicited testimony from King's assailants that depicted King repeatedly as a bear, and as emitting bearlike groans. In the eyes of the police, and then again in the eyes of the jurors, King's black body became that of a wild "Hulk-like" and "wounded" animal, whose every gesture threatened the existence of civilized society. Not surprisingly, the defense attorneys portrayed the white bodies which assailed King as guardians against the wild, and as embodying a "thin blue line" that separates civil society from the dangerous chaos which is the essence of the wild. Thus, the plot of the story which the police and their attorneys told assigned the white bodies appearing in the tape the function of holding the fort of civilization against the willful attack of a chaos-bearing wild animal. The same plot assigned the tape's protagonist and only appearing black body the role of a chaos-bearing wild animal who gives his all to attack the fort of civilization. This animal, claimed one of the jurors, echoing the words of defense attorney Michael Stone, was in complete control and directed all the action. Still, somehow, the forces of civilization prevailed, preserving intact human society as we know it.[39]

For the jurors, the story had a "happy ending." But the story was and remains an all-too-familiar one. By casting a black body in the role of a wild animal and portraying it as nemesis to civilization, the defense attorneys were producing a narrative retake of an interpreted image of black bodies that had appeared in European representations of African "others" at least since the seventeenth century.[40] Just as the character of Luke Skywalker recurs in the "to be continued" retakes of *Star Wars,* so too does the image of the Negro characterized as an uncivilized beast recur in contemporary and surely "to be continued" retakes of early modern European accounts of the behavior of black bodies.[41] The cultural legacy created by roughly three hundred years of such retakes formed the horizon of prejudices in light of which the defense attorneys asked the jurors to view the video-tape of Rodney King's beating. The implicit goal of these lawyers was to produce yet another retake of the black body whose narrative function is to incarnate a wilderness chaos inimical to civilization, and to persuade the members of the jury to see in that retake their prejudices come to life.

It is pointless to respond to the King verdicts, as did the Society for Cinema Studies, by attacking the defense lawyers for using techniques of close reading to *misread* ''powerful video evidence.''[42] Such a response succumbs again to the positivist fantasy that there are brute facts that speak for themselves. It suggests that one can simply look at the evidence and directly know what happened, unless the evidence, like some alleged criminals, is unjustly ''framed'' in advance, in this case ''freeze-framed'' so as to accommodate a detailed analysis of each of King's bodily movements. The problem here, of course, is that there are no readings, be they close or superficial, in which the construal of the evidence at hand does not admit of some prior framing by the prejudices (pre-judgments) of the reader.[43] Prejudices of *some sort* would have been operative no matter what reading of the King video the lawyers produced. And that, I believe, is why it is so important that those of us who were horrified by the verdicts in the King trial let go of our positivist fantasies, and begin carefully to attend to and to criticize the *particular* prejudices which helped to produce those verdicts.[44] This, I have been arguing, is precisely what Fanon enables us to do.

To the extent that I have been arguing that the prejudices mobilized by the defense lawyers involved interpreted images of black bodies, I have been subjecting those prejudices to *genealogical exposure*. More exactly, I have been treating them as racial representations that were constituted by the assignment of particular roles and functions to individuals who were racially classified as black. While there are many good reasons to criticize these prejudices (e.g., they promote false thinking about Rodney King and other blacks as wild animals, they are demeaning to all blacks, and they encourage the translation of complex social situations into simple minded melodramas), I want here to advance a line of reasoning that, in keeping with my conception of ideology-critique, focuses on a particular demythifying response to the socio-political allegory implicit in the defense lawyers' use of them.

Read as an allegorical commentary on American race relations, the defense attorneys' narrative of the King video goes a step further than, say, *Ghost,* because it denies that blacks can be used even to prop up and to stabilize what it, like Goldberg's movie, represents as an essentially white-American social order.[45] Indeed, the lawyers' retake of the received image of a wild and chaos-bearing black man allegorically asserted that blackness constitutes the very antithesis of that social order. The final argument of one of the defense attorneys seemed even to acknowledge this tacit assertion, when it suggested that ''the likes of Rodney King'' needed to be controlled and violently subdued if the social and political order with which the jurors identified was to be kept securely intact.[46]

Consider now another allegory. Just a few days after the Rodney King verdicts were announced, the students and faculty of Amherst College awoke to discover that the College's Black Student Union had hung by the neck, at different places on the Amherst campus, 40 black and faceless effigies. Splattered on the ground around each of these dark figures were splotches of red paint intended to symbolize blood. Accompanying each of the effigies was a copy of at least one newspaper article (some of them dating from the 1880s) reporting an act of deadly violence—in most cases a lynching—performed by white Americans on the bodies of black Americans. A lengthy statement, explaining the protest as an effort to put into historical perspective the beating of Rodney King and the exoneration of the men who beat him, was taped to the front door of the library and to a coffin placed near the entrance to the dining hall—in both cases near the effigies which were most likely to be seen by the majority of students and faculty. According to the effigy protesters, these events needed to be seen as extending America's received and continuing legacy of hideous violence against black men.

I mention here the Amherst effigy protest, because it so brilliantly demythified the allegorical vision present in the defense lawyers' representation of Rodney King. Driving into the Amherst campus and sighting the effigies for the first time, many of us (faculty and students) assumed that the black figures we saw were the product of a right-wing reaction to the L.A. uprising. Reading the effigies in light of the prejudgment that only right-wing racists would dare publicly and so blatantly to invoke the imagery of America's lynching of black men, we first saw the effigies as saying again what had been said already in the Simi Valley courtroom: that in order for American society to preserve its integrity, it must violently subjugate black bodies. Only after we walked across the Amherst campus, and so had the opportunity to read both the newspaper articles and the effigy protesters' statement, did it become clear to us that our prejudgments were false, and that the effigies were intended, not to confirm the perspective of the defense attorneys, but to demythify and refute it.[47]

An allegory in its own right, the effigy protest forced into view the "racial epidermal schemata" which haunt American society everywhere—not only in Los Angeles, but in Chicago and Philadelphia, not only in Simi Valley, but in DuBuque and Amherst itself.[48] Using historical documents (the newspaper articles) and argument (the protesters' statement) to place the King verdicts within a particular historical context, this visually shocking political act insisted that each of us remember that violence against black bodies has never not been a constitutive feature of American society. By tying faceless figures of black death to the trees and walls of privileged white Amherst, the effigy protest argued that the repressed must always return to address the forces which deny it. And by answering the defense lawyers' allegory with an historically informed and largely accurate sociopolitical allegory of its own, it placed black bodies and the mutilation of black bodies at the center of American social reality, thus denying that blackness constitutes the very antithesis of that social reality.[49]

The demythifying power of the Amherst College effigy protest brings clearly into view an especially important reason for criticizing the prejudices which enabled the Rodney King verdicts. For what that protest forces us to recognize (precisely, we have seen, by undermining the assumptions in light of which many of us first saw it) is that such prejudices promote a vision of our common history that denies the truth. We should repudiate those prejudices, because they encourage the lie that, as citizens, we can honestly assume responsibility for the present without acknowledging the pain and the injustice which link the present to the past. By casting ''the likes of Rodney King'' as external threats to American society, the defense attorneys encouraged the citizens of a mostly white jury to disown their knowledge of a history of pain and injustice that has created American society and that remains essential to its identity. In effect, these lawyers promoted a form of bad faith that enabled the Simi Valley jurors to construct black Americans as ''others,'' and then to perpetuate the history of pain and injustice from which they had so conveniently separated themselves. We should criticize and attack the prejudices which fostered this bad faith, if only to make it more difficult in the future.[50]

CONCLUSION: CITIZENSHIP AND RACIAL IDEOLOGY

Channel surfing in Berkeley during the L.A. uprising, I noticed that two views dominated the television representation of the ''rioters.'' Call the first of these ''the conservative view,'' and the second ''the liberal view.'' In essence, the conservative view saw the ''rioters'' more or less as the defense attorneys had encouraged the Simi Valley jury to see Rodney King. Thought to be primarily black (before evidence of substantial Hispanic involvement in the uprising had come to light), the people in the street were seen as embodying an uncivilized chaos that needed to be stamped out in order to restore law and order. According to this view, the ''rioting'' had nothing to do with the King verdict, and would be better seen as expressing a repressed opportunism just waiting for an excuse to flout the law.[51] The liberal view was a bit more complex, as it emphasized the social causes of the ''riots''—joblessness, poverty, and, in general, socioeconomic need—but like the conservative view, it suggested that the burning of Los Angeles had little to do with what happened to Rodney King.

By dissociating the uprising from the King verdict, both liberals and conservatives were refusing to see in it an expression of moral indignation.[52] Though ''rioters'' in the streets were readily cast as bearers of chaos, or as agents of need and deprivation, their actions simply could not be seen as involving the view that the injustice suffered by Rodney King was symbolic of a larger social injustice. While "looters" could be construed as acting from need, they could not be construed as implicitly characterizing that need as stemming from a repressive social and political order, one aspect of whose repressiveness the trial videotape seemed explicitly to have exposed, and against which they would now strike a blow.

To be sure, there is no point in romanticizing the uprising, or in losing sight of the fact that, like all complex social events, it was causally overdetermined. The motives bringing people to the streets were, no doubt, numerous. But it strains credulity to deny, as many conservative and liberal pundits immediately wanted to do, that the uprising in Los Angeles was not for many an act of political protest. The incapacity of television newscasters to see it that way points largely, I think, to their and many white Americans' general failure to regard black people, even those who have not engaged in "riotous" behavior, as fellow citizens; what they cannot admit, in other words, is that the speech and/or action of a black person might be thoughtfully entertained as making a statement about issues which concern us all as members of the same political community. Blacks can be cast as lawless opportunists, as unfortunate victims, or in any number of other roles, but rarely as persons with a reasonable point of view about their and white Americans' shared circumstances. If blacks are needy, then their neediness needs to be managed and contained; that blacks' interpretations of their and other Americans' needs might be taken seriously seems to be beyond the pale of intelligibility. Even when the media permit some respected "black leader" to speak, one worries that most white Americans will dismiss his or her voice, and that they will see the media as pandering to "special interests."

Racial ideology in contemporary America works relentlessly to exclude blacks from many white Americans' conceptions of who their fellow citizens are. The antiblack sentiment reported in a recent *New York Times* article about the Greenwood section of Chicago begins to tell the story. Putting succinctly all he claims to know about black Americans, 23-year-old William Knepper says that "they came from Africa, and they can get away with a lot of stuff because they're black, they're a minority." Peggy O'Connor, a waitress and the wife of a police officer, is a bit more blunt: "I don't want to be too close to them. I think they've been whining too long, and I'm sick of it."[53] As it turns out, the image of the whining black recurs frequently among white Americans, as according to a poll CNN reported on the weekend of the L.A. uprising, 46% of the whites queried agreed that blacks "[a]re always whining about racism."[54] For many whites, then, black speech is not the speech of fellow citizens, but the always-complaining speech of spoiled children. Casting blacks in the infantilizing role of whiners from Africa, the racial ideology of these white folk works against the possibility of recognizing blacks as partners in a broadly conceived social and political enterprise.[55]

Read as sociopolitical allegory, the remarks and thoughts of Knepper, O'Connor, and many others can be said to envision America as a white nation that has got itself beset by a bunch of whimpering interlopers who get away with too much. DuBois's words and the Amherst College effigy protest exemplify discursive strategies for demythifying and resisting this vision. Other discursive strategies are possible as well. Absent demythification and resistance, we should anticipate endless echoes of Fanon's leitmotif:

> Look at the nigger! . . . Mama, a Negro! . . . Hell, he's getting mad. . . . Take no notice, sir, he does not know that you are as civilized as we. . . .''
>
> My body was given back to me sprawled out, distorted, recolored, clad in mourning in that white winter day. The Negro is an animal, the Negro is bad, the Negro is mean, the Negro is ugly; look, a nigger. . . . [56]

Notes

1. For a clear discussion of Marx's critique of the fetishism of commodities, see Seyla Benhabib, *Critique, Norm, and Utopia: A Study of the Foundations of Critical Theory* (New York: Columbia University Press, 1986), 114–23. For an account of Freud that points implicitly to the affinity between Freud and Marx to which I have alluded, see Jürgen Habermas, ''The Hermeneutic Claim to Universality,'' in *Contemporary Hermeneutics*, ed. Joseph Bleicher (London: Routledge, 1980), 193–94. I should add, finally, that the conception of ideology critique as demystification depends on the assumption that a form of consciousness is ideological if, to borrow the words of Raymond Geuss, ''it contains essentially an 'objectification' mistake, i.e, if it contains a false belief to the effect that some social phenomenon is a natural phenomenon, or, to put it another way, human agents or 'subjects' are suffering from ideologically false consciousness if they falsely 'objectify' their own activity, i.e., if they are deceived into taking that activity to be something 'foreign' to them, especially if they take that activity to be a natural process outside their control.'' See Raymond Geuss, *The Idea of a Critical theory: Habermas and the Frankfurt School* (Cambridge: Cambridge University Press, 1981), 14.

2. Marx himself uses the figure of the hieroglyphic in his discussion of the fetishism of commodities. See Karl Marx, *Capital: A Critique of Political Economy*, vol. 1, trans. Samuel Moore and Edward Aveling (New York: International Publishers, 1967), 74.

3. My conception of allegory is the standard one, according to which an allegorical text narrates events that ''make sense in themselves . . . but also . . . signify a second, correlated order of persons, things, concepts, or events'' (see M. H. Abrams, *A Glossary of Literary Terms* (New York: Holt, Rinehart, and Winston, 1971), 4). My conceptualization of ideology as allegory and as sociopolitical imagination draws its inspiration from Frederic Jameson, *The Political Unconscious: Narrative as a Socially Symbolic Act* (Ithaca: Cornell University Press), 9–102, and Benedict Anderson, *Imagined Communities* (London: Verso, 1991), 1–7.

   For the recent use of a distinction between demystification and demythologization that differs slightly from the distinction I have drawn between demystification and demythification, see Cornel West, "The New Cultural Politics of Difference," in *Out There: Marginalization and Contemporary Cultures,* ed. Russel Ferguson, Martha Gever, Trinh T. Minh-ha, and Cornel West (New York: New Museum of Contemporary Art; and Cambridge: MIT Press, 1990), 29–32.

4. Michael Omi and Howard Winant, *Racial Formation in the United States* (New York: Routledge, 1986), 62.

5. Cf. Robert Miles, *Racism* (New York: Routledge, 1989), 69–84. Here, I also wish to emphasize that the rules of racial classification differ from place to place, and that in a single place they may change over time. For more on this, see Omi and Winant, *Racial Formation in the United States,* 60ff. I should also note here that when, in this essay, I write of "whites," "blacks," "antiblack sentiment," etc., I am myself producing racial representations and, therefore, racial ideology. Thus, my own discourse can itself be taken as an object of ideology critique as I have conceived it.

6. Some of these interpretations will be contesting received interpretations. Sometimes the object of contestation will be racial classifications themselves. (See, for example, Michael Jackson's "Black or White" MTV video.)

7. My conception of racial ideology, as a system of racial representations that can be read as interpreting the racial identities which racial classifications posit, seems to me to be logically compatible with Barbara Fields's conceptions of racial ideology as a "medium" that mediates the comprehension of social reality. See Barbara Fields, "Ideology and Race in American History," in *Region, Race, and Reconstruction: Essays in Honor of C. Vann Woodward,* ed. James Morgan Kousser and James M. Mcpherson (New York: Oxford University Press, 1982), 143–75.

8. In general, a complete analysis of any given instance of racial ideology must also take into account those analytical perspectives that focus on the interpretation of class, gender, and sexual identities in the representation of American social life. Still, it seems to me that a critique of racial ideology can be usefully undertaken as a distinct endeavor. Thus, I believe that we can approach racial ideology more or less as Eve Sedgwick suggests we should approach gender and sexuality: "[I]n twentieth-century Western culture gender and sexuality represent two analytic axes that may productively be imagined as distinct from one another as, say, gender and class, or class and race. Distinct, that is to say, no more than minimally, but nonetheless usefully." See Eve Kosofsky Sedgwick, *Epistemology of the Closet* (Berkeley: University of California Press, 1990), 30.

9. Friedrich Nietzsche, *On the Genealogy of Morals,* trans. Walter Kaufmann and R. J. Hollingdale, in *On the Genealogy of Morals and Ecce Homo* (New York: Random House, 1969), 76–9.

10. Cf. Nietzsche, *On the Genealogy of Morals,* 79–81.

11. Toni Morrison, *Playing in the Dark: Whiteness and the Literary Imagination* (Cambridge, MA: Harvard University Press, 1992), 6.

12. Ibid., 1

13. Ibid., 16

14. Ibid., 51–53

15. Ibid., 76

16. Here, I want to emphasize that genealogical exposure and the critique of racial ideology need not restrict themselves, as does Morrison's discussion, to works by whites. Wilson Moses, for example, discusses the figures of the black Messiah and the Uncle Tom as they appear in literary representations of blacks produced by blacks as well as whites. (See Wilson Jeremiah Moses, *Black Messiahs and Uncle Toms: Social and Literary Manipulations of a Religious Myth* (University

Park: Pennsylvania State University Press, 1982). For a helpful historical perspective on some of the issues Morrison raises, see George Frederickson, *The Black Image in the White Mind* (Middletown: Wesleyan University Press, 1987). For an interesting and provocative attempt to raise similar issues as regards children's literature about black children, see Keith Millner, ''By the Color of Their Skin *and* the Content of Their Character: Representing Race for Children in African-American Picture Books,'' Senior Thesis, Amherst College, 1992.

17. Morrison, *Playing in the Dark,* 82.

18. Ibid., 82ff.

19. The reading of *Ghost* I sketch below derives from an essay in progress, entitled ''Black Cupids, White Desires: A Reading of *Casablanca* and *Ghost.*'' For a brief but helpful discussion of *Ghost* that begins to address some of the issues I think important, see Tania Modleski, *Feminism without Women: Culture and Criticism in a ''Postfeminist'' Age* (New York: Routledge, 1991), 131–34. Modleski's treatment of *Ghost* comes at the end of an insightful chapter (''Cinema and the Dark Continent: Race and Gender in Popular Film'') on the interplay of racial and gender ideologies in a number of well-known American films. For an older but still-useful analysis of the representation of race in American film, see James Baldwin's *The Devil Finds Work* (New York: Dell, 1976). See also Thomas Cripps, *Slow Fade to Black: The Negro in American Film, 1900–1942* (New York: Oxford University Press, 1977).

20. A fuller reading would also take into account issues of gender and sexuality.

21. The paradigmatic cinematic expression of this claim is the portrait of the black ''good souls'' in D. W. Griffith's *The Birth of a Nation.*

22. The tendency to overlook issues of race in allegorical readings of popular film is striking. Consider, for example, Frederic Jameson's reading of *Something Wild,* which completely ignores the film's obsession with figures of racial blackness, including its deployment of black cupid figures. Jameson's discussion of *Something Wild* is contained in chapter 9 of his *Postmodernism, or, The Cultural Logic of Late Capitalism* (Durham: Duke University Press, 1991). For a helpful corrective to his racially blind reading of the film, see Cameron Bailey, ''Nigger Lover—The Thin Sheen of Race in 'Something Wild,' '' *Screen* 4 (Autumn 1988): 28–40.

23. Here, I mean to leave open the possibility that not *all* allegorical commentaries or messages are false. See, for example, my discussion below of the Amherst College effigy protest.

24. The claims set forth by a demythifying critique will vary with the allegorically expressed claims under consideration. Thus, a demythifying critique of the Cosby show would proceed along different lines than a demythifying critique of *Ghost.*

25. W. E. B. DuBois, *The Souls of Black Folk* (New York: Bantam, 1989), 186–87.

26. As far as I can tell, DuBois's argument does *not* entail the questionable view that the history of America can be readily comprehended by means of an organic model of historical development. For more on this issue, see Robert Gooding-Williams, ''Evading Narrative Myth, Evading Prophetic Pragmatism: Cornel West's *The American Evasion of Philosophy,*'' *The Massachusetts Review* (Winter 1991–92): 517–42.

27. The Grove Press edition of *Black Skin, White Masks,* translated by Charles Lam Markmann, translates the title of chapter 5 as ''The Fact of Blackness.'' The title appearing in the original French, however, is ''L'Expérience Vécue du Noir,'' which translates literally as the ''The Lived Experience of the Black.'' See Frantz Fanon, *Black Skin, White Masks,* trans. Charles Lam Markmann (New York: Grove Press, 1967). The French text I have consulted is Frantz Fanon, *Peau Noire, Masques Blanc* (Paris: Editions du Seuil, 1965).

It is essential not to lose sight of Fanon's reference here to ''lived experience,'' as that reference (1) points explicitly to the central theme of chapter 5 and (2) brings explicitly into view Fanon's indebtedness to the phenomenological tradition of European philosophical thought, as represented primarily by Husserl, Heidegger, Sartre, and Merleau-Ponty. The influence of Sartre's masterpiece, *Being and Nothingness,* is especially strong in *Black Skin, White Masks.*

Earlier discussions of Fanon that engage the phenomenological dimension of his thought include Thomas F. Slaughter, Jr., "Epidermalizing the World: A Basic Mode of Being Black," *Philosophy Born of Struggle: Anthology of Afro-American Philosophy from 1917,* ed. Leonard Harris (DuBuque: Kendall/Hunt 1983), 283–87, and Charles Johnson, *Being and Race; Black Writing Since 1970* (Bloomington: Indiana University Press, 1988), 27.

28. Fanon, *Black Skin, White Masks,* 112. Fanon's discussion here seems to me to involve a revisionary appropriation of Sartre's famous analysis of "the look" in *Being and Nothingness.* Fanon extends Sartre's analysis by tying the experience of being seen by another human being to the experience of being the object of a linguistically performed act of racial identification. Fanon's emphasis on the way in which the experience of being seen is linguistically mediated effectively historicizes Sartre's analysis; it suggests that the experience of the look of the other always has a specific and historically constituted cultural dimension. On this analysis, one is never simply seen, but always seen in a certain light. Thus "the look" typically suffered by the Negro in negrophobic societies is a look that posits the Negro as a Negro. It is a look that says "Look, a Negro!"

29. See Jean Lhermitte, *L'Image notre corps* (Paris: Editions de la Nouvelle Revue Critique, 1939), 11, and Fanon, *Black Skin, White Masks,* 111, which has a footnote referring to Lhermitte's book.

30. Here, I have slightly altered the Markmann translation, translating "élaboration" as "elaboration" rather than as "development."

31. Fanon, *Black Skin, White Skins,* 111.

32. Ibid.

33. Ibid., 35, 116, 112. For a similar interpretation of Fanon's argument, which also uses the figure of the shadow, see Homi Bhaba, "Interrogating Identity: The Post-Colonial Prerogative," in *Anatomy of Racism,* ed. David Goldberg (Minneapolis: University of Minnesota Press, 1990), 187.

34. Fanon, *Black Skin, White Masks,* 111–12.

35. The myth of *brute* facts is the myth that experience affords us data, the character and significance of which, because they can be determined independently of our judgments and interpretations, cannot be disputed by setting forth *rival* judgments and interpretations. Cf. Charles Taylor, "Interpretation and the Sciences of Man," *Interpretive Social Science: A Reader,* ed. Paul Rabinow and William M. Sullivan (Berkeley: University of California Press, 1979), 29–30.

36. By "Eurocentric societies," I mean societies in which the dominant culture is of European origin. My argument here concerns the material efficacy of racial ideology. For a parallel argument concerning the effects on women of pornographic representations, see Monique Wittig, "The Straight Mind," *Out There,* Ferguson et al., 51–57.

37. My conception of a "retake" draws its inspiration from Umberto Eco's essay "Innovation and Repetition," *Daedelus* 114 (Fall 1985): 167. Eco writes that the "first type of repetition is the *retake.* In this case one recycles the characters of a previous successful story in order to exploit them, by telling what happened to them after the end of their first adventure. The most famous example of a retake is Dumas's *Twenty Years Later,* the most recent ones are the 'to be continued' versions of *Star Wars* or *Superman.*"

38. My conception of prejudice as prejudgment derives, of course, from the hermeneutics of Hans-Georg Gadamer as developed in his *magnum opus, Truth and Method.* For a brief but clear discussion of Gadamer's conception of prejudice as shaping all interpretation, see Georgia Warnke, *Gadamer: Hermeneutics, Tradition and Reason* (Stanford: Stanford University Press, 1987), 75–82.

39. For brief but helpful discussions of the defense lawyers' representation of Rodney King, see Patricia Williams, ''The Rules of the Game,'' *Village Voice,* 12 May 1992, and Amy Taubin, ''Control Freak,'' *Village Voice,* 19 May 1992. See also the *Los Angeles Times,* 3 April 1992, 21 April 1992, and 22 April 1992.

40. Robert Miles traces to the medieval period the European use of the figure of the aggressive and untamed ''wild man'' to characterize ''uncivilized'' peoples. In the seventeenth and eighteenth centuries, the application of this figure to black Africans came to have the added connotations of bestiality. See Miles, *Racism,* 17, 27. Also worth mentioning here is the recent media use of the term ''wilding'' to describe the actions of the black young men who were the defendants in the Central Park Jogger's trial.

41. An interesting case for consideration, I think, are the differences between the way in which, in the 1988 Winter Olympics, American sportscasters represented the white East German, Katerina Witt, and the way in which they represented the black American, Debbie Thomas, in the figure-skating competition. If Witt was all charm and grace and femininity, Thomas was the figure of the strong and athletic body that still lacked the civilizing accoutrements which allegedly characterized Witt's style.

42. Amy Taubin, ''Control Freak.''

43. Cf. Warnke, *Gadamer,* 75–82.

44. Though we cannot free ourselves from all of our prejudices all at once, since prejudice is constitutive of reading and interpretation, we can subject to criticism and reject *particular* prejudices.

45. An ideologically interesting movie that splits the difference is Sylvester Stallone's *Rocky III.* One of the two principal black characters, Apollo Creed (Carl Weathers), is cast in the role of a male nurse/sidekick. The other, Clubber Lang (Mr. T), is cast in the role of the wild man. There is some suggestion of this splitting in *Ghost,* inasmuch as the male ''henchman'' in the employ of the ''illegitimate'' patriarch is, though racially ambiguous, dark skinned. A reading of *Ghost* that insisted on this splitting would also want to pay attention to the way in which, in this case, gender differentiation mediates the distribution of the nurse and wild man roles.

   Recent discussions of the splitting of the black presence in popular film include Tania Modleski, *Feminism without Women,* 115–34. Modleski's analysis draws heavily on the writings of Homi Bhaba, especially his ''Of Mimicry and Man: The Ambivalence of Colonial Discourse,'' *October* 28 (Spring 1984): 125–34.

   For an older but equally insightful analysis of the same phenomenon as it pertains to the literary portrait of the American Indian, see Leslie Fiedler's discussion of James Fenimore Cooper novels in Fiedler's *Love and Death in the American Novel* (New York: Dell, 1960), 186ff.

46. *Los Angeles Times,* 22 April 1992.

47. I owe much in this paragraph to a conversation with Karen Sanchez-Eppler.

48. See, for example, the recent piece on the whites residing in the Greenwood section of Chicago, *New York Times,* 21 June 1992. See also the article on the racism experienced by black professional men in Philadelphia and elsewhere, *Wall Street Journal,* 8 May 1992. For a brief discussion of the sort of racism which blacks routinely experience on the streets of major American cities,

see Houston Baker, "Caliban's Triple Play," in *"Race," Writing, and Difference,* ed. Henry Louis Gates, Jr. (Chicago: University of Chicago Press, 1986), 385.

The reference to DuBuque, Iowa, is intended to recall the cross burnings and Ku Klux Klan organizing efforts there in 1991 and 1992 (see the *Quad-City Times,* 3 February 1992, and the *Des Moines Register,* 29 December 1991), and to remind the reader that the attitudes toward blacks we associate with the Ku Klux Klan are not limited to the southern supporters of David Duke who "believe in white." (In a PBS documentary, entitled "Backlash: Race and the American Dream," one of Duke's supporters is shown as saying "I am white and I want to remain an individual white person, pure white. . . . I believe in white.") Evidence of racism in Amherst includes the recent police harassment of a "suspicious" looking black man who, because he was wearing an "X" (for Malcolm X) hat, was said to resemble another black man who allegedly robbed a Springfield bank.

For a less anecdotal and more statistically satisfying account of racism in contemporary America, see chapter 1 of Gertrude Ezorsky's *Racism and Justice: The Case of Affirmative Action* (Ithaca: Cornell University Press, 1991). Among other things, Ezorsky notes the persistence of housing discrimination in the United States (two million instances a year), the fact that in states where the death penalty has been imposed "the killer of a white is three times more likely to be sentenced to death than the killer of a black," and the fact that one in three American whites still believes that racial intermarriage should be prohibited by law.

A premise of my discussion is that the continuing and pervasive incidence of racism in America is strong evidence for the continuing cultural power in America of racial epidermal schemata that represent blacks in a negative light.

49. Further arguments for the veracity of the allegorical implications of the effigy protest would pertain to the history and identity of America. These arguments, like the one DuBois makes, would be historical arguments and, like all historical arguments, would concern themselves with questions of authentication, justification, and objectivity (cf. Paul Ricoeur, *Time and Narrative,* vol. 1, trans. Kathleen McLaughlin and David Pellauer (Chicago: University of Chicago Press, 1984), 175–77). I should add that, in defending the accuracy of a particular perspective, say, on American history, one need not assume that that perspective is privileged, in the sense of being free of prejudgments or being based on "brute data" (cf. n. 35 above). Rather, one can take the view that all justificatory appeals to experience or other evidence operate within a hermeneutic circle in which one is always comparing one version of reality with a version that one treats as experience or empirical evidence in a given context. One need not, in other words, assume the possibility of appealing to an uninterpreted or unconceptualized reality (cf. Hilary Putnam, "Reflections on Goodman's *Ways of Worldmaking,*" *The Journal of Philosophy* 11 (November 1979): 611–15, and Hilary Putnam, *Reason, Truth and History* (Cambridge: Cambridge University Press, 1981), 54–56).

50. My reliance here on the language of "acknowledgment" and "disowning knowledge" draws much of its inspiration from the writings of Stanley Cavell. See, e.g., Stanley Cavell, *Disowning Knowledge: Six Plays of Shakespeare* (Cambridge: Cambridge University Press, 1987), 115–23.

51. For more on this point, see Mark Shubb's "Race, Lies, and Videotape: The L.A. Upheaval and the Media" (especially the section entitled "Thugs, Hooligans and Savages"), *Extra* 5 (July/August 1992): 8–11.

52. Appearing on *Crossfire,* William Allen of the United States Civil Rights Commission was the only person I heard dispute the liberal-conservative consensus.

53. *New York Times,* 21 June 1992.

54. The poll was taken on 30 April 1992 by the firm of Yankelovich Clancy Shulman, located in Westport, Connecticut.

55. Television media's tendency to use images of black bodies to represent people on welfare contributes substantially to the view that black people, *in general,* are clients but not citizens of the larger political community. Note also Gertrude Ezorsky's observation that ''15 to 19 percent of whites would not vote for a qualified black candidate nominated by their own party either for governor or president. According to Linda Williams, senior research associate at the Joint Center for Policy Studies, their 1986 poll showed that 'the higher the office, the more whites there were who would admit that they would never vote for a black.' '' See Gertrude Ezorsky, *Racism and Justice,* 13.

   For an insightful discussion of the ways in which the failure of whites to recognize blacks as fellow citizens has (mis)shaped contemporary policy debates about race in America, see Adolph Reed and Julian Bond, ''Equality: Why We Can't Wait,'' *The Nation* 20 (December 1991): 736. For a provocative *philosophical* discussion of the issues of recognition, membership, and citizenship which I have raised here, see Michael Walzer, *Spheres of Justice* (New York: Basic Books, 1983), 31–63.

56. Fanon, *Black Skin, White Masks,* 113.

12

The New Enclosures:
Racism in the Normalized Community

Thomas L. Dumm

There's a black person up our street and
we say "Hi," like he's a normal person.
—Resident of Simi Valley, May 1992

INTRODUCTION

The uprising that occurred in Los Angeles following the verdict in the Rodney King beating trial has been treated by many commentators as though it were the same as earlier urban riots. A special series of reports in the *Los Angeles Times,* for instance, straightforwardly compared the 1992 riots with Watts in 1965.[1] It emphasized a similar circumstance of poverty, a similar situation of overt brutality by police forces, and a similar despair over the future for the children of the city, then and now. The series noted as well the many pleas for harmony and peace at both times, and even concluded by mentioning earlier commission reports and studies on how to solve the core economic and social problems at the roots of the uprising. Conservatives repeated their usual charges as well, complaining

I wish to acknowledge the aid of Willie Epps, Jr., as a research assistant, Peter Stallybrass of the University of Pennsylvania for a helpful conversation on the European Enclosures, and Michael Shapiro of the University of Hawaii, for suggestions concerning technologies of vision. Bob Gooding-Williams and Austin Sarat of Amherst College made valuable suggestions on a late draft. Nancy Board meticulously proofed this essay. I am grateful to the participants in the seminar on homelessness being conducted at Princeton University, especially Tom Keenan and Pat Morton, for inviting me to lead a discussion concerning the riots on short notice, a discussion which yielded the initial outline of this essay.

about a lack of respect for law by those who rioted, calling for tougher prosecution of those unworthy urbanites who would loot and burn.

But this time, as opposed to last time, there is one major difference, perhaps so obvious that it has not been explored as carefully as it might otherwise have been. It can be put in the form of a question: The entire country knows the name of Rodney King, but who remembers Marcus Frye, the young man whose arrest on 11 August 1965 for speeding and reckless driving was the catalyst for the Watts riots?

That the video representation of Rodney (not Martin Luther) King in March of 1991, and the events that followed its broadcast, led to the uprising that occurred at the end of April 1992 is uncontested. I wish to explore the why and the how of the power of the image that has been associated with the name of Rodney King. To do so requires an acknowledgement that there has been a certain kind of "overdetermination" of the meaning of the image itself. Moreover, to discuss the power of the image in this case necessarily implicates the events concerning the King beating in a large, but as yet largely unarticulated crisis in the politics of representation in the United States.

I wish to argue that the image of King developed out of three interrelated perspectives, each of which contributed to a powerfully racist mode of under-standing King's circumstance, each of which connected the example of King to a more general category of "person," one who is a criminal "type." To explore this argument, first I survey briefly the "scientific" racism which implicitly informed the primary representation of King. Then, I turn to a discussion of the particular disciplines of observation which operated to convey that racism and are associated with contemporary monitoring techniques. Finally, I outline what I call the strategy of normalization which operated to encourage the internment of black minorities. The strategy of normalization could not have emerged had it not been for the correlational use of "scientific" racism and monitoring. Together they sustained an ensemble of forces that allowed the beating of King to occur and provided its *post hoc* justification. These forces operate in Los Angeles, as they do increasingly in other urban areas of the United States. Each has a history, yet their coming together in Los Angeles is perhaps a new event. And if it is not totally new, it is at least the most developed instance of these forces operating together. If so, Los Angeles may be the first city to experience in full measure the political crisis brought about by the establishment of lines of representational power that are likely to predominate through the remainder of this decade in the United States.

"SCIENTIFIC" RACISM

How did the members of the jury in Simi Valley reach their verdict to acquit the Los Angeles police officers who beat Rodney King? An old answer might suffice. They did so because they suffer racist fears of people who are different from themselves in skin color and other surface characteristics. The jurors had a simple wish to see Rodney King beaten, and they expressed a simple approval of what the police did, a simple desire to send a message to the world that the police should be allowed to beat black men who act suspiciously, especially outside of their own neighborhoods.

Generally speaking, in this view racism can be easily comprehended as an atavism, a simple hatred of others based upon the fear of what is unknown. The background chatter on the LAPD Mobile Data Terminals (MDTs) which referred to African Americans as "gorillas in the mist" and "mo fos," which casually mentioned beatings inflicted ("I obviously didn't beat this guy enough . . .") and the presumed lack of pain felt by people with black skin, can all be assimilated to this simple racism.[2] Alternative explanations advanced by the police for these communications, appealing to irony, black (sic) humor, and the siege mentality that afflicts police in dangerous chase situations could, from this perspective, be explained as a cynical cover for racial hatred. The jurors who voted to acquit could be understood as racist sympathizers from a community ignorant of minority experience and fearful of others.

There is much to be said for such an explanation. It is undoubtedly true that this raw hatred is still endemic to American culture. The relevant question concerning such an explanation, however, is how much does this overt racism explain? Might there be more than a cynical conspiracy of racial hatred at work in the Simi Valley verdict? If all of the jurors voted simply out of a fear of a black planet, then the only problem with their verdict would be that it was motivated by racism in what we presume is an era of racial enlightenment. Indeed, it is possible that if evidence of such racism were concealed by the prosecutors, then the verdict itself might be thrown out on grounds of fraud. Moreover, if only this form of racism were at work, a more careful screening process, better education concerning difference and similarity, and more vigorous enforcement of laws forbidding racial discrimination would eventually make such atavistic behaviors become as marginal as they are meant to be.

But an explanation that bases itself exclusively on this sort of racism, while probably necessary for understanding at least some of the events surrounding the King affair, is nonetheless not sufficient. Contemporary racism is not simply a stupid hatred. It may be based upon the ignorance that breeds hatred, but it is every bit as dependent upon a form of knowledge. That knowledge, sometimes wittingly used, sometimes unwittingly, operates to reinforce the fear and hatred of others by providing rationales for hierarchizing differences.

This hierarchizing became especially intense in the late nineteenth century, after the emergence of Darwinian evolutionary theory led to its specious application to different human groups under the guise of social Darwinism.[3] In the United States, one might trace "scientific" racism back to the American Enlightenment. An early and instructive instance of "scientific" racism can be located in the theory of race advanced by Doctor Benjamin Rush. Rush, a leading figure in the American Enlightenment of the late eighteenth century, posited that the color of the skin of black people was a form of leprosy.[4] He rooted his theory in his desire to *ameliorate* the condition of African Americans. He suggested that if the leprosy that made skin dark and hair wooly were to be cured (through purges, bleeding, sexual abstinence, psychological shock cures, and chemical bleaching), the problem of prejudice against those suffering the condition of black skin (which contributed toward their enslavement) would no longer hold. He suggested that even those black people who thought they liked being black really would prefer to be white. Finally Rush suggested, "We shall render the belief of the whole human race being descended from one pair, easy, and universal, and thereby not only add weight to the Christian revelation, but remove a material obstacle to the exercise of that universal benevolence with is inculcated by it."[5]

Rush's universalism obliterated difference in the name of benevolence. His theory is a utopian fantasy of peace achieved through "sameness." It predated more malevolent theories that would insist upon the preservation of difference in the name of the superiority of one group over another. It also, with its adumbration of the idea of the "normal," anticipated the general trajectory American social policy has taken in the late twentieth century.

With the emergence of both evolutionary theory and the science of genetics in the nineteenth century, biological theories of race with their specious logic of genetic inferiority came to the fore and dominated "scientific" discussions of racial difference. The credence that such theories enjoyed in the sciences, however, ended after the Second World War, when they were decisively disproved.[6] Since then, theories of biological inferiority have migrated to the social sciences, where the logic of strict causality is abandoned and statistical-probability tests are used to validate claims concerning inferiority. In these theories, deep explanations based upon the mechanisms of genetics have been displaced by arguments concerning the representations of racialized characteristics of appearance. The work of earlier geneticists who employed cranial measures to try to infer genetic characteristics is now used for a different end. Physical characteristics are freed from arguments about essential racial inferiority, and are simply associated with whatever behavior the racist wishes to attribute to the other, whether it be passivity and laziness or violent hyperactivity. "Race," in this newer sense, becomes a marker tied to a series of associated social phenomena. Its attachments to the body are not connected through a logic of strict causality, but an alternative logic of statistically valid correlation. Race becomes a normalizing category that uses a shorthand of visible markers to communicate its separations.[7]

To illustrate how this process operates, I turn briefly to the theory of criminality advanced during the 1980s by two of the most prominent conservative students of criminal behavior, James Q. Wilson and Richard Herrnstein.[8] Their work is the contemporary epitome of what I mean by "scientific" racism. Like most theories of crime, their theory ignores most crime that doesn't involve violence, and then, focusing on racial variations in violent crime rates, implicitly suggests that people of color are more likely to be violent than white majorities. More generally, by characterizing criminal proclivities in terms of pathology, Wilson and Herrnstein follow the lead of (or perhaps they, themselves, lead) mainstream modern criminology, dividing populations into the normal and the pathological, reinforcing views of the "abnormality" of minorities, and intensifying a general interpretive frame for criminalizing "otherness." Their book provides a justification for the police beating of King by suggesting that such a response might be reasonable in the face of the positive information concerning the allegedly, statistically valid, violent proclivities of the type of person they faced.

While Wilson and Herrnstein offer a variety of explanations of the etiology of criminal behavior, their most startling contribution to this literature is their explanation of how physical shape and appearance might contribute to criminal behavior. In a section entitled "Anatomical Correlates of Crime," they suggest that "character" is shaped by physical characteristics. While they argue that the "constitutional traits" associated with criminal behavior cannot ultimately predict what any one person will do every time, they suggest that, nonetheless, such "constitutional criminal predispositions,"[9] make it likely that someone will behave in a particular way, thus moving the focus of study from strict causality to a more general predictability. Historically revising the work of the nineteenth-century physician Cesare Lombroso, they suggest that there exist strong genetic correlates of crime, and go so far as to conclude that

> [t]he average offender tends to be constitutionally distinctive, though not extremely or abnormally so. The biological factors whose traces we see in faces, physiques, and correlations with the behavior of parents and siblings are predispositions toward crime that are expressed as psychological trait and activated by circumstances. . . . The existence of biological predispositions means that circumstances that activate criminal behavior in one person will not do so in another, that social forces cannot deter criminal behavior in 100 percent of a population, and that the distribution of crime within and across societies may, to some extent, reflect underlying distributions of constitutional factors.[10]

Wilson and Herrnstein argue here in a biological mode, but they augment their essentialism throughout in their attempts to explain how it might be that biological factors could be associated causally with criminal behavior. They suggest, for instance, that low intelligence would make one less aware of the dangerous consequences of lawbreaking.

But it is their understanding of the connections between visible features and underlying biological traits that makes Wilson and Herrnstein's work an important contribution to "scientific" racism. In outlining the constitutional factors that contribute to criminal behavior, they emphasize the use of "somatotyping" as a way of measuring a propensity for criminal behavior. A somatotype is a set of measures of a person's physique according to endomorphy (roundness, or chubbiness), mesomorphy (muscularity, or heavy-bonedness), and ectomorphy (linearity, or thinness). Referring to the work of W. H. Sheldon in the mid-1950s, which established seven-point scales on each of these measures, Wilson and Herrnstein suggest that it might be possible to measure *according to physique for criminal "traits."* According to them, those more likely to be criminals are those who are "mostly mesomorphs deficient in ectomorphy" (that is, heavily muscled people who are not thin and tall), and who have a characteristic called "andromorphy," which, they explain, is having "such masculine traits as a broad chest flaring toward the shoulders, low waist, relatively large arms, prominent muscle relief, large bones and joints, fat distributed throughout the body, etc."[11]

When summarizing their explanation of crime, Wilson and Herrnstein write the following sentence: "An impulsive person can be taught greater self-control, a low-IQ individual can engage in satisfying learning experiences, and extroverted mesomorphs with slow autonomic nervous system response rates may earn honest money in the National Football League instead of dishonest money robbing banks."[12] One might apply their racist understanding to the beating of Rodney King. Since he is not a professional football player, Rodney King, an "endormorphic mesomorph" of a size and shape and skin color *correlated* with a propensity to behave violently, probably impervious to pain, not likely to be very intelligent, undoubtedly has followed the path that leads to robbing banks. Vicious consequences follow from this logic. Because Wilson and Herrnstein only predict a probability of King behaving in a particular way, there remains an element of volition or choice. The degree of freedom associated with any statistical correlation still holds King (at least partly) responsible, responsible enough to be imprisoned.

King's responsibility extends not only to what he does, but to who he is, in Wilson and Herrnstein's *constitutional* sense. His body might be said to have informed on him to the police. Even in its inability to be perfectly still, King's body showed the police that he was a dangerous criminal.[13] But finally, and most insidiously, even though his body made manifest his criminal propensity, he nonetheless had a choice in his behavior. He could have played football in the NFL.

This is the double bind of free will and determinism imposed by Wilson and Herrnstein.

When they develop this sort of racist representational schema, contemporary criminologists move the categorization of the dangerous individual to a new level. Even if the criminal does not speak on his own behalf, even if his motives are not explained by investigation and confession, the body of the criminal itself speaks the "truth" of the criminal's character. Such a strategic move returns the relationship of criminal and sovereign power to an earlier moment in the history of crime, when the role of the spectacle of public punishment was crucial to determining the meaning of crime and its punishment.[14] But there is one difference. Now, instead of a liturgy of punishment in front of an assembled crowd, the representation of the body of the least-condemned person is conveyed through television, reinforced by television's repetitions, its slowing down of imagery, and its use of stereotypes, to convey the reassurance of serial continuity.[15]

Wilson and Herrnstein could not be said to hate Rodney King, any more than they could hate any unfortunate person who possessed a body of the "wrong" somatotype. "Scientific" racism is not about hate in such a primitive sense. But in its concern to establish a certainty about identity, and to render judgments concerning the social capacities of people on the basis of those certain distinctions, it seems to make little difference whether the damage to those who are subjected to its judgments originates in hate or not.

FROM SURVEILLANCE TO MONITOR

As I noted above, a common theme in the posttrial interviews of jurors was an insistence that "King was in control" of the events that unfolded the night of the beating.

> "He refused to get out of the car," said one juror who was interviewed by the *Times*. "His two companions got out of the car and complied with the orders and he just continued to fight. So the Police Department had no alternative. He was obviously a dangerous person. . . . Mr. King was controlling the whole show with his actions."[16]

This understanding of King's control over events was received with astonishment by many, who saw it as clear evidence of racist hatred at work. A simple and disingenuous excuse was created for blaming the victim and excusing the victimizers. However true that might be, the evocation of *movement* as a synonym for control shifts the terms of understanding from the level of King's body to its place in a larger system of representation. While Wilson and Herrnstein characterize dangerous criminals as hyperactive, there is a deep historical concern about movement and lack of control that is recapitulated symbolically in the concern about King's unwillingness to be still.

How is one to achieve a secure place? This question reaches the heart of the issue concerning King's movement. It has its historical precedent during the great Enclosures of the seventeenth century in Europe, when various attempts were made by those in power to control the movement of "masterless men" by establishing poor laws to criminalize vagabondage, a condition which was simply the state of being in transit.[17] For masterless men, freedom was deeply associated with mobility and the accompanying lack of legal requirements to be accountable to a superior. In the sixteenth and seventeenth centuries, peasants who were thrown off the land as a consequence of the Enclosures flocked to the cities, as their less numerous predecessors, during the feudal era, had retreated to green woods in search of anonymity.[18] The response of political authorities to the growth of these populations was to establish poorhouses and the early gaol houses, predecessors to modern penitentiaries.[19] Masterless men came to be understood as dangerous to political order, especially as the shift to market values made property more important, and they engaged in crimes against property to sustain themselves. As Michel Foucault put it, "The illegality of rights, which often meant the survival of the most deprived, tended, with the new status of property, to become an illegality of property."[20]

For the jurors from Simi Valley, Rodney King was "obviously a dangerous person." Why? Because his movement was an indicator of his control. More specifically, King was mobile. He was stopped in the Valley, in the neighborhood of Lake View Terrace, not in South Central Los Angeles. Allegedly, he was driving his car (an inexpensive Hyundai) at an excessive speed. His presence on the freeways of Los Angeles, moreover, was a sign of the free circulation available to even the poorer residents of Los Angeles, a city that relies first and foremost on the automobile as its mode of transportation. King was but one more acolyte in one of the most potent cults of twentieth-century America—the cult of the automobile. Los Angeles has always been the headquarters of this cult. But that cult is generally not perceived as belonging to black men. Indeed, one of the terrifying visions of white suburbanites is that of the migration of drive-by shootings of gang-bangers in South Central to the more prosperous (white) peripheral neighborhoods. This nightmare came true in December of 1987 when a young white woman was caught in the cross fire of a gang drive-by shooting in the posh neighborhood of Westwood, on the border of UCLA, close to Santa Monica.[21] That shooting contributed mightily to the creation of Operation Hammer, Police Chief Daryl Gates's major gang intervention program, which used the model of war to round up young people in South Central. Especially in southern California, then, Rodney King's mobility, his movement on the streets of suburban Los

Angeles as a dangerous young black man carried enormous demonological symbolic significance.[22] A desire to assert control over his mobility thus transferred,
through the medium of the representation of his body as an archetype, from the
movement of his automobile to the movement of his singular body. This mediation
of his body is yet another twist on the old theological figure of the King's two
bodies, this time rendered through a body that carried the name "King."[23]

Michael Stone, who served a defense counsel for Laurence Russell, the officer
who delivered the most blows on King's body, restated his defense strategy after
the verdict: "We got the jurors to look at the case not from the eye of the camera
or the eye of a video cameraman, but from the eyes of the officers who were out
there that night."[24] In moving from the singular "eye" to the plural "eyes,"
Stone implicitly was suggesting a move from the singular vision of panopticism,
with its idea of an objective vision of control through visibility, to the stereoscopic
vision of more pluralistic techniques of observation that have emerged in the
twentieth century. These techniques of the observer suggest that perspective can
be multiple.[25] The defense tactics relied upon resetting the video footage of the
beating in a larger temporal frame (what happened prior to the time that the
camera was turned on), slowing down the speed of the video and freezing different
moments of it (so as to give plausible alternative interpretations of the spatial
relations and the movements of the various viewed persons), and repetition of
the video during the course of the trial (so as to habituate the jurors to the use
of force). All of these tactics were techniques for disciplining the viewing of the
jurors so that they could plausibly "see from the eyes of the officers." Issued as
an invitation, the notion of envisioning deployed by Stone was a sophisticated
one. In short, he confronted the notion of objective truth (and guilt) with per-
spectivism (and reasonable doubt).

This attempt to position the jurors as stereoscopic viewers might be understood
as the result of a complex strategy which could not succeed without a widespread
shift in the "viewing habits" of modern subjects. From a way of seeing largely
based upon the ubiquitousness of *surveillance,* there has been, though this century,
a shift to a way of seeing based upon the *monitor.* It is not as though surveillance
has ended.[26] But the earlier modern connection of surveillance with the idea of a
perfect visibility, the idea that there could be an objective visibility which would
disclose the subjective status of the individual, no longer is the hegemonic discipline of observation that it once was. It is the more modest task of the monitor
to provide partial coverage of dangerous spaces, not to pretend to make surveillance perfect, but only to ensure that in protected zones defensive actions might
be taken in response to invasions.[27] Jonathan Crary suggests that the observing
subject, one who has the skills to "deobjectify" the power of surveillance, begins
to come into its own in the nineteenth century through the emergence of new

disciplines of vision. Thus, he suggests that surveillance and spectacle cannot be as clearly separated as someone like Foucault would wish. The objectification of the viewed subject is the product of a *discipline* of observation which has its own history as well.[28]

The move from surveillance to monitor is consistent with the emergence of the spectacle in the twentieth century.[29] The politics of the contemporary spectacle, as opposed to the classical spectacle of the scaffold, are strongly influenced by the fact the contemporary spectacle is mediated by cinematic and electronic technologies of representation. Because of the expenses and the organizational powers that are entailed in the proliferation of these technologies, state institutions and corporate powers are, at a very general level, usually able to act as gateways for the appearance of things that otherwise would not rise to the level of visibility. They do so not in the simple role of censor, but in the role of creating the contexts of visibility through which images are observed. The "real" scandal of the entire King affair might be that it began as a spectacle not controlled by those powers. The privately shot video was a new phenomenon, and not yet subject to the scrutiny of the sort of editorial judgments to which such videos are likely to be subjected in the future. In the proper order of things, the police would be able to monitor public spaces with their helicopters, patrol cars, and video cameras. The appearance of a video, which monitored the monitors, resonated as a latter-day instance of the Carnivale of the European Middle Ages.

Like the crowds toward the end of the classical age of public punishment, the spectators of the King beating became unruly and threatened the sovereign power on display. The highly publicized investigation and findings of the Independent Commission on the Los Angeles Police Department (popularly called the Christopher Commission), and the trial of the police officers (which was given complete coverage by the Los Angeles Fox Network news affiliate—a maverick network which specializes in "reality-based" television shows such as "Cops"), became exercises in damage control by those in authority who realized that their authoritative interpretation of the meaning of events was out of sync with the unruly mob. In the venues of commission and court there could be a reassertion of the power of the government and of the government's corporate sponsors to reshape and recuperate the prevailing discourse of political subjectivity.

THE NORMALIZED COMMUNITY

This process of readjusting the techniques of the observer is not unusual. It can instead be considered an inevitable part of the history of the disciplines of the eye. But I would suggest that the current readjustment is part of a larger process through which American society is becoming more reliant on observational techniques of monitoring and less reliant on surveillance as the primary channel of power. As policy makers in the United States deploy techniques of social control that are free from individuating disciplines, the disallowance of the perspective of the victim of police violence suggests not a mere corruption, but a radical and frightening transformation in the activity of policing. The techniques of surveillance which gave rise to modern police forces were designed to individuate even as they normalized. They accompanied a regime of rights. When policing moves from surveillance to monitoring, a move is made from the correction of individuals to the control of populations. Rights become anachronistic.

There are powerful ambiguities at work in such a process which make the move to monitoring potentially explosive politically. First, the continued reliance on a discourse of personal responsibility, as, for instance followed by Wilson and Herrnstein (King could choose to be a football player), when coupled with the withdrawal of the individuating discipline of surveillance, puts unbearable pressure on those who are designated as marginal. They are damned, and then they are damned for being damned, as the logic of Wilson and Herrnstein shows. Second, the technique of monitoring, which substitutes a passive control over protected space for a corrective and interventionist surveillance of individuals, forces the development of public policies to handle what could be called the waste products of social control, the ever-growing numbers of people who cannot be integrated into the "normal" social order.[30]

Of course, the other side of this process of "normalization" is the development of new modes of inclusion, in this case the development of communities of consumption. In such communities, television monitors are used extensively to observe the ingress and egress of persons who live in private housing developments. Mike Davis reports on one such community in Los Angeles, Forest City Enterprises. "As a spokeswoman for the owners observed, 'it's a trend in general to have enclosed communities.'"[31] These communities privatize what would once have been considered public spaces by erecting gates of entry and departure to provide security for those who can afford to live inside of them. Monitors provide a continuous flow of information which shows who has entered and who has left, who is in and who is out. Those within constitute communities of consumption. As Davis suggests,

> [T]he designers of malls and pseudo-public space attack the crowd by homogenizing it. They set up architectural and semiotic barriers to filter out "undesirables." They enclose the mass that remains, directing its circulation with behaviorist ferocity. . . . This Skinnerian orchestration, if well conducted, produces a veritable commercial symphony of swarming, consuming monads moving from one cash point to another.[32]

Or, as Arend Collen, a manager of a McDonald's in Simi Valley put it, "It's one of the few communities left where you can go shopping and not get hit up by people wanting money."[33]

Normalization through consumption is consistent with key elements in the Marxist critique of consumer capitalism.[34] But normalization proceeds through techniques governing the allowance and disallowance of activities beyond consumption as well. François Ewald, among others, has noted some of the elements by which populations are constituted in relation to risk and insurance. These are categories of norms which allow and disallow not only consumption, but activities of production as well.[35] Normalization, at its most general level, is a technique that permits withdrawal from the special interventions of discipline by directly manipulating populations at large. Through the establishment of norms, people become parts of systems of equivalence that substitute, for an equality based upon particularity, an inequality based upon comparison to a standard which is based upon an average. No single person is ever average, and hence no one is ever completely normal. One's place in such a system is determined by the attributes one shares with others. Each attribute places a dimension of one's life on a specific continuum. Personhood itself is fragmented, and elements of it become signs of one's place in reference to a norm.

In Simi Valley, the expression of normative values is closely associated with the practices of normalization. The mayor, for instance, is quick to note: "There is no question, in this community, that somebody out of the ordinary sticks out quickly. And people are very quick to report anything suspicious, very quick to call the police, and expect them to be there."[36] In the minds of the residents of Simi Valley, it is a lifestyle that separates those who live in the suburbs from urban others. Those who are different are perceived as dangerous.

> Residents insist that what binds them is not their common race or ethnicity, but a shared middle-class life style. "We like living in a place with educated people, people who believe as we do," said Brian Arkin. . . . "But I don't believe skin color is a criteria."
>
> "There's a black person up our street and we say 'Hi' like he's a normal person," Mr. Arkin continued. "This isn't about race. It's about whether you let your property run down."
>
> "Or whether you sell drugs out of your house," his wife, Valerie, interjected.[37]

In the normalized community, the best that a minority can be is "like a normal person." There is a range of deviations from the norm that only those who are "like" normal people will fall into; such people will not quite be inside the allowable range of the norm, whether because they don't quite succeed in maintaining their property or because they end up turning their homes into crack houses or because they *look* like people who would turn their homes into crack houses. And those who are *within* the range of the "normal" are likely to be discomfited by the very presence of those *outside* the "normal" for one other reason. By their presence (metaphorically more than physically), the nonnormal remind the normal of their own deviations from the law of the norm.

The normalized community is itself an enclosed space, as Davis notes, with sharply delineated points of entry and exit. Simi Valley is described as a very safe place, in part because of its plan. "The geographic configuration of the 12-mile-long valley, and its carefully planned street grid, makes a safe place safer. Just as each subdivision in Simi Valley is a self-contained web of cul-de-sacs, so the whole city can, in effect, be cordoned off simply by blocking four highway exits."[38] Such a system of streets encloses Simi Valley from the dangerous people of the outside world. People feel safe because they are surrounded with a familiar sameness. Those who are different are far away, spatially. Those who invade will be contained and removed.

What happens to those who are cast out of these enclosed communities? The nonnormal face of normalization is that of the deviant. If it is true that techniques of normalization are becoming less discipline centered than ever before, then those who are considered deviant from norms are not left to their own devices. Instead, they are threatened with a loss of the standing they may still enjoy as citizens.[39] In the end they remain subject to the recently rejuvenated, repressive power of the juridical apparatuses of the United States.

In the American version of normalized society, the least normal (and most despised) group of people are young black men. From 1980 to 1990, the prison and jail population of the United States exploded (from 350,000 to 1,200,000). Young black men are extremely overrepresented in the ranks of those in the arms of the law. A Sentencing Project Report, using U.S. Department of Justice and Census Bureau data, has shown that as of 1990 23% of black men between the ages of 18 and 30 in the United States were in prison, in jail, or on probation or parole, versus 6% of white men in the same age category. The report noted, "The number of *young* black men under the control of the criminal justice system—609,690— is greater than the *total* number of Black men of *all ages* enrolled in college—436,000 as of 1986. For white males, the comparable figures are 4,600,000 total in higher education and 1,054,508 age 20–29 in the criminal justice system."[40] A second study conducted by the National Center on Institutions and Alternatives found that 42% of black men in Washington, D.C. between the ages of 18 and 35 were in jail, on probation or parole, or awaiting trial or sentencing. The study noted that as many as 70% of black men in the city have been arrested by the time they turn 35, and as high as 85% of black men in Washington, D.C., face arrest at some time in their lives.[41]

The dramatic shift in the scale of punishment has turned prisons into internment centers. There is less effort than ever to engage in the discipline of an earlier era, in what was once called "rehabilitation." Since the middle of the 1970s, what Leon Radzinowitz labeled the "neoclassical revival" in punishment has gained ground in the United States.[42] It was in 1975, in the conclusion of *Thinking about Crime,* that James Q. Wilson suggested the path that would be followed in subsequent decades. He wrote, "Wicked people exist. Nothing avails except to set them apart from innocent people."[43] The ideas for determining what constitutes wickedness and innocence that Wilson subsequently advanced are inextricably connected to the latest techniques of normalization. The categories which determine dangerousness versus harmlessness, based as they are in the "scientific" racism which makes being a black male a criminal proclivity, can reasonably be seen as having contributed to the deep injustices that have resulted in 85% of the black men of Washington, D.C. facing arrest in their lifetimes. Once such a fundamental theological category as wickedness is reintroduced to provide a justification for the infliction of punishment on "abnormal others," the normalized community has moved into an ominous zone, where lives might collectively be condemned as wicked and eventually be taken, all in the name of justice. When "scientific" racists such as James Q. Wilson turn into moralists, people like Rodney King become a bearers of a new mark of Cain.

CONCLUSION

The representation of the normalized community that I have presented here is white, suburban, middle-class, male, straight, and law-abiding.[44] But norms themselves are particular. Each one flows along a specified dimension of existence. The threat of a normalized society does not rest with the existence of norms, but precisely in the ways in which the norms coalesce into operations of enclosure and internment. The vision of enclosed space—tightly controlled, perfectly monitored—has long been the beau ideal of Los Angeles, home of Disneyland. In a meditation about Los Angeles, the urban geographer Edward Soja notes this, and also notes that "when all that is seen is so fragmented and filled with whimsy and pastiche, the hard edges of the capitalist, racist, and patriarchal landscape seem to disappear, melt into air."[45] Just so. And yet it is important to avoid the sorts of reductions too common to the Marxist critical tradition which would make those hard edges blunt through overuse. Contemporary racism in the United States has several dimensions. Class cannot be a substitute for race, and the visions of politics associated with and sometimes resistant to the new Enclosures are not reducible to the analysis of the distribution of goods, any more than they can be the result of a pseudotheological explanation based upon the growth of evil in the hearts of criminal beings.

The new Enclosures cannot endure because they cannot sustain themselves. While suburban life is not an oxymoron, it will become one if those excluded from its peace are given only the miserable and incommodious lives of exclusion to live. That alternative future is upon us in the United States. It can and will result in the replication of the Los Angeles riot. But at the same time it is possible for the emergence of a politics of deterritorialization and reconnection, a politics in which arguments over space—its enclosures, exclusions, and internments—become subjects for debate and discussion, and more important, for resistances and transgressions. The initiation of such a politics is a short step in the long journey to beginning the process of ameliorating the current problem. Can Americans, for so long lacking a need to think about space, begin to think in spatial terms? Can they begin to act upon those thoughts?

After the rioting began, Rodney King went on television to plead with his fellow citizens. Most Americans remember that he asked, "Can we all get along?" But he added, "We all can get along. We've just go to, just got to. *We're all stuck here for awhile.*"[46] King recognized the finitude of the space of Los Angeles. He resisted the temptation to separate, to enclose, to substitute for the messy and open qualities of heterogeneous urban spaces the closed and deadened spaces of the suburbs. In making his plea he implicitly endorsed an ill-defined notion of toleration and plurality. He gave us all a moment to reflect upon the possibility of a democratic existentialism. The world is worlding. The forces of normalization operate to constrain, to separate, to exclude, and to intern. Our hope is precisely phrased. We're all stuck here for awhile.

Notes

The passage cited in the epigraph comes from Jane Gross, "In Simi Valley, Defense of a Shared Way of Life," *New York Times*, 4 May 1992, A15. Simi Valley was the site of the trial of the police officers who beat Rodney King. The trial was moved there in response to a request for a change of venue. With a population of about 100,000, it is located in Ventura County, the population of which is 65.9% white (non-Hispanic) and 2.2% black. Los Angeles County's population is 44% white (non-Hispanic) and 10.5% black. Simi Valley itself has a population that is 80% white and 2% black. It is also the home of the Ronald Reagan Presidential Library.

1. See "Understanding the Riots" (special series), *Los Angeles Times*, 11–15 May 1992, section T.

2. Throughout this essay, I rely on the *Report of the Independent Commission on the Los Angeles Police Department* (Los Angeles: Independent Commission on the Los Angeles Police Department, 1991). For references to the Mobile Digital Terminal (MDT) communications, see 48–55. For specific references to MDT communications by officers who beat King, see 14–15.

3. See Robert Miles, *Racism* (New York: Routledge, 1989), especially 36–38.

4. Benjamin Rush, "Observations intended to favour a supposition that the Black Color (as it is called) of the Negroes is derived from LEPROSY," *Transactions of the American Philosophical Society* 4 (1799): 289–97. For a powerful discussion of Rush, see Ronald Takaki, *Iron Cages: Race and Culture in Nineteenth-Century America* (New York: Alfred Knopf, 1979), 16–35.

5. Ibid., 297.

6. Miles, *Racism,* 37.

7. This theme is developed in great detail in Robert Gooding-Williams's analysis of Frantz Fanon's *Black Skin, White Masks.* See "Look, a Negro!" in this volume.

8. See James Q. Wilson and Richard Herrnstein, *Crime and Human Nature* (New York: Simon and Schuster, 1985). Wilson, it should be mentioned was an expert witness (and served as an advisor) to the Mayor of Los Angeles's special commission to investigate police brutality, known as the Christopher Commission, which was organized in the wake of the beating of Rodney King (see *Report of the Independent Commission,* table 2A–2). Herrnstein currently is working on a study of the relationship between "race and I.Q." with Charles Murray, a scholar better known for advancing the idea that welfare creates poverty by encouraging a "culture of dependence."

   I focus on this book because it is a standard in the field of criminology. In 1985, it summarized the literature in an attempt to develop a general theory of criminal behavior. I also chose it because Wilson has been exceedingly influential on the direction of criminal-punishment policy in the United States, a leader in what has been termed the "neoclassical" revival in criminal punishment, which has led to theoretical justification for greater punitiveness in sentencing and the explosive growth in prison populations. Finally, Wilson is not considered merely a "popularizer" of ideas. His work on the study of policy is respected enough in the discipline of political science so that the American Political Science Association has named him its president for 1992.

9. Ibid., 71–72.

10. Ibid., 102–3.

11. Ibid., 85–86. More generally, see the entire section, 81–90. The development of a "scientific" understanding of what a criminal is, one that cuts it loose from the mooring of law, has long been a eugenically inspired utopian impulse in modern criminal discourse. These attempts to reach some essential understanding of "who the criminal is" underlay what Michel Foucault referred to as the establishment of both general categories of "delinquency," and the more specific establishment of specific persons as "dangerous individuals," in which the question comes to focus not on criminal acts but on individualized behavior. See Michel Foucault, *Discipline and Punish: The Birth of the Prison,* trans. Alan Sheridon (New York: Pantheon, 1977), especially 290–92. Also see Michel Foucault, "The Dangerous Individual," translated by Alan Baudot and Jane Couchman, with reference to a translation by Carol Brown, in Lawrence Kirtzman, ed., *Michel Foucault: Politics, Philosophy, Culture* (New York: Routledge, 1988), 125–51.

12. Wilson and Herrnstein, *Crime and Human Nature,* 66. A "slow autonomic nervous system" implies an imperviousness to pain.

13. I will return to the this theme of "stillness" later in this essay.

14. Foucault, *Discipline and Punish,* especially 28–31.

15. For an analysis of television that influences the one I use here, see Stanley Cavell, *Themes Out of School* (Chicago: University of Chicago Press, 1988), for an essay entitled, "The Fact of Television," 235–68. I discuss the politics of the spectacle further in the next section of this essay.

16. See Richard A. Serrano and Tracy Wilkinson, "All Four in King Beating Acquitted," *Los Angeles Times,* 30 April 1992, 2.

17. See Christopher Hill, *The World Turned Upside Down: Radical Ideas During the English Revolution* (Baltimore: Penguin, 1975), especially chapter 3.

18. Ibid., 40–41. Also see Foucault, *Discipline and Punish,* 291.

19. Hill, *The World Turned Upside Down,* 40–41.

20. Foucault, *Discipline and Punish,* 85.

21. See Mike Davis, *City of Quartz: Excavating the Future in Los Angeles* (New York: Verso, 1991), 270.

22. On minority inversions of the dominant automobile culture in the American southwest, see Brenda Bright, "Mexican American Lowriders: An Anthropological Approach to Popular Culture," dissertation, Department of Anthropology, Rice University, 1993.

23. On the political theology of the medieval monarchy, see Ernst Kantorowicz, *The King's Two Bodies: A Study in Medieval Political Theology* (Princeton: Princeton University Press, 1957). This book is put to great use by Foucault in *Discipline and Punish,* 28–29.

24. Serrano and Wilkinson, "All Four in King Beating Acquitted."

25. See Jonathan Crary, *Techniques of the Observer: On Vision and Modernity in the Nineteenth Century* (Cambridge, MA: MIT Press, 1990).

26. See Davis, *City of Quartz,* especially 223–63, the chapter entitled "Fortress L.A." By this title Davis himself implicitly is acknowledging a shift in the form and function of surveillance, which is not to provide an individuating power, but instead to establish a citadel for those inside, and, as he noted in the next chapter, "The Hammer and the Rock," 267–322, to enable the redeployment of militarizing tactics of control for the remainder of the population.

27. See the next section of this essay for an elaboration on this theme.

28. Crary, *Techniques of the Observer,* especially 17–19.

29. This is one of Crary's important points. Also see the most important theorization of this perspective, Guy Debord, *The Society of the Spectacle,* trans. Donald Nicholson-Smith (Detroit: Red and Black, 1983).

30. The metaphor of the waste product is a dangerous one, implying as it does the disposability of those who are waste. I first encountered its use in a review essay by John Langbein, *"Albion's Fatal Flaws,"* *Past and Present* 98 (February 1983): 96–120.

31. Davis, *City of Quartz,* 246.

32. Ibid., 257.

33. Gross, "In Simi Valley, Defense of a Shared Way of Life."

34. The classic critique of this form of normalization is Herbert Marcuse, *One-Dimensional Man* (Boston: Beacon Press, 1964).

35. See François Ewald, "Norms, Discipline and the Law," trans. and adapted by Marjorie Beale, *Representations* 10 (Spring 1990): 138–61. See also, Jonathan Simon, "The Ideological Effects of Actuarial Practices," *Law and Society Review* 22, no. 4 (1988): 771–800.

36. Gross, "In Simi Valley, Defense of a Shared Way of Life."

37. Ibid.

38. Ibid.

39. On the erosion of citizen rights of standing in the United States, see my forthcoming book, *United States: Representing American Political Experience,* especially chapter 2, "Fear of Liberalism."

40. Marc Mauer, *Young Black Men and the Criminal Justice System: A Growing National Problem* (Washington: The Sentencing Project, February 1990), 3.

41. See Jason DeParle, "Young Black Men in Capital Study Finds 42% in Courts," *New York Times,* 18 April 1992, A1.

42. See Sir Leon Radzinowitz and Marvin Wolfgang, ed., *Crime and Justice: The Criminal in the Arms of the Law,* vol. 3 (New York: Basic Books, 1977), especially, "Ideologies and Crime," by Radzinowitz and Joan King, 442–49.

43. James Q. Wilson, *Thinking about Crime* (New York: Basic Books, 1975), 235.

44. I have been silent on the issue of gender in this essay, primarily for reasons having to do with my own unpreparedness to address it as fully as it deserves to be addressed here. But the issue of gender in regard to normalizing discourse and race is an enormous one. The presumption of the criminal as a black *man* has much to do with the sexual insecurities of men in powerful positions. The core of the demonological shift in the representation of black men in "The Birth of a Nation" was associated most convincingly by Michael Rogin with fears of miscegenation and male misogyny. See Michael Rogin, " 'The Sword Became a Flashing Vision,' " *Ronald Reagan, the Movie and Other Episodes in American Political Demonology* (Berkeley: University of California Press, 1987), pages 190–235. I address questions of race and gender in this context more thoroughly in my forthcoming, *United States.* See chapter 2 of that book, "George Bush, or Sex in the Superior Position."

45. Edward Soja, *Postmodern Geographies: The Reassertion of Space in Critical Social Theory* (New York: Verso, 1989), 246.

46. "Rodney King's Statement," *Los Angeles Times,* 2 May 1992, 3.

13

Korean Americans vs. African Americans: Conflict and Construction

Sumi K. Cho

The violence and destruction that followed the Rodney King verdict again exploded the myth of a shared consensus around American justice and democracy. The blind injustice of the Simi Valley "not guilty" verdict produced a rainbow coalition of people—old, young, of all colors—who had few or no reservations about looting stores owned primarily by Koreans and Latinos. It soon became clear that the nation's professional, academic, political, and business elite were ill-equipped to deal with the complexity of issues before them, captured in the simple but straightforward plea by Rodney King: "Can we all get along?"

King's question hints at the real question confronting U.S. society: Who is the "we" that must get along? For too long, the political and academic tradition has defined U.S. race relations in terms of a Black/white binary opposition. For example, a CNN–*Time Magazine* poll taken immediately after the verdict surveyed "Americans" on their opinions regarding the verdict and the violence that followed. Yet the poll only sought the views of African Americans and whites regarding the future of race relations. The Black/white framing of race issues must give way to a fuller, more differentiated understanding of a multiracial, multiethnic society divided along the lines of race, class, gender, and other axes in order to explicate effectively the Los Angeles explosion and to contribute to

I would like to thank Gil Gott, Pedro Noguera, Susan Lee, Ronnie Stevenson, Ann Park, and Bob Gooding-Williams for their helpful comments on this essay.

the long-term empowerment of those who, for a short time, exercised the power of their own agency.

Dominating the current debate within the Black/white racial paradigm are, on the one hand, the human-capital theorists[1] who assert that the degradation of "family values" caused the fires in L.A. Dan Quayle's now infamous Murphy Brown speech, for example, pointed the finger at a television sitcom for contributing to the social and moral decay which lie behind the problems in South Central L.A. by portraying the single motherhood of a white woman from the professional class. On the other hand, there are structuralists[2] proposing that the U.S. adopt a "Marshall Plan" for its cities to address the institutional lockout of people of color from economic development.

While the structural explanations provide more illuminating insights than human-capital theories, they cannot fully explain the myriad of events in Los Angeles, particularly those that affected the Korean-American community. The portrayal of Asian Americans as the paragons of socioeconomic success contributed to the targeting of Korean Americans as a scapegoat by those above and below Koreans on the socioeconomic ladder during the L.A. riots. The King verdict and the failure of the U.S. economy to provide jobs and a decent standard of living for all of its peoples, the ostensible root causes of the rioting, were not the fault of Korean (or Latino) shopowners. If, as some have suggested, the Willie Horton imagery[3] is the myth and Rodney King's beating the practice, then likewise, the casting of Asian Americans as a model minority is the myth, and the looting and burning of Koreatown and Korean-owned stores is the practice.

Manipulation of Korean Americans into a "model minority" contributed to their "triple scapegoating" following the King verdict. The first layer of attack came from those who targeted Korean-owned stores for looting and arson. The second layer consisted of those in positions of power who were responsible for the sacrifice of Koreatown, Pico Union, and South Central Los Angeles to ensure the safety of wealthier, whiter communities. The final scapegoating came at the hands of the media, eager to sensationalize the events by excluding Korean perspectives from coverage and stereotyping the immigrant community. These three forces combined to blame the Korean-American community for the nation's most daunting economic and sociopolitical problems.

Rodney King's spontaneous reaction upon seeing the varied groups of color pitted against each other in L.A. reflected a deeper understanding of the commonalities among those groups than many intellectuals and politicians have shown. "I love people of color," he declared, although almost all the mainstream edited out this statement. Further, his plea can be read as a challenge to the academic community and intellectual activists of racial and ethnic politics: "We're all stuck here for awhile. . . . Let's try to work it out."

Race-relations theorists must accept this challenge and go beyond the standard structuralist critique of institutional racism to incorporate the most difficult issues presented by the aftermath of the not-guilty verdicts in the Rodney King case. Specifically, intellectual activists must devise a new approach to understanding interethnic conflict between subordinated groups and work toward a proactive theory of social change. Such a theory would examine the structural conditions that influence patterns of conflict or cooperation between groups of color, racial ideologies and how they influence group prejudices, as well as the roles of human agency, community education, and political leadership and accountability. Such a theory should strive to explain and resolve interethnic conflicts to unite subordinated groups.

KOREAN AMERICANS IN L.A.: MODEL MINORITY MYTH AND PRAXIS

The View from Below: The Politics of Resentment

The deteriorated socioeconomic conditions of neglected inner cities have led scholars to compare ghettos like South Central Los Angeles (which includes the Southeast and South Central city-planning areas) to South African "bantustans" that serve solely as "holding space for blacks and browns no longer of use to the larger economy."[4] African Americans constitute 73.9 percent of South Central's residents, and Latinos account for 22.9 percent (with a quickly growing undocumented population). Only 3.6 percent of the total land mass is zoned for industry.[5] South Central residents lack self-determination and political-economic power. In this context, Korean Americans who open stores in the neighborhood are resented by long-deprived residents and are seen as "outsiders" exerting unfair control and power in the community. The interaction between the two racial groups is structured strictly by market relationships: one is the consumer, the other is the owner. This market structuring of group relations has influenced the "Korean/Black conflict" and contributed to the course of events following the not-guilty verdicts.

Koreans first were scapegoated by rioters of all colors who looted stores and later set them afire. Reports of the early activity following the not-guilty verdict in the Rodney King beating centered around a crowd that had gathered in front of Tom's Liquor Store at Florence and Normandie in the late afternoon of 29 April 1992. One of the first targets of the group was the "swap meets" because they were Korean-owned. The swap meets were essentially indoor flea markets that operated every day during the week and offered discounted prices on consumer items such as electronics and clothing. Whether these stores provided a service to an underserved community by offering low-priced goods where mega-retailers refused to tread or whether they shamelessly promoted consumerism to an economically disadvantaged population was not at issue. The most oft-stated reason for the targeting of these stores and Korean stores in general was a familiar refrain: Korean owners were rude to African-American and Latino customers. One Latino interviewed on television was asked why people were looting Koreans. "Because we hate 'em. Everybody hates them," he responded.

Much has been said about the rudeness of Korean owners. Some of the major media outlets that covered the tensions between African Americans and Korean Americans attempted to reduce the conflict to "cultural differences" such as not smiling enough, not looking into another person's eyes, not placing change in a person's hands. Although Koreans wanted very badly to believe in this reductionism, one making an honest assessment must conclude that far too many Korean shopowners had accepted widespread stereotypes about African Americans as lazy, complaining criminals.

The dominant U.S. racial hierarchy and its concomitant stereotypes are transferred worldwide to every country that the United States has occupied militarily. Korean women who married American GIs and returned to the United States after the Korean War quickly discovered the social significance of marrying a white versus an African-American GI. American racial hierarchies were telegraphed back home. When Koreans immigrate to the U.S., internationalized stereotypes are reinforced by negative depictions of African Americans in U.S. films, television shows, and other popular forms of cultural production. This stereotype, combined with the high crime rate inherent in businesses such as liquor or convenience stores (regardless of who owns them), produced the prejudiced, paranoid, bunker mentality of Soon Ja Du who shot Latasha Harlins, a 15-year-old African-American girl, in the back of the neck during a dispute over a bottle of orange juice. Since 1 January 1990, at least 25 Korean merchants have been killed by non-Korean gunmen.[6]

On the other hand, many African Americans also internalize stereotypes of Korean Americans. Asian Americans walk a fine line between being seen as model minorities and callous unfair competitors. The result is a split image of success and greed that goes together with callousness and racial superiority. Distinctions between Asian ethnicities are often blurred as are distinctions between Asians and Asian Americans. "Sins of the neighbor" are passed on to Koreans in the United States. For example, when then prime minister Yasuhiro Nakasone of Japan made his blundering remarks in 1986 that "the level of intelligence in the United States is lowered by the large number of Blacks, Puerto Ricans, and Mexicans who live there,"[7] this comment was often applied generally to represent the views of all Asians, including Koreans, although Korea has a long history of colonization at the hands of the Japanese.

In rationalizing the violence that followed the verdict, African-American leaders often repeated the myth that Korean immigrants unfairly compete with aspiring entrepreneurs from the Black community because Korean Americans receive preferential treatment over African Americans for bank and government loans. "Until banks make loans available to blacks as much as other people, there's going to be resentment," observed John Murray of Cal-Pac, a Black liquor-store-owners' association.[8] In reality, however, banks and government lenders uniformly reject loan applications for businesses located in poor, predominantly minority neighborhoods such as South Central Los Angeles, regardless of the applicant's color. Korean immigrants rarely receive traditional financing. Those who open liquor stores and small businesses often come over with some capital and/or borrow from family and friends. At times, groups of Koreans will act as their own financial institutions through informal rotating credit associations known as "kyes" (pronounced "keh").

Thus, the ability to open stores largely depends upon a class variable, as opposed to a racial one. In fact, Korean merchants most often purchased their liquor and grocery stores from African-American owners. Prior to the Watts riot in 1965, most of the liquor-store owners in South Central Los Angeles were Jewish. After the riots, many Jewish owners wanted out. The easing of government-backed loans and the low selling price of the stores in the mid-1960s—roughly two times monthly gross sales or $80,000—opened the way for African-American entrepreneurs. The labor-intensive, high-risk nature of work combined with the deregulation of liquor pricing in 1978 and subsequent price wars that drove many small stores out of business led to a sell-off of liquor stores by African Americans in the late 1970s and early 1980s. The sell-off coincided with a large increase in Korean immigration to the U.S. during the same time period. African-American merchants made a handsome profit selling to Koreans for five times monthly gross sales, or about $300,000.[9] Korean immigrants, many of whom held college degrees, could not find jobs commensurate with their training and education in the new country due to structural discrimination, occupational downgrading, and general antiforeign sentiment. A disproportionate number of Korean families turned to small businesses as a living. According to U.S. Census Bureau statistics, the rate of self-employment among Koreans is higher than that of any other ethnic group.[10] This self-employment, or "self-exploitation" as some have termed the practice, extends not only to the "head of the household," but often to the entire family, including children. Given the high educational background of this group, high self-employment rates in mom-and-pop grocery stores can hardly be viewed as "success."[11]

Nevertheless, the politics of resentment painted Koreans as callous and greedy invaders who got easy bank loans. As this depiction ran unchecked, it became increasingly easy to consider violence against such a contemptible group. The popular rap artist, Ice Cube, warned Korean shopowners in his song entitled "Black Korea" (on his *Death Certificate* album) to "pay respect to the black fist, or we'll burn your store right down to a crisp." The scene was set for disaster and required simply a spark to ignite a highly flammable situation. When the scorching injustice of the verdict was announced, Korean-owned businesses were scapegoated as the primary target for centuries of racial injustice against African Americans—injustice that predated the bulk of Korean immigration which occurred only after the lifting of discriminatory immigration barriers in 1965.

The View from Above: "Racist Love" and the Model Minority

The police nonresponse to the initial outbreak of violence represented a conscious sacrificing of South Central Los Angeles and Koreatown, largely inhabited by African Americans, Chicanos, Latinos, and Korean Americans, to ensure the safety of affluent white communities. The LAPD's intentional neglect in failing to respond to the initial outbreak of rioting set up a foreseeable conflict between African Americans, Chicanos, Latinos, and Korean Americans with destructive and deadly consequences. When it became evident that no police would come to protect Koreatown, Koreans took up arms in self-defense against other minority groups. Rather than focus on whether these actions by the Korean community were right or wrong, one should question the allocation of police-protection resources and the absolute desertion of Koreatown and South Central L.A. by the police. When Deputy Chief Matthew Hunt, who commands officers in South Los Angeles, asked Chief of Police Daryl Gates for greater preparation prior to the announcement of the verdicts, the chief refused, claiming smugly that such preparations were unnecessary.

It was a badly kept secret that angry mobs bent upon destruction and violence would be descending on Koreatown. When Korean Americans called the LAPD and local and state officials for assistance and protection, there was no response. It was very clear that Koreatown was on its own. In the absence of police protection, the community harnessed its resources through Radio Korea (KBLA) in Los Angeles to coordinate efforts to defend stores from attack. People from as far away as San Bernadino and Orange County came to help. Radio Korea reported on the movement of the crowds and instructed volunteers where to go. In short, the radio station and individual volunteers served as the police force for Koreatown. It is bitterly ironic that some Koreans defending stores were later arrested by police for weapon-permit violations.

In stark contrast, when looters began to work over major shopping malls such as the Fox Hills Mall in Culver City, they were quickly stopped by the police, with "merchants and residents praising [police] efforts."[12] Likewise, the police made sure that the downtown business interests were secured. The west-side edition of the *Los Angeles Times* even boasted that the police forces in the predominantly white communities of Santa Monica, Beverly Hills, and West Hollywood "emerged remarkably unscathed by the riots."[13] Other areas, especially communities of color such as South Central, Pico Union, and Koreatown, effectively became a "no-person's-land." Enter at your own risk. There was no protection for these areas. Although residents paid taxes for police protection, the LAPD made a conscious choice to stay out of the neighborhoods of color that were most at risk during the postverdict rioting.

Although Korean Americans donated substantial amounts of money to the election campaigns of state and local officials, no political assistance was forthcoming in their time of need. "We've made significant contributions to the city council, as well as county, state and federal politicians, and they failed us," said Bong Hwan Kim, executive director of the L.A. Korean Youth Center.[14] Attempts to contact Governor Wilson for help from the National Guard were in vain. The National Guard did not arrive on the scene until there was little left to do. Wilson's explanation was that the National Guard was late because they had run out of ammunition.[15] During the initial outbreak of violence, it is now known Chief Gates was attending an expensive fundraiser on the west side while these communities burned. In response, he later stated at his first press conference following the verdict that police were needed to protect the firefighters. Unfortunately, the fire department was unwilling to go along with this excuse. In a stinging report to the Fire Commission, L.A. Fire Chief Donald Manning complained that the LAPD dismissed their requests for protection during the outbreak of violence as "not a top priority," thereby delaying fire-department responses to the fires.[16] Moreover, Gates was stumped by an *L.A. Times* reporter who pressed him about the hours prior to the arsons, when some of the most sensationalized violence occurred outside of Tom's Liquor Store.

Many Koreans mistakenly believed that they would be taken care of if they worked hard, did not complain, and contributed handsomely to powerful politicians such as Governor Wilson and local officials. One hard lesson to be learned from the aftermath of the King verdict and the Korean-American experience is that a model minority is expediently forgotten and dismissed if white dominance or security is threatened. This point was also demonstrated through the Asian-American admissions scandals at the nation's premier institutions of higher education when Asian-American students began to outperform white students on SATs and GPAs. The rules of the game of "meritocracy" had to be changed to put a ceiling on Asian-American admissions, thereby producing the largest unstated affirmative-action policy benefiting whites.

The easy dismissal of Korean-American pleas for help is rooted in the relationship between the dominant power brokers and the model-minority group. The model-minority "thesis," popularized during the late 1960s and the mid-1980s during the Reagan administration, represents a political backlash to civil rights struggles. It is critical to understand that the model-minority thesis is no compliment for Asian Americans. It has been historically constructed to discipline activists in the Black Power, Black Panther, American Indian, United Farm Workers, and other radical social movements demanding institutional change.[17] Because it has this genesis, the embrace of Asian Americans as a model minority is an embrace of "racist love."[18] The basis of that love has a racist origin: to provide a public rationale for the ongoing subordination of non-Asian people of color. Because the embrace or love is not genuine, one cannot reasonably expect the architects truly to care about the health or well-being of the model minority.

The View from Afar: Media Ignorance, Media Sensationalism

The exclusion of Korean Americans and Asian Americans from mainstream media analysis allows distorted stereotypes to be perpetuated. Stereotypic media portrayals of Koreans as smiling, gun-toting vigilantes and African Americans as vandals and hoodlums trivialize complex social and economic problems. A reasoned Korean perspective would help to balance the picture of hardship and frustration felt by all communities. It would be too simplistic, however, to relegate all of the media to a monolithic mind-set in the coverage. The coverage and stereotypes varied and reflected different political perspectives.

For conservative journalists, Korean Americans were held up as hard-working, law-abiding citizens rightfully taking matters into their own hands. The widespread imagery of the armed shopkeeper confronting young African-American males may represent a wish fulfillment on the part of conservative reporters. Korean immigrant shopkeepers were a surrogate army acting out the white suburban male's American dream—bearing arms against Black men. Korean Americans, as a model minority, were depicted as the "legitimate victims" (along with Reginald Denny) and singled out in the media for praise and sympathy.

For liberal members of the media, Korean Americans were manipulated as dangerous vigilantes who were directly responsible for the plight and oppression of African Americans. Already anguished by the not-guilty verdicts of the four white police officers, liberal journalists sought to redeem themselves by providing critical coverage of Korean Americans. From this angle, Korean Americans, not white Americans, became the primary instigators of racism against African Americans. Korean aggression against African Americans was the focus, with depictions of armed shopkeepers and the last seconds of the videotape showing

Soon Ja Du shooting Latasha Harlins repeatedly taking center stage to deflect white guilt.

The treatment of Korean Americans in the media may reflect more about relations between white and Black America than about relations between African Americans and Korean Americans. The embrace of the model-minority myth by the media becomes a bear hug particularly at times when Black/white tensions intensify and white America wishes to discipline African Americans. For example, Korean Americans were sympathetically represented during the racial tensions in New York following racist white violence and the African-American deaths in Howard Beach and Bensonhurst. The boycott of the Korean-owned Family Red Apple grocery store in Brooklyn provided a welcome opportunity to discredit the African-American community as "racist," linking the Red Apple boycott to the African-American responses to Howard Beach and Bensonhurst.

Other times Korean Americans will be sacrificed to communities of color to salve white consciences. In Los Angeles, the Black/white tensions resulting from the Rodney King beating and verdict became the filter through which the Latasha Harlins killing was mediated. It is possible that the leadership organizing the African-American community around the Latasha Harlins case was viewed by the mainstream media as less visible and threatening, as opposed to Sonny Carson and Al Sharpton in New York. In this sense, conflicts between Korean Americans and African Americans in Los Angeles may have provided a safe opportunity to portray Korean "racism," deflect attention away from white racism, while not risking the legitimization of problematic (to whites) Black leadership.

Clearly, Soon Ja Du's killing of Latasha Harlins was wrong, as was Judge Karlin's failure to incarcerate her. The point here is not to provide an excuse for what Du did, but to question why the individual actions of one store owner are attributed to an entire race. Du can hardly be seen as a "typical store owner." Many in the Korean-Angeleno community state that she was mentally unbalanced. The media chose to indict the entire Korean-American population over the actions of one woman whose mental stability was questionable. Headlines in the *San Francisco Examiner* and the *Los Angeles Times* on 16 November 1991 blared "Korean Shopowner Freed" or "Korean Grocer Receives Probation." Such identification of ethnic backgrounds in criminal cases violates standard journalistic practices. As Dr. Taeil Bai observed, there are no headlines trumpeting "Italian Businessman Jailed" or "Jewish Shop Owner Convicted." Perhaps the images of white police officers savagely beating a helpless Rodney King were so damaging to the white journalists' psyches that the depiction of Korean aggression against African Americans provided a needed release, a transferral of their guilt.

THEORETICAL CHALLENGES FOR COMMUNITY-BASED RESEARCHERS

The fact that few academics were sought out to provide insight into the riots reflects the general public's estimation of the intellectual class's ability to provide answers to the serious problems of race in the United States. Part of the reason for such a perception may lie in the priorities which guide the production of knowledge and the definition of theory. With respect to the issues at hand, the shortcomings of race-relations theory can be separated into at least two categories.

Beyond the Black/White Dichotomy

Recent books on race, such as Andrew Hacker's *Two Nations: Black and White, Separate, Hostile, Unequal*, and Studs Terkel's *Race: How Whites and Blacks Think and Feel about the American Obsession*, further embed the construction of U.S. race relations as a binary opposition. Although the theoretical framing of race relations in Black/white terms has substantial historical and contemporary grounding, the recent events in Los Angeles reveal that such an essentialism misses many of the factual complexities in contemporary, urban politics. Latinos suffered nearly one-third of the 58 casualties related to the riot. About one-third of those arrested following the verdict were Latino (mostly for curfew violations, not for looting), although the media portrayed African Americans as the primary participants. At least 1,000 of the Latinos arrested were undocumented immigrants who were immediately scheduled for deportation by the Immigration and Naturalization Service. A substantial number (estimated between 30 and 40 percent) of stores that were lost were Chicano- or Latino-owned. Over 300 Chinese businesses were looted and burned. Vietnamese-owned stores were targeted in Long Beach. Filipino-owned stores were also lost. These facts are overlooked due to the dominant racial framing of the explosion. Although Chicanos, Latinos, and Asian-Pacific Americans are the fastest-growing immigrant groups in the United States, the oppositional Black/white character of the race-relations debate excludes discussion of the colors in the middle, now inexorable parts of the Black/white spectrum.

Many race-relations and civil rights scholars, situated on the East Coast, may share a lived experience of an oppositional Black/white racial dynamic. The Asian-American and Chicano populations are much smaller in the East than on the West Coast. Moreover, white-liberal or progressive guilt has been focused largely on the historic exploitation of African Americans by whites. While there are important structural and historical bases for this concentration, the contemporary realities and demographics of racial groups in the U.S. necessitate a broader discussion. Undoubtedly, many scholar-activists' direct involvement with the civil rights movement has been confined to struggles waged by the African-American community. However, uncritical acceptance of the dichotomous Black/white character of U.S. race relations by such scholars obscures the role of Asian Americans, Native Americans, Chicanos, and Latinos to the detriment of a more differentiated understanding of contemporary race relations and struggles.

Typically, non–African American people of color are categorized as either Black or white if they are discussed at all. Native Americans, Chicanos, and Latinos are often summarily included with African Americans under the people of color rubric. The ubiquitous internalization of the model-minority myth by the general population and academics leads to the invisibility of Asian Americans in the racial landscape. An awkward silence has descended upon liberal and progressive circles analyzing the events in Los Angeles around the role and fate of Korean Americans and Asian Americans generally. Many leftist publications avoided discussion of Asian Americans altogether, thereby sidestepping the troubling interracial conflicts among Korean Americans, Chicanos, Latinos, and African Americans.[19]

Some boldly categorized Korean Americans with a contempt usually reserved for the dominant majority, characterizing the immigrant shopkeepers as a primary antagonist of African Americans and Latinos. Sadly, the neoconservatives' embrace of Korean Angelenos, combined with liberal and progressive neglect or contempt, may trigger a self-fulfilling prophecy of the model-minority myth. Korean Americans do not identify with European Americans and see themselves as very distinct. Yet the cold reception that they and other Asian Americans receive from community organizers, coalition-minded politicians, and progressive intellectuals excludes them from the people of color organizing and theoretical models.

Even in the so-called "Black/Korean conflict," although Koreans are necessarily included in the discussion, the conflict is viewed through the lens of Black/white relationships. In other words, how Korean relationships with African Americans are represented and interpreted often depends upon the latter group's relationship to whites. Korean Americans are instrumentalized in a larger public-relations campaign on behalf of Euro-Americans. Moreover, important class and gender dynamics become obscured by the emphasis on racial differences.[20]

The conflict between Korean Americans and African Americans contains definite cultural differences and racial animosities. But many of the tensions may be class-, rather than racially, based, actually reflecting differences between the store-owning Korean immigrants and the African-American customers. Violence between shopkeepers and residents exists in inner cities regardless of which racial group owns the majority of stores. John Murray, a former African-American liquor-store owner, stated that he fled the liquor business because of the violence: "I stared down the barrel of a gun nine times."[21]

The interests of the entrepreneurial class transcend racial differences in South Central Los Angeles. Cal-Pac, the African-American liquor-store-owners association, and KAGRO, the Korean-American grocers association, stand together on the issues of liquor-store rebuilding and permit issuance. Both organizations oppose grass-roots community efforts to limit the number of liquor stores in South Central to one-half of their original preverdict number. Nationalism may be used by members of the entrepreneurial or more privileged classes to obscure community interests upon whose behalf they ostensibly act. Ice Cube, for example, has directed a Black-nationalist critique against Korean-American liquor-store owners. Whether his actions have generally benefitted the South Central community are questionable, given his lucrative endorsement contract of St. Ides malt liquor, an alcohol-fortified beer widely marketed in poor communities of color.

Nonbusiness activists stand on the same side of many issues. African-American and Korean-American community organizers are united in the call for a reduction of liquor stores, high-alcohol-content liquors, and public assistance with conversion from liquor retailing to other types of business or liquor-store buyouts. More similarities across racial boundaries may emerge as an increasing number of Korean shopkeepers who lost everything in the riots are facing financial ruin and homelessness, problems they share with other residents of South Central.

Scholars of ethnic and racial politics must confront head on the challenges of racial theory for the twenty-first century. In order to do this, a serious effort must be made to incorporate the histories and the contemporary experiences of people of color between the two poles of Black and white on the racial spectrum, especially those of the new and rapidly expanding immigrant groups such as Salvadorans Guatemalans, Vietnamese, Hmong, Mien, Palestinians, Pacific Islanders, and Koreans, among many others. Intellectual activists must grapple openly and critically with the position of each community of color within the complexities of race, ethnicity, class, and gender relations in a post-industrial society. For example, scholars must address the question of class in the L.A. context. What are Korean "mom and pop" store owners? Petty bourgeoisie? Capitalist exploiters? Self-exploited? Owning poor? Middle class?[22] Diversity within ethnic and racial groups must be acknowledged and incorporated into theoretical analyses to avoid essentializing race and obscuring important differences and contradictions.

Structure, Agency, and Theories for Action and Social Change

Much of the theoretical construction of race relations has employed structural analysis that incorporate a critique of institutional discrimination, historical racism, and modes of economic production. While these factors are important and necessary to understanding the state of contemporary race relations in the

U.S., an excessively structural analysis presents those subordinated under oppressive systems as "victims" with little or no recourse. Structuralist social scientists often face problems in contextually understanding their subjects as actors possessing agency. As Michael Burawoy points out,

> Such [objective and systemic] analyses, whether critical or complacent, have a tendency to degenerate into pessimistic overestimations of the power of the welfare state, the capitalist economy, or 'the system." Too often, the system is seen as all-determining, so that forms of resistance such as innovation, negotiation, and rebellion are not taken seriously.[23]

Scholars of ethnic studies, urban politics, and race relations can work to build toward a theory for action, a theory for social change. Such a theory would emphasize the experiences and conditions of the oppressed and of those working directly to improve those conditions. In order to do so, intellectual activists must know the people and live the experience—the pains, the challenges, and the realities—of racism. They must measure the success of theories by their ability to explain racial problems and to provide solutions to difficult problems. If abstract theories do not prove useful to the folks most affected by riots, they should be abandoned. A respectful and informed partnership must be created in the Freirian tradition to create more relevant research, pedagogy, and theory to assist those suffering in the affected communities. Intellectual activists must know which leadership is respected and acknowledged in different communities; how change comes about in different neighborhoods; what relationships exist between structures and individuals. In short, intellectuals must leave their offices and go to where the problems are in order to understand that about which they claim to be "experts."

The roles of political leadership, individual accountability, and community education must be addressed in order to make the transition from rigid, structure-induced victim perspectives to progressive, activist-based perspectives. Some of the worst problems faced by subordinated communities cannot be resolved or addressed simply by reciting the standard critiques of "the system" or "the man." Serious problems such as drugs, crime, domestic violence, and interracial conflict clearly do have structural roots. But afflicted communities must seek solutions to the toughest problems here and now, since the system will not disappear tomorrow. As Karen Bass, a community organizer against substance abuse in L.A., states, "We cannot afford to avoid problems like drugs and crime by saying these issues will get resolved when we change society."

In this spirit, Korean-American organizers and intellectuals must work with communities to reject prejudices and stereotypes about other people of color that have been adopted from the mainstream culture. Korean Americans must address seriously the complaints that too many store owners are rude and disrespectful to darker skinned customers, and search for ways to improve relations. The community cannot use the reality of high crime rates that shopowners face to rationalize unacceptable behavior, but must openly communicate with the residents they serve regarding the numerous deaths of Korean merchants before and after the Harlins killing. There must be a better understanding of the fearful, bunker mentality of all shopkeepers, regardless of color. While Koreans may not have constructed the international racial hierarchy, they can educate one another as to its fallacies. Each community, likewise, can do some soul-searching and admit the truths that could produce a stronger foundation for coalition politics and the seizing of L.A.'s transformative potentials.

Similarly, members of the academic community must critically assess their roles, passive or otherwise, in relation to the events in Los Angeles. Intellectuals of color failed miserably at mediating the conflict between Korean Americans and African Americans. Because Korean- and Asian-American academics failed to speak up and condemn the light sentence that Judge Karlin rendered in the Du case *before* the riots forced this reckoning, we were complicit in the sentencing as well. Likewise, African-American scholars could have taken a position on the blatant promotion of hate violence against Korean Americans in Ice Cube's lyrics but failed to do so. Activist scholars must be willing to take a stand on issues and immerse themselves in the problem-solving task. Specific opportunities to intervene to help solve conflicts should not be lost but grasped.

A more open-ended, qualitative approach is required to conduct such community-based research. Many traditional methodologies, which emphasize quantitative methods and analysis in order to posit predictions, are not useful in resolving problems. Politics is not a hard science. Even the hard sciences no longer consider themselves "hard." Scholars of ethnic studies and urban politics must capture the human, not the mathematical, element in politics. Problem solving must become the focus. Theory must draw from activists and organizers as the generative sources of themes and solutions. If academics cite Foucault, Cornel West, and bell hooks, they should also cite community organizers, such as Joe Hicks, Gloria Romero, and Marcia Choo, and privilege their insights, too, as "expert."

In the analysis of racial consciousness and politics in the twenty-first century, researchers face new challenges currently unaddressed by both conservative and progressive scholars. A new era recognizing the autonomy and strength of people of color will depend largely on our ability to listen to the voices of the subjects being studied, to position people of color as actors in the research who can provide real insight into the diversity and contingencies constitutive of communities of color. The new scholarship can subvert pervasive perceptions of people of color as either the faceless, downtrodden victims or as romanticized, oppressed revolutionaries carrying out an inevitable historical task and, in so doing, perhaps contribute to a new theory and praxis of empowerment.

Notes

1. The human-capital model is a variant of neoclassical economic theory applied to labor-market economics. The model attempts to explain a dependent variable such as income inequality as derivative of independent variables such as educational attainment, work experience, total number of hours worked per year, marital status, and English proficiency, among others. It explains Asian Americans' advancement by foregrounding their investments in human capital such as educational attainment. It would also explain the lack of mobility of certain groups such as Southeast Asians or African Americans who had not yet invested appropriately in human capital.

2. Structuralists emphasize the basic characteristics or "structures" of a social system. For example, internal colonial theory places the U.S. historical and contemporary actualities of race in the context of international colonialism that connects the Third World abroad with the Third World within the U.S. This framework emphasizes similarities in the patterns of racial domination and exploitation experienced by people of color and distinguishes their incorporation into the U.S. from the processes of immigration and assimilation by which European Americans are incorporated into a nation. See Robert Blauner, "Colonized and Immigrant Minorities," *Racial Oppression in America* (New York: Harper and Row, 1972), 51–82.

3. President Bush's 1988 television campaign centered around an ad attacking Michael Dukakis for being "soft on crime." To support this claim, the TV ads played upon white fears by focusing on close-up "mug" shots of Willie Horton, an African-American convict who committed subsequent crimes while on an early-release program implemented by Dukakis, then governor of Massachusetts.

4. Cynthia Hamilton, *Apartheid in an American City: The Case of the Black Community in Los Angeles* (Van Nuys, CA: Labor Community Strategy Center, 1991), 1.

5. Ibid. Internal colonial theory is useful in viewing South Central as a Third World colony, within a First World nation, that lacks political and economic self-determination, similar to the relationship between Third World nations abroad and First World ones.

6. Eui-Young Yu, "We Saw Our Dreams Burn for No Reason," *San Francisco Examiner*, 24 May 1992, editorial page.

7. Robert C. Toh, "Blacks Pressing Japanese to Halt Slurs, Prejudice," *Los Angeles Times*, 13 December 1990.

8. Susan Moffat, "Shopkeepers Fight Back," *Los Angeles Times*, 15 May 1992.

9. Ibid.

10. At 17 percent, self-employment rates of foreign-born Korean men top those of white men (10 percent) and other people of color. U.S. Bureau of the Census, 1980 Census of Population, vol. 2, Subject Reports, *Asian and Pacific Islander Population in the United States: 1980*, table 45A. A 1990 survey conducted by California State University sociologist Eui-Young Yu found that nearly 40 percent of Korean families own a business.

11. The long hours worked by more members of the family under dangerous conditions, combined with the high educational levels of those owning businesses, calls into question the definition of success applied to Korean Americans. Some have suggested that a blue-collar union job offers better working conditions and a more reliable income than engaging in small businesses.

12. Nancy Hill-Holtzman and Mathis Chazanov, "Police Credited for Heading Off Spread of Riots," *Los Angeles Times*, 7 May 1992.

13. Ibid.

14. Steven Chin, "Innocence lost: L.A.'s Koreans Fight to be Heard," *San Francisco Examiner*, 9 May 1992.

15. California National Guard Brigadier General Daniel Brennan stated that bullets and grenades were not loaded for transport to L.A. because there were no lights on the parade ground where the ammunition is stored. Daniel Weintraub, "National Guard Official Cites Series of Delays," *Los Angeles Times*, 7 May 1992.

16. Rich Connell and Richard Simon, "Top LAPD Officer, Fire Chief Cite Flaws in Police Response," *Los Angeles Times*, 8 May 1992.

17. *At a time when it is being proposed that hundreds of billions be spent to uplift Negroes and other minorities*, the nation's 300,000 Chinese are moving ahead on their own . . . with no help from anyone else. Still being taught in Chinatown is the old idea that people should depend on their own efforts . . . not a welfare check . . . in order to reach America's 'promised land' " (emphasis added). "Success Story of One Minority Group in U.S.," *U.S. News and World Report*, 26 December 1966, 73. Similarly, scholar Thomas Sowell argues in *Race and Economics* (New York: McKay and Co., 1975) that historic exclusion from U.S. political institutions paradoxically benefits Jews and Asian Americans. "[T]hose American ethnic groups that have succeeded best politically have not usually been the same as those who succeeded best economically. . . . [T]hose minorities that have pinned their greatest hopes on political action—the Irish and the Negroes, for example—have made some of the slower economic advances."

18. Frank Chin and Jeffrey Paul Chan, "Racist Love," in *Seen through Shuck* ed. Richard Kostelanetz (New York: Ballantine Books, 1972), 65–79.

19. For example, see Linda Burnham, "A Sledgehammer Message from L.A.," *Crossroads* (June 1992): i, as well as this author's critique of that issue, "Contradictions and Challenges from L.A.," *Crossroads* (July/August 1992):28–30.

20. Gender dynamics are also ignored in nationalistic constructions of the Korean/Black conflict. Protection of women and children has often been used as the rationale for violence initiated by men from both communities.

21. Moffat, "Shopkeepers Fight Back."

22. Other important questions we need to ask include: What are the differences and similarities between Latino and Chicano in Los Angeles? Why was the elected Chicano leadership silent on the fate of the Latino population during the riots? In what class are the often exploited Salvadorans who work menial jobs at day-labor rates? How does the Latino undocumented class compare to the African-American residents in South Central?

23. Michael Burawoy, "The Extended Case Method," *Ethnography Unbound*, ed. Michael Burawoy et al. (Berkeley and Los Angeles: University of California Press, 1991), 284.

Part Six

The Fire This Time

———————————

14

Home is Where the *Han* Is:
A Korean American Perspective on the
Los Angeles Upheavals

Elaine H. Kim

About half of the estimated $850 million in estimated material losses incurred during the Los Angeles upheavals was sustained by a community no one seems to want to talk much about. Korean Americans in Los Angeles, suddenly at the front lines when violence came to the buffer zone they had been so precariously occupying, suffered profound damage to their means of livelihood.[1] But my concern here is the psychic damage which, unlike material damage, is impossible to quantify.

I want to explore the questions of whether or not recovery is possible for Korean Americans, and what will become of our attempts to "become American" without dying of *han*. *Han* is a Korean word that means, loosely translated, the sorrow and anger that grow from the accumulated experiences of oppression. Although the word is frequently and commonly used by Koreans, the condition it describes is taken quite seriously. When people die of *han*, it is called dying of *hwabyong*, a disease of frustration and rage following misfortune.

I am deeply indebted to the activists in the Los Angeles Korean American community, especially Bong Hwan Kim and Eui-Young Yu, whose courage and commitment to the empowerment of the disenfranchised, whether African American, Latino, or Korean American, during this crisis in Los Angeles have been a continuous source of inspiration for me. I would also like to thank Barry Maxwell for critically reading this manuscript and offering many insightful suggestions; my niece Sujin Kim, David Lloyd, and Caridad Souza for their encouragement; and Mia Chung for her general assistance.

Situated as we are on the border between those who have and those who have not, between predominantly Anglo and mostly African American and Latino communities, from our current interstitial position in the American discourse of race, many Korean Americans have trouble calling what happened in Los Angeles an "uprising." At the same time, we cannot quite say it was a "riot." So some of us have taken to calling it *sa-i-ku*, April 29, after the manner of naming other events in Korean history—3.1 (*sam-il*) for March 1, 1919, when massive protests against Japanese colonial rule began in Korea; 6.25 (*yook-i-o*), or June 25, 1950, when the Korean War began; and 4.19 (sa-il-ku), or April 19, 1960, when the first student movement in the world to overthrow a government began in South Korea. The ironic similarity between 4.19 and 4.29 does not escape most Korean Americans.

Los Angeles Koreatown has been important to me, even though I visit only a dozen times a year. Before Koreatown sprang up during the last decade and a half,[2] I used to hang around the fringes of Chinatown, although I knew that this habit was pure pretense.[3] For me, knowing that Los Angeles Koreatown existed made a difference; one of my closest friends worked with the Black-Korean Alliance there,[4] and I liked to think of it as a kind of "home"—however idealized and hypostatized—for the soul, an anchor, a potential refuge, a place in America where I could belong without ever being asked, "Who are you and what are you doing here? Where did you come from and when are you going back?"

Many of us watched in horror the destruction of Koreatown and the systematic targeting of Korean shops in South Central Los Angeles after the Rodney King verdict. Seeing those buildings in flames and those anguished Korean faces, I had the terrible thought that there would be no belonging and that we were, just as I had always suspected, a people destined to carry our *han* around with us wherever we went in the world. The destiny (*p'aljja*) that had spelled centuries of extreme suffering from invasion, colonization, war, and national division had smuggled itself into the U.S. with our baggage.

African American and Korean American conflict. As someone whose social consciousness was shaped by the African American–led civil rights movement of the 1960s, I felt that I was watching our collective dreams for a just society disintegrating, cast aside as naive and irrelevant in the bitter and embattled 1990s. It was the courageous African American women and men of the 1960s who had redefined the meaning of "American," who had first suggested that a person like me could reject the false choice between being treated as a perpetual foreigner in my own birthplace, on the one hand, and relinquishing my identity for someone else's ill-fitting and impossible Anglo American one on the other. Thanks to them, I began to discern how institutional racism works and why Korea was never mentioned in my world-history textbooks. I was able to see how others besides

Koreans had been swept aside by the dominant culture. My American education offered nothing about Chicanos or Latinos, and most of what I was taught about African and Native Americans was distorted to justify their oppression and vindicate their oppressors.

I could hardly believe my ears when, during the weeks immediately following *sa-i-ku*, I heard African American community leaders suggesting that Korean American merchants were foreign intruders deliberately trying to stifle African American economic development, when I knew that they had bought those liquor stores at five times gross receipts from African American owners, who had previously bought them at two times gross receipts from Jewish owners after Watts.[5] I saw anti-Korean flyers that were being circulated by African American political candidates and read about South Central residents petitioning against the reestablishment of swap meets, groups of typically Korean immigrant-operated market stalls. I was disheartened with Latinos who related the pleasure they felt while looting Korean stores that they believed "had it coming" and who claimed that it was because of racism that more Latinos were arrested during *sa-i-ku* than Asian Americans.[6] And I was filled with despair when I read about Chinese Americans wanting to dissociate themselves from us. According to one Chinese American reporter assigned to cover Asian American issues for a San Francisco daily, Chinese and Japanese American shopkeepers, unlike Koreans, always got along fine with African Americans in the past.[7] "Suddenly," admitted another Chinese American, "I am scared to be Asian. More specifically, I am afraid to be mistaken for Korean."[8] I was enraged when I overheard European Americans discussing the conflicts as if they were watching a dogfight or a boxing match. The situation reminded me of the Chinese film "Raise the Red Lantern," in which we never see the husband's face. We only hear his mellifluous voice as he benignly admonishes his four wives not to fight among themselves. He can afford to be kind and pleasant because the structure that pits his wives against each other is so firmly in place that he need never sully his hands or even raise his voice.

Battleground legacy. Korean Americans are squeezed between black and white and also between U.S. and South Korean political agendas. Opportunistic American and South Korean presidential candidates toured the burnt ruins, posing for the television cameras but delivering nothing of substance to the victims. Like their U.S. counterparts, South Korean news media seized upon *sa-i-ku*, featuring sensational stories that depicted the problem as that of savage African Americans attacking innocent Koreans for no reason.[9] To give the appearance of authenticity, Seoul newspapers even published articles using the names of Korean Americans who did not in fact write them.[10]

Those of us who chafe at being asked whether we are Chinese or Japanese as if there were no other possibilities or who were angered when the news media sought Chinese and Japanese but not Korean American views during *sa-i-ku* are sensitive to an invisibility that seems particular to us. To many Americans, Korea is but the gateway to or the bridge between China and Japan, or a crossroads of major Asian conflicts.[11]

It can certainly be said that, although little known or cared about in the Western world, Korea has been a perennial battleground. Besides the Mongols and the Manchus, there were the *Yŏjin* (Jurched), the *Koran* (Khitan), and the *Waegu* (Wäkö) invaders. In relatively recent years, there was the war between China and Japan that ended in 1895 and the war between Japan and Russia in 1905, both of which were fought on Korean soil and resulted in extreme suffering for the Korean people. Japan's 36 years of brutal colonial rule ended with the U.S. and what was then the Soviet Union dividing the country in half at the 38th parallel. Thus, Korea was turned into a Cold War territory that ultimately became a battleground for world superpowers during the conflict of 1950–53.

Becoming American. One of the consequences of war, colonization, national division, and superpower economic and cultural domination has been the migration of Koreans to places like Los Angeles, where they believed their human rights would be protected by law. After all, they had received U.S.-influenced political educations. They started learning English in the seventh grade. They all knew the story of the poor boy from Illinois who became president. They all learned that the U.S. Constitution and Bill of Rights protected the common people from violence and injustice. But they who grew up in Korea watching "Gunsmoke," "Night Rider," and "McGyver" dubbed in Korean were not prepared for the black, brown, red, and yellow America they encountered when they disembarked at the Los Angeles International Airport.[12] They hadn't heard that there is no equal justice in the U.S. They had to learn about American racial hierarchies. They did not realize that, as immigrants of color, they would never attain political voice or visibility but would instead be used to uphold the inequality and the racial hierarchy they had no part in creating.

Most of the newcomers had underestimated the communication barriers they would face. Like the Turkish workers in Germany described in John Berger and Jean Mohr's *A Seventh Man*,[13] their toil amounted to only a pile of gestures and the English they tried to speak changed and turned against them as they spoke it. Working 14 hours a day, six or seven days a week, they rarely came into sustained contact with English-speaking Americans and almost never had time to study English. Not feeling at ease with English, they did not engage in informal conversations easily with non-Koreans and were hated for being curt and rude. They did not attend churches or do business in banks or other enterprises where English was required. Typically, the immigrant, small-business owners utilized unpaid family labor instead of hiring people from local communities. Thanks to Eurocentric American cultural practices, they knew little or nothing good about African Americans or Latinos, who in turn and for similar reasons knew little or nothing good about them. At the same time, Korean shopowners in South Central and Koreatown were affluent compared with the impoverished residents, whom they often exploited as laborers or looked down upon as fools with an aversion to hard work.[14] Most Korean immigrants did not even know that they were among the many direct beneficiaries of the African American–led civil rights movement, which helped pave the way for the 1965 immigration reforms that made their immigration possible.

Korean-immigrant views, shaped as they were by U.S. cultural influences and official, anticommunist, South Korean education,[15] differed radically from those of many poor people in the communities Korean immigrants served: unaware of the shameful history of oppression of nonwhite immigrants and other people of color in the U.S., they regarded themselves as having arrived in a meritocratic "land of opportunity" where a person's chances for success are limited only by individual lack of ability or diligence. Having left a homeland where they foresaw their talents and hard work going unrecognized and unrewarded, they were desperate to believe that the "American dream" of social and economic mobility through hard work was within their reach.

Sa-i-ku. What they experienced on 29 and 30 April was a baptism into what it really means for a Korean to "become American" in the 1990s.[16] In South Korea, there is no 911, and no one really expects a fire engine or police car if there is trouble. Instead, people make arrangements with friends and family for emergencies. At the same time, guns are not part of Korean daily life. No civilian in South Korea can own a gun. Guns are the exclusive accoutrement of the military and police who enforce order for those who rule the society. When the Korean Americans in South Central and Koreatown dialed 911, nothing happened. When their stores and homes were being looted and burned to the ground, they were left completely alone for three horrifying days. How betrayed they must have felt by what they had believed was a democratic system that protects its people from violence. Those who trusted the government to protect them lost everything; those who took up arms after waiting for help for two days were able to defend themselves. It was as simple as that. What they had to learn was that, as in South Korea, protection in the U.S. is by and large for the rich and powerful. If there were a choice between Westwood and Koreatown, it is clear that Koreatown would have to be sacrificed. The familiar concept of privilege for the rich and powerful would have been easy for the Korean immigrant to grasp if only those exhortations about democracy and equality had not obfuscated the picture. Perhaps they should have relied even more on whatever they brought with them from Korea instead of fretting over trying to understand what was going on around them here. That Koreatown became a battleground does seem like the further playing out of a tragic legacy that has followed them across oceans and continents. The difference is that this was a battle between the poor and disenfranchised and the invisible rich, who were being protected by a layer of clearly visible Korean American human shields in a battle on the buffer zone.

This difference is crucial. Perhaps the legacy is not one carried across oceans and continents but one assumed immediately upon arrival, not the curse of being Korean but the initiation into becoming American, which requires that Korean Americans take on this country's legacy of five centuries of racial violence and inequality, of divide and rule, of privilege for the rich and oppression of the poor. Within this legacy, they have been assigned a place on the front lines. Silenced by those who possess the power to characterize and represent, they are permitted to speak only to reiterate their acceptance of this role.

Silencing the Korean American voice. Twelve years ago, in Kwangju, South Korea, hundreds of civilians demonstrating for constitutional reform and free elections were murdered by U.S.-supported and -equipped South Korean elite paratroopers. Because I recorded it and played it over and over again, searching for a sign or a clue, I remember clearly how what were to me heartrendingly tragic events were represented in the U.S. news media. For a few fleeting moments, images of unruly crowds of alien-looking Asians shouting unintelligible words and phrases and wearing white headbands inscribed with unintelligible characters flickered across the screen. The Koreans were made to seem like insane people from another planet. The voice in the background stated simply that there were massive demonstrations but did not explain what the protests were about. Nor was a single Korean ever given an opportunity to speak to the camera.

The next news story was about demonstrations for democracy in Poland. The camera settled on individuals' faces which one by one filled the screen as each man or woman was asked to explain how he or she felt. Each Polish person's words were translated in a voice-over or subtitle. Solidarity leader Lech Walesa, who was allowed to speak often, was characterized as a heroic human being with whom all Americans could surely identify personally. Polish Americans from New York and Chicago to San Francisco, asked in man-on-the-street interviews about their reactions, described the canned hams and blankets they were sending to Warsaw.

This was for me a lesson in media representation, race, and power politics. It is a given that Americans are encouraged by our ideological apparatuses to side with our allies (here, the Polish resisters and the anti-communist South Korean government) against our enemies (here, the communist Soviet Union and protesters against the South Korean government). But visual-media racism helps craft and reinforce our identification with Europeans and whites while distancing us from fearsome and alien Asiatic hordes.

In March of last year, when two delegates from North Korea visited the Bay Area to participate in community-sponsored talks on Korean reunification, about 800 people from the Korean American community attended. The meeting was consummately newsworthy, since it was the first time in history that anyone from North Korea had ever been in California for more than 24 hours just passing through. The event was discussed for months in the Korean-language media—television, radio, and newspapers. Almost every Korean-speaking person in California knew about it. Although we sent press releases to all the commercial and public radio and television stations and to all the Bay Area newspapers, not a single mainstream media outfit covered the event. However, whenever there was an African American boycott of a Korean store or whenever conflict surfaced between Korean and African Americans, community leaders found a dozen microphones from all the main news media shoved into their faces, as if they were the president's press secretary making an official public pronouncement. Fascination with interethnic conflicts is rooted in the desire to excuse of minimize white racism by buttressing the mistaken notion that all human beings are "naturally" racist, and when Korean and African Americans allow themselves to be distracted by these interests, their attention is deflected from the social hierarchies that give racism its destructive power.

Without a doubt, the U.S. news media played a major role in exacerbating the damage and ill will toward Korean Americans, first by spotlighting tensions between African Americans and Koreans above all efforts to work together and as opposed to many other newsworthy events in these two communities, and second by exploiting racist stereotypes of Koreans as unfathomable aliens, this time wielding guns on rooftops and allegedly firing wildly into crowds.[17] In news programs and on talk shows, African and Korean American tensions were discussed by blacks and whites, who pointed to these tensions as the main cause of the uprising. I heard some European Americans railing against rude and exploitative Korean merchants for ruining peaceful race relations for everyone else. Thus, Korean Americans were used to deflect attention from the racism they inherited and the economic injustice and poverty that had been already well woven into the fabric of American life, as evidenced by a judicial system that could allow not only the Korean store owner who killed Latasha Harlins but also the white men who killed Vincent Chin and the white police who beat Rodney King to go free, while Leonard Peltier still languishes in prison.

As far as I know, neither the commercial nor the public news media has mentioned the many Korean and African American attempts to improve relations, such as joint church services, joint musical performances and poetry readings,

Korean merchant donations to African American community and youth programs, African American volunteer teachers in classes for Korean immigrants studying for citizenship examinations, or Korean translations of African American history materials.

While Korean immigrants were preoccupied with the mantra of day-to-day survival, Korean Americans had no voice, no political presence whatsoever in American life. When they became the targets of violence in Los Angeles, their opinions and views were hardly solicited except as they could be used in the already-constructed mainstream discourse on race relations, which is a sorry combination of blaming the African American and Latino victims for their poverty and scapegoating the Korean Americans as robotic aliens who have no "real" right to be here in the first place and therefore deserve whatever happens to them.

The Newsweek *experience.* In this situation, I felt compelled to respond when an editor from the "My Turn" section of *Newsweek* magazine asked for a 1000-word personal essay.[18] Hesitant because I was given only a day and a half to write the piece, not enough time in light of the vastness of American ignorance about Koreans and Korean Americans, I decided to do it because I thought I could not be made into a sound bite or a quote contextualized for someone else's agenda.

I wrote an essay accusing the news media of using Korean Americans and tensions between African and Korean Americans to divert attention from the roots of racial violence in the U.S. I asserted that these lie not in the Korean-immigrant-owned corner store situated in a community ravaged by poverty and police violence, but reach far back into the corridors of corporate and government offices in Los Angeles, Sacramento, and Washington, D.C. I suggested that Koreans and African Americans were kept ignorant about each other by educational and media institutions that erase or distort their experiences and perspectives. I tried to explain how racism had kept my parents from ever really becoming Americans, but that having been born here, I considered myself American and wanted to believe in the possibility of an American dream.

The editor of "My Turn" did everything he could to frame my words with his own viewpoint. He faxed his own introductory and concluding paragraphs that equated Korean merchants with cowboys in the Wild West and alluded to Korean/African American hatred. When I objected, he told me that my writing style was not crisp enough and that as an experienced journalist, he could help me out. My confidence wavered, but ultimately I rejected his editing. Then he accused me of being overly sensitive, confiding that I had no need to be defensive—because his wife was a Chinese American. Only after I had decided to withdraw the piece did he agree to accept it as I wrote it.

Before I could finish congratulating myself on being able to resist silencing and the kind of decontextualization I was trying to describe in the piece, I started receiving hate mail. Some of it was addressed directly to me, since I had been identified as a University of California faculty member, but most of it arrived in bundles, forwarded by *Newsweek*. Hundreds of letters came from all over the country, from Florida to Washington state and from Massachusetts to Arizona. I was unprepared for the hostility expressed in most of the letters. Some people sent the article, torn from the magazine and covered with angry, red-inked obscenities scratched across my picture. "You should see a good doctor," wrote someone from Southern California, "you have severe problems in thinking, reasoning, and adjusting to your environment."

A significant proportion of the writers, especially those who identified themselves as descendants of immigrants from Eastern Europe, wrote *Newsweek* that they were outraged, sickened, disgusted, appalled, annoyed, and angry at the magazine for providing an arena for the paranoid, absurd, hypocritical, racist, and childish views of a spoiled, ungrateful, whining, bitching, un-American bogus faculty member who should be fired or die when the next California earthquake dumps all of the "so-called people of color" into the Pacific Ocean.

I was shocked by the profound ignorance of many writers' assumptions about the experiences and perspectives of American people of color in general and Korean and other Asian Americans in particular. Even though my essay revealed that I was born in the U.S. and that my parents had lived in the U.S. for more than six decades, I was viewed as a foreigner without the right to say anything except words of gratitude and praise about America. The letters also provided some evidence of the dilemma Korean Americans are placed in by those who assume that we are aliens who should "go back" and at the same time berate us for not rejecting "Korean-American identity" for "American identity."

> How many Americans migrate to Korea? If you are so disenchanted, Korea is still there. Why did you ever leave it? Sayonara.

> Ms. Kim appears to have a personal axe to grind with this country that has given her so much freedom and opportunity. . . . I should suggest that she move to Korea, where her children will learn all they ever wanted about that country's history.

> [Her] whining about the supposedly racist U.S. society is just a mask for her own acute inferiority complex. If she is so dissatisfied with the United States why doesn't she vote with her feet and leave? She can get the hell out and return to her beloved Korea—her tribal afinity [sic] where her true loyalty and consciousness lies [sic].

> You refer to yourself as a Korean American and yet you have lived all your life in the United States . . . you write about racism in this country and yet you are the biggest racist by your own written words. If you cannot accept the fact that you are an American, maybe you should be living your life in Korea.

> My stepfather and cousin risked their lives in the country where your father is buried to ensure the ideals of our country would remain. So don't expect to find a sympathetic ear for your pathetic whining.

Many of the letter writers assumed that my family had been the "scum" of Asia and that I was a college teacher only because of American justice and largesse. They were furious that I did not express gratitude for being saved from starvation in Asia and given the opportunity to flourish, no doubt beyond my wildest dreams, in America.

> Where would she be if her parents had not migrated to the United States? For a professor at Berkeley University [sic] to say the American dream is only an empty promise is ludicrous. Shame, shame, shame on Elaine!

> [Her father and his family] made enough money in the USA to ship his corpse home to Korea for burial. Ms. Kim herself no doubt has a guaranteed life income as a professor paid by California taxpayers. Wouldn't you think that she might say kind things about the USA instead of whining about racism?

At the same time some letters blamed me for expecting "freedom and opportunity":

> It is wondrous that folks such as you find truth in your paranoia. No one ever promised anything to you or your parents.

Besides providing indications of how Korean Americans are regarded, the letters revealed a great deal about how American identity is thought of. One California woman explained that although her grandparents were Irish immigrants, she was not an Irish American, because "if you are not with us, you are against us." A Missouri woman did not seem to realize that she was conflating race and nationality and confusing "nonethnic" and "nonracial," by which she seems to have meant "white," with "American." And, although she insists that it is impossible to be both "black" and "American," she identifies herself at the outset as a "white American."

> I am a white American. I am proud to be an American. You cannot be black, white, Korean, Chinese, Mexican, German, French, or English or any other and still be an American. Of course the culture taught in schools is strictly American. That's where we are and if you choose to learn another [culture] you have the freedom to settle there. You cannot be a Korean American which assumes you are not ready to be an AMERICAN. Do you get my gist?

The suggestion that more should be taught in U.S. schools about America's many immigrant groups and people of color prompted many letters in defense of Western civilization against non-Western barbarism:

You are dissatisfied with current school curricula that excludes Korea. Could it possibly be because Korea and Asia for that matter has [*sic*] not had . . . a noticeable impact on the shaping of Western culture, and Korea has had unfortunately little culture of its own?

Who cares about Korea, Ms. Kim? . . . And what enduring contributions has the Black culture, both here in the US and on the continent contributed to the world, and mankind? I'm from a culture, Ms. Kim, who put a man on the moon 23 years ago, who established medical schools to train doctors to perform open heart surgery, and . . . who created a language of music so that musicians, from Beethoven to the Beatles, could easily touch the world with their brilliance forever and ever and ever. Perhaps the dominant culture, whites obviously, "swept aside Chicanos . . . Latinos . . . African-Americans . . . Koreans," because they haven't contributed anything that made—be mindful of the cliche—a world of difference?

Koreans' favorite means of execution is decapitation . . . Ms. Kim, and others like her, came here to escape such injustice. Then they whine at riots to which they have contributed by their own fanning of flames of discontent. . . . Yes! Let us all study more about Oriental culture! Let us put matters into proper perspective.

Fanatical multiculturalists like you expect a country whose dominant culture has been formed and influenced by Europe . . . , nearly 80% of her population consisting of persons whose ancestry is European, to include the history of every ethnic group who has ever lived here. I truly feel sorry for you. You and your bunch need to realize that white Americans are not racists. . . . We would love to get along, but not at the expense of our own culture and heritage.

Kim's axe-to-grind confirms the utter futility of race-relations—the races were never meant to live together. We don't get along and never will. . . . Whats [*sic*] needed is to divide the United States up along racial lines so that life here can finally become livable.

What seemed to anger some people the most was their idea that, although they worked hard, people of color were seeking handouts and privileges because of their race, and the thought of an ungrateful Asian American siding with African Americans, presumably against whites, was infuriating. How dare I "bite the hand that feeds" me by siding with the champion "whiners who cry 'racism' " because to do so is the last refuge of the "terminally incompetent"?

The racial health in this country won't improve until minorities stop erecting "me first" barriers and strive to be Americans, not African-Americans or Asian-Americans expecting privileges.

Ms. Kim wants preferential treatment that immigrants from Greece-to-Sweden have not enjoyed. . . . Even the Chinese . . . have not created any special problems for themselves or other Americans. Soon those folk are going to express their own resentments to the insatiable demands of the Blacks and other colored peoples, including the wetbacks from Mexico who sneak into this country then pilfer it for all they can.

The Afroderived citizens of Los Angeles and the Asiatic derivatives were not suffering a common imposition. . . . The Asiatics are trying to build their success. The Africans are sucking at the teats of entitlement.

As is usual with racists, most of the writers of these hate letters saw only themselves in their notions about Korea, America, Korean Americans, African Americans. They felt that their own sense of American identity was being threatened and that they were being blamed as individuals for U.S. racism. One man, adept at manipulating various fonts on his word processor, imposed his preconceptions on my words:

Let me read between the lines of your little hate message:

. . ."The roots . . . stretch far back into the corridors of corporate and government offices in Los Angeles, Sacramento, and Washington, D.C."

All white America and all American institutions are to blame for racism.

. . . "I still want to believe the promise is real."

I have the savvy to know that the American ideals of freedom and justice are a joke but if you want to give me what I want I'm willing to make concessions.

Ms. Kim, . . . if you want to embody the ignorant, the insecure, and the emotionally immature, that's your right! Just stop preaching hate and please, please, quit whining.

Sincerely, A proud White-American teaching
my children not to be prejudicial

Especially since my essay had been subdued and intensely personal, I had not anticipated the fury it would provoke. I never thought that readers would write over my words with their own. The very fact that I used words, and English words at that, particularly incensed some: one letter writer complained about my use of words and phrases like "manifestation" and "zero-sum game," and "suzerain relationship," which is the only way to describe Korea's relationship with China during the T'ang Dynasty. "Not more than ten people in the USA know what [these words] mean," he wrote. "You are on an ego trip." I wondered if it made him particularly angry that an Asian American had used those English words, or if he would make such a comment to George Will or Jane Bryant Quinn.

Clearly I had encountered part of America's legacy, the legacy that insists on silencing certain voices and erasing certain presences, even if it means deportation internment, and outright murder. I should not have been surprised by what happened in Koreatown or by the ignorance and hatred expressed in the letters to *Newsweek*, any more than African Americans should have been surprised by the Rodney King verdict. Perhaps the news media, which constituted *sa-i-ku* as news, as an extraordinary event in no way continuous with our everyday lives, made us forget for a moment that as people of color many of us simultaneously inhabit two Americas: the America of our dreams and the America of our experience.

Who among us does not cling stubbornly to the America of our dreams, the promise of a multicultural democracy where our cultures and our differences might be affirmed instead of distorted in an effort to destroy us?

After *sa-i-ku*, I was able to catch glimpses of this America of my dreams because I received other letters that expressed another American legacy. Some people identified themselves as Norwegian or Irish Americans interested in combating racism. Significantly, while most of the angry mail had been sent not to be but to *Newsweek*, almost all of the sympathetic mail, particularly the letters from African Americans, came directly to me. Many came from Korean Americans who were glad that one of their number had found a vehicle for self-expression. Others from Chinese and Japanese Americans who wrote that they had had similar experiences and feelings. Several were written in shaky longhand by women fervently wishing for peace and understanding among people of all races. A Native American from Nashville wrote a long description of cases of racism against African, Asian, and Native Americans in the U.S. criminal-justice system. A large number of letters came from African Americans, all of them supportive and sympathetic—from judges and professors who wanted better understanding between Africans and Koreans to poets and laborers who scribbled their notes in pencil while on breaks at work. One man identified himself as a Los Angeles African American whose uncle had married a Korean woman. He stated that as a black man in America, he knew what other people feel when they face injustice. He ended his letter apologizing for his spelling and grammar mistakes and asking for materials to read on Asian Americans. The most touching letter I received was written by a prison inmate who had served twelve years of a 35-to-70-year sentence for armed robbery during which no physical injuries occurred. He wrote:

> I've been locked in these prisons going on 12 years now . . . and since being here I have studied fully the struggles of not just blacks, but all people of color. I am a true believer of helping ''your'' people ''first,'' but also the helping of all people no matter where there at or the color of there skin. But I must be truthful, my struggle and assistance is truly on the side of people of color like ourselves. But just a few years ago I didn't think like this.
>
> I thought that if you wasn't black, then you was the enemy, but . . . many years of this prison madness and much study and research changed all of

this. . . . [I]t's not with each other, blacks against Koreans or Koreans against
blacks. No, this is not what it's about. Our struggle(s) are truly one in the
same. What happened in L.A. during the riot really hurt me, because it was
no way that blacks was suppose to do the things to your people, my people
(Koreans) that they did. You're my sister, our people are my people. Even
though our culture may be somewhat different, and even though we may
worship our God(s)   different . . . white-Amerikkka [doesn't] separate us.
They look at us all the same. Either you're white, or you're wrong. . . . I'm
just writing you to let you know that, you're my sister, your people's struggle
are my people's struggle.

This is the ground I need to claim now for Korean American resistance and
recovery, so that we can become American without dying of *han*.

Although the sentiments expressed in these letters seemed to break down
roughly along racial lines—that is, all writers who were identifiably people of
color wrote in support—and one might become alarmed at the depth of the
divisions they imply, I like to think that I have experienced the desire of many
Americans, especially Americans of color, to do as Rodney King pleaded on the
second day of *sa-i-ku*: "We're all stuck here for awhile. . . . Let's try to work
it out."

In my view, it's important for us to think about *all* of what Rodney King said
and not just the words "we all can get along," which have been depoliticized
and transformed into a Disneyesque catchphrase for Pat Boone songs and roadside
billboards in Los Angeles. It seems to me the emphasis is on the being "stuck
here for awhile" together as we await "our day in court."[19]

Like the African American man who wrote from prison, the African American
man who had been brutally beaten by white police might have felt the desire to
"love everybody," but he had to amend—or rectify—that wish. He had to speak
last about loving "people of color." The impulse to "love everybody" was there,
but the conditions were not right. For now, the most practical and progressive
agenda may be people of color trying to "work it out."

Finding community through national consciousness. The place where Korean and
American legacies converge for Korean Americans is the exhortation to "go home
to where you belong."

One of the letters I received was from a Korean American living in Chicago.
He had read a translation of my essay in a Korean language newspaper. "Although
you were born in the U.S.A.," he wrote, noticing what none of the white men
who ordered me to go back to "my" country had, "your ethnical background
and your complexion belong to Korea. It is time to give up your U.S. citizenship
and go to Korea."

Some ruined merchants are claiming that they will pull up stakes and return
to Korea, but I know that this is not possible for most of them. Even if their

stores had not been destroyed, even if they were able to sell their businesses and take the proceeds to Korea, most of them would not have enough to buy a home or business there, since both require total cash up front. Neither would they be able to find work in the society they left behind because it is plagued by recession, repression, and fierce economic competition.

Going back to Korea. The dream of going back to Korea fed the spirit of my father, who came to Chicago in 1926 and lived in the United States for 63 years, during which time he never became a U.S. citizen, at first because the law did not allow it and later because he did not want to. He kept himself going by believing that he would return to Korea in triumph one day. Instead, he died in Oakland at 88. Only his remains returned to Korea, where we buried him in accordance with his wishes.

Hasn't the dream of going back home to where you belong sustained most of America's unwanted at one time or another, giving meaning to lives of toil and making it possible to endure other people's hatred and rejection? Isn't the attempt to find community through national consciousness natural for people refused an American identity because racism does not give them that choice?

Korean national consciousness, the resolve to resist and fight back when threatened with extermination, was all that could be called upon when the Korean Americans in Los Angeles found themselves abandoned. They joined together to guard each other's means of livelihood with guns, relying on Korean-language radio and newspapers to communicate with and help each other. On the third day after the outbreak of violence, more than 30,000 Korean Americans gathered for a peace march in downtown L.A. in what was perhaps the largest and most quickly organized mass mobilization in Asian American history. Musicians in white, the color of mourning, best traditional Korean drums in sorrow, anger, and celebration of community, a call to arms like a collective heartbeat.[20] I believe that the mother of Edward Song Lee, the Los Angeles–born college student mistaken for a looter and shot to death in the streets, has been able to persevere in great part because of the massive outpouring of sympathy expressed by the Korean-American community that shared and understood her *han*.

I have been critical lately of cultural nationalism as detrimental to Korean Americans, especially Korean American women, because it operates on exclusions and fosters intolerance and uniformity of thought while stifling self-criticism and encouraging sacrifice, even to the point of suicide. But *sa-i-ku* makes me think again: what remains for those who are left to stand alone? If Korean Americans refuse to be victims or political pawns in the U.S. while rejecting the exhortation that we go back to Korea where we belong, what will be our weapons of choice?

In the darkest days of Japanese colonial rule, even after being stripped of land and of all economic means of survival, Koreans were threatened with total erasure when the colonizers rewrote Korean history, outlawed the Korean language, forced the subjugated people to worship the Japanese emperor, and demanded that they adopt Japanese names. One of the results of these cultural-annihilation policies was Koreans' fierce insistence on the sanctity of Korean national identity that persists to this day. In this context, it is not difficult to understand why nationalism has been the main refuge of Koreans and Korean Americans.

While recognizing the potential dangers of nationalism as a weapon, I for one am not ready to respond to the antiessentialists' call to relinquish my Korean American identity. It is easy enough for the French and Germans to call for a common European identity and an end to nationalisms, but what of the peoples suppressed and submerged while France and Germany exercised their national prerogatives? I am mindful of the argument that the resurgence of nationalism in Europe is rooted in historical and contemporary political and economic inequality among the nations of Europe. Likewise, I have noticed that many white Americans do not like to think of themselves as belonging to a race, even while thinking of people of color almost exclusively in terms of race. In the same way, many men think of themselves as "human beings" and of women as the ones having a gender. Thus crime, small businesses, and all Korean-African American interactions are seen and interpreted through the lens of race in the same dominant culture that angrily rejects the use of the racial lens for viewing yellow/white or black/white interactions and insists suddenly that we are all "American" whenever we attempt to assert our identity as people of color. It is far easier for Anglo Americans to call for an end to cultural nationalisms than for Korean Americans to give up national consciousness, which makes it possible to survive the vicious racism that would deny our existence as either Korean Americans or Americans.

Is there anything of use to us in Korean nationalism? During one thousand years of Chinese suzerainty, the Korean ruling elite developed a philosophy called *sadaejui*, or reliance of the weak on the strong. In direct opposition to this way of thought is what is called *jaju* or *juche sasang*, or self-determination.[21] Both *sadaejui* and *juche sasang* are ways of dealing with unequal power relationships and resisting the transformation of one's homeland into a battlefield for others, but *sadaejui* has never worked any better for Koreans than it has for any minority group in America. *Juche sasang*, on the other hand, has the kind of oppositional potential needed in the struggle against silence and invisibility. From Korean national consciousness, we can recover this fierce refusal to accept subjugation, which is the first step in the effort to build community, so that we can work with others to challenge the forces that would have us annihilate each other instead of our mutual oppression.

What is clear is that we cannot "become American" without dying of *han* unless we think about community in new ways. Self-determination does not mean living alone. At least for now, that may mean mining the rich and haunted lode of Korean national consciousness while we struggle to understand how our fate is entwined with the fate of others lying prostrate before the triumphal procession of the winners of History.[22] During the past fifteen years or so, many young Korean nationalists have been studying the legacies of colonialism and imperialism that they share with peoples in many Asian, African, and Latin American nations. At the same time that we take note of this work, we can also try to understand how nationalism and feminism can be worked together to demystify the limitations and reductiveness of each as a weapon of empowerment. If Korean national consciousness is ever to be such a weapon for us, we must use it to create a new kind of nationalism-in-internationalism to help us call forth a culture of survival and recovery, so that our *han* might be released and we might be freed to dream fiercely of different possibilities.

NOTES

1. According to a September 1992 Dun and Bradstreet survey of 560 business owners in Korea-town in South Central Los Angeles, an estimated 40 percent of the businesses damaged during *sa-i-ku* have closed their doors permanently. Moreover, almost 40 percent had no insurance or were insured for 50 percent or less of their total losses ("L.A. Riot Took Heavy Toll on Businesses," *San Francisco Chronicle*, 12 September 1992).

2. Following quota changes in U.S. immigration laws in 1965, the Korean population in America increased more than eightfold to almost one million. Between 1970 and 1990, Los Angeles Koreatown grew from a few blocks of stores and businesses into a community base for all sorts of economic and cultural activities.

3. Pretense, of course, because I was only passing for Chinese. The temporary comfort I experienced would come to an end whenever it was discovered that I could speak no Chinese and that I had no organic links to Chinese Americans, who frequently underscored both our commonalities and our differences by telling me that everything Korean—even *kimchi*, that quintessentially Korean vegetable eaten at every Korean meal—was originally Chinese.

4. The Black-Korean Alliance (BKA) was formed, with the assistance of the Los Angeles County Human Relations Commission, to improve relations between the Korean and African American communities after four Korean merchants were killed in robberies during the month of April 1986. The BKA sponsored activities and events, such as joint church services, education forums, joint cultural events, and seminars on crime prevention and community economic development. The BKA never received political or financial support from the public or private sectors. The organization had neither its own meeting place nor a telephone. Grass-roots participation was not extensive, and despite the good intentions of the individuals involved, the BKA was unable to prevent the killing of a dozen more Korean merchants in southern California between 1990 and *sa-i-ku*, or to stop the escalation of tensions between the two communities after the shooting of 15-year-old Latasha Harlins by Korean merchant Soon Ja Du in March, 1991. By June of that year, after police declared the killing of an African American man by a Korean liquor-store owner "justifiable homicide," African American groups began boycotting the store, and the BKA failed to convince African American boycotters and Korean merchants to meet together to negotiate an end to the conflict. Nor were the members of the BKA successful in

obtaining the help of members of the Los Angeles City Council or the California State Legislature, who might have been instrumental in preventing the destructive violence of *sa-i-ku* if
they had had the integrity and farsightedness to address the intensifying hostilities before it was
too late. After *sa-i-ku*, the BKA was in disarray, and as of this writing, its members are planning
to dissolve the group.

5. According to John Murray, founder of the southern California chapter of Cal-Pac, the black
   beverage and grocers' association, African American liquor-store owners "sold stores they had
   bought in the mid-1960s for two times monthly gross sales—roughly $80,000 at the time,
   depending on the store—for five times monthly gross, or about $300,000." After the Jews
   fled in the wake of the Watts riots, African Americans were enabled by civil rights legislative
   mandates to obtain for the first time credit from government-backed banks to start a number
   of small businesses. But operating liquor stores, although profitable, was grueling, dangerous,
   and not something fathers wanted their sons to do, according to interviews with African
   American owners and former owners of liquor stores in African American communities. Former
   liquor merchant Ed Piert exclaimed: "Seven days a week, 20 hours a day, no vacations, people
   stealing. That's slave labor. I wouldn't buy another liquor store." When liquor prices were
   deregulated in 1978 and profit margins shrank in the face of competition from volume buyers,
   many African American owners sold out to Korean immigrants carrying cash collected in
   rotating credit clubs called *kye* (Susan Moffat, "Shopkeepers Fight Back: Blacks Join with
   Koreans in a Battle to Rebuild Their Liquor Stores," *Los Angeles Times*, 15 May 1992).

6. In a newspaper interview, Alberto Machon, an 18-year-old junior at Washington Preparatory
   High School who had moved to South Central Los Angeles with his family from El Salvador
   ten years ago, said that he was laughing as he watched every Korean store looted or burned
   down because "I felt that they deserved it for the way they was treatin' people . . . the money
   that we are giving to the stores they're taking it to their community, Koreatown." Thirty-
   two-year-old Arnulfo Nunez Barrajas, served four days in the Los Angeles County jail for
   curfew violation. He was arrested while going from Santa Ana to Los Angeles to see his aunt,
   whose son had been killed during the upheavals. According to Nunez, "[T]he ones they've
   caught are only from the black race and the Latin race. I haven't seen any Koreans or Chinese.
   Why not them? Or white? Why only the black race and the Latinos? Well, it's racism" (*Los
   Angeles Times*, 13 May 1992).

7. L. A. Chung, "Tensions Divide Blacks, Asians," *San Francisco Chronicle*, 4 May 1992.

8. *Los Angeles Times*, 5 May 1992.

9. They were also given to gloating over the inability of American authorities to maintain social
   order as well as the South Korean government can. In an interview, a South Korean diplomat
   in Los Angeles remarked to me that he was astonished at how ill-prepared the Los Angeles
   police and the National Guard were for "mass disturbances." They did not react quickly
   enough, they were very inefficient, they had no emergency plan, and even their communications
   network broke down, he observed. He could not imagine "riots" getting out of control in
   South Korea, which was ruled by the military from 1961 to 1987; there, he commented, "the
   police are very effective. They work closely with the military."

10. For example, a story about the "black riots" in the 6 May 1992 *Central Daily News* in Seoul
    listed the writer as Korean-American sociologist Edward T'ae-han Chang, who was astonished
    when he saw it because he hadn't written it (personal communication).

11. In 1913, a group of Korean-American laborers was run out of Hemet Valley, California by a
    mob of anti-Japanese whites. The Koreans responded by insisting that they were Korean, not
    Japanese. What might seem a ludicrous response to racist expulsion has to be viewed in light

of the fact that the U.S. sanctioned Japan's 1909 annexation of Korea, closing all Korean delegations and placing Korean immigrants under the authority of Japanese consulates. Since they were classified as Japanese, Korean Americans were subject to the Alien Land Acts that targeted Japanese by denying them the right afforded all others regardless of race, nativity, or citizenship: the right to own land in California and nine other states. Also, foreign-born Koreans were able to become naturalized U.S. citizens only after the McCarran-Walter Act of 1952 permitted naturalization of Japanese. I have heard some Asian Americans equate the Chinese- and Japanese-American use of signs and buttons reading "I Am Not Korean" during *sa-i-ku* with the Korean American (and, not coincidentally, Chinese American) practice of wearing buttons saying "I Am Not Japanese" during World War II. But, in light of the specificities of Korean and Korean American history, this cannot be a one-to-one comparison.

12. In a 23 July 1992 interview, a 50-year-old Korean immigrant woman whose South Central Los Angeles corner grocery store had been completely destroyed during *sa-i-ku* told me, "The America I imagined [before I arrived here] was like what I saw in the movies—clean, wide streets, flowers everywhere. I imagined Americans would be all big, tall . . . with white faces and blond hair. . . . But the America here is not like that. When I got up to walk around the neighborhood the morning after we arrived in Los Angeles from Korea, it was as if we had come to Mexico."

13. John Berger and Jean Mohr, *A Seventh Man: A Book of Images and Words about the Experiences of Migrant Workers in Europe* (New York: Penguin Books, 1975). I want to thank Barry Maxwell for bringing this work to my attention.

14. I am not grappling directly with social class issues here because, although I am cognizant of their crucial importance, I am simply not qualified to address them at the present time. The exploited "guest workers" in Europe described by Berger and Mohr, unlike the Korean immigrants to the U.S., brought with them their laboring bodies but not capital to start small businesses. Because they are merchants, the class interests of Korean American shopowners in Los Angeles differ clearly from the interests of poor African American and Latino customers. But working with simple dyads is impossible, since Korean American shopowners are also of color and mostly immigrants from a country colonized by the United States. At the same time, it seems to me that class factors have been more important than race factors in shaping Korean-American immigrants' attitudes toward African American and Latino populations. Perhaps because of the devastation caused by Japanese colonization and the Korean War, many Koreans exhibit intensely negative attitudes toward the poor and indeed desperately fear being associated with them. I have often marveled at the importance placed on conspicuous consumer items, especially clothing, in South Korean society, where a shabbily dressed person can expect only shabby treatment. In the 1960s, a middle class American could make a social statement against materialistic values by dressing in tattered clothing without being mistaken for a homeless person. Now that this is no longer true, it seems to me that middle class Americans exhibit some of the fears and aversions that I witnessed in South Korea. Ironically, in the society where blackness and brownness have historically been almost tantamount to a condemnation to poverty, prejudice against the poor brought from Korea is combined with home-grown U.S. racism, and the results have been explosive.

At the same time, I have also noticed among Korean merchants profound empathy with the poor, whose situation many older immigrants know from first-hand past experiences. I personally witnessed many encounters between Korean merchants who lost their stores and African American neighbors in South Central during July 1992, when I accompanied the merchants as they visited their burned-out sites. None of the encounters were hostile. On the contrary, most of the African American neighbors embraced the Korean shopowners and expressed concern for them, while the merchants in turn asked warmly after the welfare of their neighbors' children. Although Korean–African American interaction has been racialized in the dominant culture, the quality of these relationships, like the quality of all human relationships, proved far more individual than that racial schematizing allows for.

15. Every South Korean middle school, high-school, and college student is required to take a course in "National Ethics," formerly called "Anticommunism." This course, which loosely resembles a civics class on Western civilization, government, constitutionalism, and political ideology, emphasizes the superiority of capitalism over communism and the importance of the national identity and the modern capitalist state. From the early 1960s through the 1970s, when most of the Los Angeles Korean immigrant merchants studied "Anticommunism" or "National Ethics," they were taught that "capitalism" and "democracy" are the same, and that both are antithetical to "communism" or "socialism." According to this logic, criticisms of the U.S., a "democracy," are tantamount to praise of "communism." Such a view left little room for acknowledgment of racism and other social problems in American society. Indeed, the South Korean National Security Law formerly prosecuted and jailed writers who depicted Americans negatively and film makers who portrayed North Koreans as good-looking or capable of falling in love. Today, however, the interpretation of what constitutes antistate activity is far narrower than in former decades, and although the South Korean government maintains that "pro–North Korea" activities are against the law, anti-U.S. sentiments have been common in South Korea since the mid-1980s.

16. I cannot help thinking that these violent baptisms are an Asian American legacy of sorts, for in some sense it was the internment that forced the Japanese Americans to "become American" half a century ago.

17. Many Korean Americans have criticized the *Los Angeles Times* and local television news, and the ABC network in particular, for repeatedly running stories about Soon Ja Du shooting Latasha Harlins (the tape was the second-most-played video during the week of the riots, according to the media-watch section of *A Magazine: An Asian American Quarterly* 1, no. 3, 4). They complained that the Los Angeles ABC affiliate aired the store videotape in tandem with the King footage. ABC even inserted the Du-Harlins tape segment into its reportage of the height of the *sa-i-ku* upheavals. Korean Americans have also protested the media focus on armed Korean American merchants. In particular, they objected to the repeated use of the image of a Korean merchant pointing a gun at an unseen, off-camera target. They knew that he was being shot at and that he was firing only at the ground, but they felt that the image was used to depict Korean immigrants as violent and lawless. They argued that by blocking out the context, the news media harmed Korean Americans, about whom little positive was known by the American public. Tong S. Suhr wrote in a Korean American newspaper:

> The Harlins killing is a tragic but isolated case. . . . This is not to condone the Harlins killing; nor is it to justify the death by countering with how many merchants in turn have been killed. Our complaint is directed to the constant refrain of "the Korean-born grocer killing a black teen-ager," which couldn't help but sow the seeds of racial hatred . . . [and make me wonder]: Was there any conspiracy among the . . . white-dominated media to pit one ethnic group against another and sit back and watch them destroy one another? . . . Why were the Korean American merchants portrayed as gun-toting vigilantes shooting indiscriminately when they decided to protect their lives and businesses by arming themselves because no police protection was available?

Why wasn't there any mention of the fact that they were fired upon first? Why such biased reporting? ("Time for Soul Searching by Media," *Korea Times*, 29 June 1992).

I would challenge representatives of the news media who argue that visual images of beatings and shootings, especially when they are racialized or sexualized, are "exciting" and "interesting," even when they are aired hundreds or thousands of times, when compared with "boring" images of the everyday. Three months after *sa-i-ku*, I visited a videotape brokerage company in search of generic footage that could be used in a documentary about the Korean immigrant experience of losing their means of livelihood. Almost every inch of the stringers' footage contained images of police cars, fire engines, and uniformed men heroically wiping their brows as they courageously prepared to meet the challenges before them. Since there were neither police nor firemen anywhere in sight in South Central or Koreatown during the first three days of *sa-i-ku*, none of this footage was of use to me. No doubt the men who shot these scenes chose what seemed to them the most "interesting" and "exciting" images. But if I, a woman and a Korean American, had had a camera in my hands, I would have chosen quite different ones.

18. *Newsweek*, 18 May 1992.

19. The text of King's statement was printed in the *Los Angeles Times* (2 May 1992) as follows:

> People I just want to say . . . can we all get along? Can we get along? Can we stop making it horrible for the older people and the kids? . . . We've got enough smog here in Los Angeles, let alone to deal with the setting of those fires and things. It's just not right. It's not right, and it's not going to change anything.
>
> We'll get our justice. They've won the battle but they haven't won the war. We will have our day in court and that's all we want. . . . I'm neutral. I love everybody. I love people of color. . . . I'm not like they're . . . making me out to be.
>
> We've got to quit. We've got to quit. . . . I can understand the first upset in the first two hours after the verdict, but to go on, to keep going on like this, and to see a security guard shot on the ground, it's just not right. It's just not right because those people will never go home to their families again. And I mean, please, we can get along here. We all can get along. We've just got to, just got to. We're all stuck here for awhile. . . . Let's try to work it out. Let's try to work it out.

20. The news media that did cover this massive demonstration invariably focused on the Korean musicians because they looked and sounded alien and exotic. Ironically, most of them were young, American-born or at least American-educated Korean Americans who learned traditional music as a way to recover their cultural heritage. They perform at many events: I remember them in the demonstrations against the 1991 Gulf War.

21. *Juche sasang,* the concept of self-determination, was attractive to Koreans before the division of the country after the defeat of Japan in World War II. However, since the term *juche* is central to the official political ideology in communist North Korea, the synonym *jaju* is used in South Korean officialdom.

22. I borrow this image from Walter Benjamin, "Theses on the Philosophy of History," *Illuminations* (New York: Schocken Books, 1969), 256. I would like to thank Shelley Sunn Wong for helping me see its relevance to Korean Americans in the 1990s.

15

Reflections on the Rodney King Verdict and the Paradoxes of the Black Response

Jerry G. Watts

It appears almost trivial, if not belittling, today to claim that Afro-American urban communities are in crisis. The word "crisis" just does not adequately capture the catastrophic doom that pervades so much of contemporary black life. One need only confront the myriad of statistics about urban black life: high rates of unemployment; malnutrition; Third World levels of infant mortality; the return of polio and other immunizable diseases among elementary school children; the phenomenal spread of AIDs, particularly among intravenous drug users; homelessness; widespread substandard housing; underfunded public schools; frightening rates of illiteracy; rates of incarceration exceeding rates of college enrollment; alcoholism; epidemics in drug addiction, particularly crack cocaine; unwanted children; teenage parenthood; commonplace child abuse and the routine abuse of the dependent elderly. Black urban communities are engulfed in an everyday violence unheard of in the history of humankind except during periods of extended warfare. For instance, in Washington, D.C., and neighboring Prince Georges County, Maryland, which has a sizable poor black population, 3,000 murders have been officially recorded in the last five years. The murderers and murder victims were overwhelmingly young blacks, particularly young black men. To fathom the murder of approximately 3,000 young people within a five-year span,

I would like to thank emphatically Farah Griffin and Traci C. West for sharing their thoughts about the Rodney King episode and for helping me to sharpen some of my ideas.

one might want to imagine this death toll as the equivalent of two Washington, D.C., high schools disappearing from the face of the earth.[1] However, the violence in poor black neighborhoods is far more extensive than murder statistics convey. Armed robbery, wife battering, rape, assault with intent to kill, and simple assault occur at staggering rates. The *Washington Post* reported that 75% of all black men in Washington, D.C., will at some point in their lives have some type of formal interaction with the city's criminal-justice system.[2] Stabilizing elements in poor communities are being overwhelmed by state callousness and racist indifference to the lives of the black and Hispanic poor.[3] As a result, a nihilism has grown in the black community.[4] Anomie reigns in some small but growing sectors.[5] Black urban communities are simultaneously under assault and self-destructing. Yet, given the tremendous odds against escaping the impact of the violence, drugs, and social decay, most inner-city blacks cling to deeply held humane values and lifestyles.[6]

Yes, black America is in crisis, but life goes on in the republic. Amid the utter devastation of the South Bronx, nightly baseball games are played in the lavishness of a renovated Yankee Stadium; newlyweds continue to honeymoon in Bermuda; new versions of white robber barons make overnight fortunes through the Savings and Loan rip-offs; black fraternities and sororities like Delta Sigma Theta hold garish annual conventions; discussions in luncheonettes center around why Susan Lucci has failed to win an Emmy; "The Price Is Right" continues to "give away" gaudy prizes; and Jet Magazine publishes weekly, mindless stories about the talentless Latoya Jackson. Americans in search of vicarious identities purchase sleek new cars. The weekly incomes of the poor and working classes are sometimes squandered in state lotteries while the more affluent attend diet centers or surgically endure "tummy tucks." Bourgeois life goes on in the United States. A few beats are missed out of concern for safety and health but otherwise it is an exciting time to be alive. Instead of confronting the urban poor as a humane concern, bourgeois Americans try either to move farther and farther away from the city or to develop coping strategies for ignoring the inconvenience of these people's existence. After a while, the homeless are not seen, just stepped over. When they become too numerous to step over, as is the case in Grand Central Station during the winter, we expect our paid public servants (i.e., the police) to remove them from the premises. The black American urban crisis is an American typicality. Americans accept the destitute plight of the black poor as potentially unchangeable by any human effort. The refrain is no longer that "they don't want a job" but that "we tried in the sixties and it just did not work." The black poor are a given, relegated to the scrap heap of human inevitabilities like "death and taxes."

I recently attended a gathering of black political thinkers and activists from around the country. We were called together in part because of a sense of urgency following the Rodney King verdict and the rioting in Los Angeles. Our mission was to consider ways of breaching the dome of public silence concerning the human needs of black American citizens and breaking out of the prevailing political malaise that has captured so much of black America and white progressive circles as well. The coordinator for the gathering was a very prominent black leftist social theorist, who continually raised some interesting questions and tried to steer our discussions in a fruitful, directed manner. On the whole, the conference was quite energizing. Despite trying to cope with problems far beyond their means, progressive activists throughout the United States are continuing to wage the "good fight."

At one of the sessions, the coordinator stated that one of the major weaknesses in the Afro-American political community was the absence of a progressive black think tank. There was, he claimed, no central institution that had, as its mission, the issuance of critiques of prevailing policies as well as the dissemination of information concerning viable alternatives. Such a think tank could provide local black activists with help in forecasting the impact of a public-policy option being debated in their specific locale. Such a center could be a clearinghouse for disseminating information documenting the impact of reactionary public policies on black American lives. Moreover, the existence of a black think tank could provide the legitimate imprimatur for the entry of progressive black policy analysts into national media forums. I agreed with his formulations concerning the need for a black progressive think tank for I have long bemoaned the weakness of the Afro-American political and intellectual infrastructures. Yet, when talking about the absence of a progressive black presence in media talk shows (i.e., "Washington Week in Review") this radical thinker added, "Had we had such a think tank, we could have better explained Los Angeles, for we could have explained the difference between a riot and a rebellion."

I was dumbfounded by the statement. Though I continue to believe that the recent Los Angeles disturbances constituted a riot, it was not his attempt to distinguish a riot from a rebellion that puzzled me. Instead, I was puzzled by his hidden assumption that such distinctions would be politically significant to the television viewing audience. To whom were we supposed to explain the difference between riots and rebellions? To the Latino and black rioters? To whites looking at television? What difference was our explanation supposed to make? The presuppositions of his rather innocent desire "better to explain" hold some revealing yet problematic insights into the psyche of black Americans.

I was struck by the ease with which one of black America's most prominent radical intellectuals presumed that there was a vast television audience that would care whether the L.A. episode was discussed as a riot or a rebellion. My assumption has been that if there was such a substantial caring audience among television viewers, the black urban crisis would not exist and thus there would have been no Rodney King episode. My point is not merely to label the statement as naive but to bring to bear the degree to which a resilient, naive faith in America is often present even in the most informed and radical black Americans.

His statement reminded me of a press conference held by the National Urban League during the latter part of Reagan's first term in office. The Urban League held yearly press conferences to coincide with the publication of their annual report, *The State of Black America*. At these press conferences, the various policy experts who authored chapters of the report commented on their findings. As the conclusion of what can only be considered strident indictments of the callousness of the state, John Jacobs usually speaks. On this one occasion, among other things, Jacobs stated that it was important to bring the facts (of the report) to the attention of the Reagan presidency because he thought that President Reagan did not actually grasp the impact of his policies on black America. Such a statement led me to reflect on the psyche of black American political leaders and black Americans in general. What vested interests did Jacobs have in wanting to believe that Reagan did not understand that his policies were devastating black Americans? Why was Jacobs incapable of confronting an obvious possibility that, at best, Reagan was indifferent to the plight of poor blacks and, at worst, willed their destruction? Furthermore, he did so with the apparent approval of most Americans.

Why is it that many blacks continue to hold on to the belief that all that prevents white America or bourgeois black America from intervening on behalf of the black poor is the "correct" information? Such faith assumes that white America and bourgeois black America are progressives-in-waiting, waiting, that is, for the right political figure or argument to energize their good will toward blacks. This naiveté is quite dangerous for it refuses to comprehend the extent to which the black poor are hyperpariahs in American society. While I have neither systematic empirical data nor survey research to support this claim, I emphatically believe that there is something in the political culture of Afro-Americans that precludes us from confronting our plight in America in all of its naked honesty. Perhaps evasiveness is a survival instinct to ward off despair. Maybe the impact of our resilient Christian beliefs prevents us from recognizing that hell has arrived for many blacks. Yet, at this utterly destitute moment, stark honesty necessitates that progressive whites and blacks face up to the fact that sufficiently large sectors of the American populace are both pleased and/or indifferent to the destruction of large sectors of black urban America. Must such a realization lead to political paralysis and despair? Perhaps, but I think not. Contrary to the pop psychology that often pervades American political discourse, recognition of the authentic parameters of the subjugation of the black poor will not necessarily embed them or their allies in a collective, paralyzing depression. It will certainly increase anxieties, but so what? As a prerequisite for political engagement, hope does not necessitate the creation of a fictitious America. Hope is useless to a political opposition if it suffocates or sidetracks a rigorous critique of one's political condition. Strategic politics always rest on realistic assessments, however dreadful.

The resilient kernel of black American hope in the ultimate justness of white American goodwill is not merely confined to the affluent sectors of black America. An important telltale of the escapist ethos of large sectors of poor black Americans lies in the fact that the recent rioting in Los Angeles did not begin immediately following the airing of the video film of the Rodney King beating over Los Angeles television. Would-be rioters waited under the hope that American justice, whatever that is, would prevail. Certainly, the video which showed numerous white policemen mercilessly beating on a black man generated an intense anger in the black populace. It resonated with widespread beliefs concerning the racist nature of the Los Angeles police force. Throughout the entire nation, blacks, particularly black men, recognized themselves and their local police forces in the videotaped assault. Were cops in Philadelphia, New York, Chicago, or New Haven any different?

It has long been a belief in urban black America that white Americans do not understand the viciousness and criminality of urban white police forces. But underlying this belief in white ignorance is a corollary belief that "things would be different" if whites knew the truth. Still, the white cops of Los Angeles must be deemed unique given their open, enduring, and cowboylike commitment to racist brutality. After all, Rodney King was beaten without any police apprehension about the utterly public nature of the event. Their racist legacy goes as far back as the 1950s under Police Chief William Parker, an avowed white supremacist.[7] During the 1960s and 1970s, the racist brutality of the Los Angeles police force was matched by the racist antics of the Chicago police department; the brazenness of the Oakland cops in their dealings with the Black Panthers; the pre–Coleman Young, Detroit police department's unstated license to kill blacks; the racist brutality of various southern police departments; and the almost impenetrable racist corruption of New York City's finest. Yet, during this period, the masters of high-profile racist policing were Philly's finest, under the direction of Big Frank Rizzo. Rizzo, if the reader will recall, first as police chief and later as mayor, gave a new meaning and vitality to white-ethnic racist resentment.[8] By the 1980s, Los Angeles under Police Chief Daryl Gates replaced Philadelphia as the national beacon point for white-racist police repression. At a time when many urban police forces were engaged in efforts to better police/black relations, usually in response to the emergence of sizable black electorates, the Los Angeles

Police Department (LAPD) remained stuck in racist time. Under the direction of Chief Gates, one of America's most explicit advocates of Gestapolike police tactics, the Los Angeles police force of the 1980s and 1990s emerged as the popularly acknowledged national leader in the field of racist aggression. After numerous blacks had been murdered by Los Angeles police using a "choke hold," Gates claimed that their deaths were the result of their flawed racial anatomy. He stated, "We may be finding that in some blacks when the carotid choke hold is applied the veins or arteries do not open up as fast as they do on normal people."[9] Black movie stars were routinely stopped, frisked, and forced to kiss the earth while lying flat on their faces. The rule in Los Angeles was that black men, by their very existence, were valid suspects and that black men driving around in expensive cars were obviously guilty of something. The racism of the Los Angeles cops, when coupled with their class resentments, led them to pull their guns on any black celebrity from the Lakers' Jamal Wilkes to movie star Wesley Snipes, television actor Blair Underwood, and Olympic medal winner and coach Al Joyner. Recently news has leaked concerning a secret investigatory unit that Gates had established. Gates was clearly protofascist.

Given the history of the Los Angeles Police Department's open violation of blacks' citizenship rights, many residents were not shocked by the video of the King beating. Yet, one cannot grasp the absence of rioting unless one realizes that many of the very black Americans who had been victimized by the Los Angeles police believed that the videotape of the beating would once and for all educate white America about a form of racist repression that black Americans endure in everyday life. In effect, the film was viewed by many blacks as moral capital in a racial struggle. The immediacy and accuracy of the video in an age of television, when coupled with the fact that it was filmed unrehearsed by a white American, persuaded blacks that whites could no longer hide from the truth. It was there in black and white for all to see.

But what was expected of whites? Specifically, nothing less than a conviction of the gangster cops and public condemnations of such behavior. Perhaps some blacks even entertained the idea that this video could lead to changes in police behavior toward blacks. Generally speaking, blacks expected whites to be appalled by the divergence between professed American democratic values and the black urban reality. Various forms of this expectation have been at the center of black political thought since the days of slavery.

The question remains, How was it that blacks living in South Central Los Angeles could have ever come to have faith in the ability of the criminal-justice system to convict white cops for beating a black man when the very same system did not convict white cops for killing blacks? The very lives of the residents of South Central spoke to the absence of constitutional safeguards. By what stretch of the imagination did they come to believe that the judicial and political system cared about their rights?

In part, their faith in the criminal-justice system was predicated on two phenomena. First, blacks, like all Americans, had come to invest power in the truth of the television screen. The existence of a videotape was irrefutable proof. Second, given the peculiarity of this incident and the national attention that it commanded, many blacks had come to believe in the potential for the criminal-justice system to function in a just manner in this one instance. "Maybe this once, they will act right." The sense of being both subjugated and citizens of "a land of laws and not men" is a profound paradox in black life. In effect, W.E.B. DuBois's metaphor of the "twoness" of Afro-American consciousness still seems valid. Blacks, however marginal, are still fundamentally steeped in American ideology, even in some instances when it appears utterly divorced from their lived experience.

Ironically, the jury verdict in the King trial was steeped in authentic American values as much as the King beating itself and black American optimism in the judicial system. Once the verdict of complete acquittal of the cops was announced, many blacks felt naive and foolish. They had dared to believe that the existence of the videotape ensured justice. Now they had to recognize themselves as having been "suckers" to a white-racist scam. Moreover, their naiveté was publicly forced down their own throats. It was racially humiliating. As such, the verdict in the trial of the police officers was a crystallizing event that prevented blacks from effectively shielding themselves from their own social marginality in America. Many blacks were obviously hurt by the verdict. Yet, there was little in their lives that made the hurt seem anything but weak and stupid. Blacks were ashamed of their hurt and gullibility. In effect, blacks were ashamed of their Americanness. It was no wonder some people rioted!

There will perpetually be blacks who claim not to be surprised or hurt by anything that white Americans do to black people. Such individuals will claim that they always knew that the racist Los Angeles cops would be acquitted. While some blacks have acquired a rather matter-of-fact, stoic grasp of the viciousness of racism in American politics, most of us have not. We can still be surprised by certain acts of white racism and undoubtedly were surprised by the verdict. It is an extraordinary task, perhaps superhuman, to try to live in such a manner that the expectations of racially fair treatment do not enter one's mind even at some moment of weakness. Even if one could live in such a cold and calculating fashion, the decision to do so would be in many respects a surrender of one's autonomy to racism. Unsurprisingly, many of the blacks who claim to have been neither surprised nor hurt by acquittal of the four Los Angeles cops are probably individuals who have been at some point so thoroughly devastated by American racism and subsequently ashamed of that hurt, that they now try to shut down their emotions in a pathetic attempt to shield themselves from the possibility of further racial humiliation. Usually, such strategies do not ultimately work.

The rioting in Los Angeles brought into question the viability of ethnic-based electoral politics as a vehicle for the protection of the interests of the black poor. Los Angeles is a fascinating locale to study the limitations of black urban electoral politics precisely because it is one of the few cities in the United States that was not on the verge of fiscal bankruptcy when a black was elected mayor. Mayor Tom Bradley is now in his fourth term as mayor of the city. Yet, Bradley's tenure as mayor has had an incredibly minute positive impact on the lives of the city's most economically marginal residents, many of whom are black and Latino.[10] Whether the marginal impact of Bradley's mayoralty stems from his lack of initiative and concern or from the absence of sufficient resources, it became evident to many blacks in Los Angeles that local electoral politics were irrelevant to their plight. Moreover, it is clear that Bradley was not a legitimate leader in the eyes of the black residents of South Central Los Angeles. Yet, Bradley and black mayors like him throughout America have done little to stimulate effective indigenous leadership for they fear that such persons and their groups will become the source of pressure. In effect, the 1992 Los Angeles riot was uniquely undisciplined and parapolitical, characteristics which resemble the organic state of much of everyday life in these communities.

During the riots of the 1960s, like the one that occurred in my hometown of Washington, D.C., in 1968 (following Martin Luther King's assassination), ethnic consciousness was sufficiently high among the black rioters that black store owners that had been "friends" of the local black community were not burned out. In fact, some friendly white businesses were spared. Signs in the windows of stores standing intact following nights of arson and looting read, "I'm a Soul Brother." Unlike the riots of the 1960s, in Los Angeles the race of the store owner appears to have had little impact on the arson selection. Black businesses were burned out along with those of whites and Korean Americans. The media made a point of showing black store owners crying or stunned by the loss of their enterprises.[11] The willingness to burn out black store owners in the face of what appeared to have been a protest against white racism may signal the rise of a festering black nihilism. Los Angeles rioters appear to have been generally far less politicized than the black rioters of the 1960s. A contrasting analysis might argue that the reason black store owners were burned out alongside white owners is that the blacks were owners. In effect, this interpretation views the Los Angeles riot as a class riot and not a race riot. Support for this argument stems from the multiethnic composition of the rioters. Some reports indicate that there may have been more Latino rioters than black ones. It might appear that the only traits which all of the rioters shared were their class locations and festering class resentments. Both interpretations might be partially true.

However, it is not surprising that ethnic solidarity meant little to the black Los Angeles rioters. What could ethnic unity possibly mean in a community where blacks killing blacks may be the number-one killer of black people? Racist white cops, however vicious, are ultimately minor irritants when compared to the viciousness of the black gangs and wanton black violence. Black-on-black violence is thoroughly debilitating to many blacks for it signals an inculcation of racism and the breakdown of communal sensibilities. It is such an ethnically traumatizing phenomenon that few black intellectuals want to talk about it in public arenas. In effect, the value of black life is not only minuscule in the eyes of white racists but equally worthless in the eyes of many other blacks.

Much like black New York, in its response to the Howard Beach and Yusef Hawkins murders, the black community of Los Angeles seems capable of generating vehement protests only when whites kill or beat blacks. Have blacks also come to accept black-on-black violence and murder as American typicalities? Yet, if the racist violence of white-ethnic youths and cops was the only violence confronting blacks, our communities would have reached the millennium. However, there are occasional mass marches, demonstrations, and public outcries when blacks kill other blacks. Black communities do at times march against street violence, drugs, and murder, but their efforts do not usually receive the publicity that they merit. Black-on-black murder is simply not as big a spectacle as white-on-black or black-on-white murder.

But why arson? Why do politically disenfranchised and despairing blacks gut and burn down their own neighborhoods? In this age of pervasive historical amnesia, it is ridiculous to expect today's would-be rioters to understand that rioting makes even a marginally endurable life that much more unendurable. Of those inner-city black neighborhoods that were destroyed during the urban riots of the 1960s, few, if any, were ever substantially rebuilt for the use of the indigenous peoples. In some cities, there have been efforts to rebuild these areas but only via gentrification and the requisite removal of their indigenous poor black residents. Now, on one level, it is quite understandable for poor people to desire to burn down their own neighborhoods since these neighborhoods are rat-infested, poor, dilapidated, filthy, and ultimately remindful of their devalued status in America. One can easily imagine that the residents of such a neighborhood harbor a great deal of aggression toward their living environment. Through arson, aggression and rage are released. A momentary feeling of empowerment takes root. But, even these moments of supposed empowerment are but swindles. Though highly cathartic, arson and looting are false empowerments. The highs that they give last only as long as the building burns. The fact is, the poor obtain no benefit from a burned-out structure or an empty lot. Such urban spaces in poor inner-city neighborhoods eventually lead to further decay and social disintegration.[12] Ressentiment reigns. Through destruction, one obtains empowerment. Yet destruction is an incomplete form of human agency and appears to reinvigorate nihilism, for it may make the socially marginal think that they are capable only of destroying what others have built. Herein may lie some of the origins of the antagonism between blacks and Korean Americans.

The mere presence of Korean-American businesses in this black urban community may have generated feelings of black-ethnic inadequacy. While I have no doubt that Korean Americans can be as racist as any other Americans, the intensity of the rioters' desire to destroy Korean-American businesses may indicate naked envy or misplaced aggression. After all, Korean Americans do not numerically dominate the Los Angeles police force nor do they constitute the power elite of the city. Moreover, the mere fact that one Korean-American businesswoman had recently murdered a black customer in cold blood does not implicate the entire Korean-American business community in race genocide. Yet, during moments of high stress, Americans, white and black, become quite skillful at generating paranoid-style objectifications of "others." This phobic response is directed at an imaginary enemy in the guise of real people; yet, it is subconsciously responding to a growing sense of disorder and lack of control. The acquittal of the four police in the Rodney King beating had nothing specifically to do with the Korean-American business community, and yet it was partially singled out for destruction as the enemy. Not surprisingly, Korean-American businesses were a much more vulnerable target than the judicial system or the police department. Ironically, the Korean-American business community, which was viewed as powerful by local blacks, was unable to generate protection from the Los Angeles police. Was this racism?

What lessons did progressive intellectuals learn from the urban riots of the 1960s? To many bourgeois, progressive black and white intellectuals, this question may appear absurd. I will probably be told that the sense of frustration is so high and the lack of state concern so thorough that cathartic rage is all that can be expected. But, if this is all that can be expected, how can we posit the possibility of a politicized poor black urban stratum? The issue before us is neither to blame nor to absolve the rioters for their actions. However, rioters must be held accountable for rioting and not primarily before the law. Rioters must be held accountable before their very own communities. Rioting is not a democratic act. The arsonists and rioters did not take the pulse of their local communities before setting fire to stores. They acted on their own. Everyone else is forced to accept the consequences of their actions. Had the rioters polled their neighbors they may have discovered that the majority of the local residents, who were not participants in the rioting, did not want their neighborhood burned down.

As traditional intellectuals, it behooves us not to weave hyperpoliticized counterhegemonic narratives around any and all actions taken by poor people living in poor neighborhoods. In the face of poverty, many South Central residents did not have numerous options for effective political engagement. Yet, rioting also is not efficacious. The problem is that so-called white and black progressives had done little to open up possibilities for new politics among the black urban poor. We, too, participate in the marginalization of the black urban poor. They become intellectual capital that we can use to bolster our critiques of American vulgarity in the age of Reagan-Bush, but we don't, by and large, interact personally with them.

This is not a call for all progressive intellectuals to drop their texts and to run to local community organizing. The task of demarginalizing the urban poor demands struggles waged on turfs far beyond the local communities. Furthermore, we certainly have a vital role to play in countering the various hegemonic ideologies which construct the black urban poor as American "throwaways." In this regard, we cannot let the nonsense of Housing and Urban Development Secretary Jack Kemp go unchallenged. Kemp has used the moment to reinvigorate time-worn calls for "black capitalism." He has argued that the key to the prevention of future riots lies in the black ownership of businesses in the black community. Kemp would have us believe that individual black-owned businesses are inherently and collectively owned by all members of that black community. Such claims attempt to mask intraracial class differences.

Instead of calling for an expansive democratic process that substantively includes the black poor, Kemp offered them a vision of more commodities. In this vision, the fact that the commodities are owned and distributed by black businesses is supposed to soothe the naked inequalities in the purchasing power of the local black consumers. Obviously, some black residents aren't buying this vision. After all, some black business owners were burned out during the riots. Yet, sadly enough, there are large sectors of the black poor and working classes who may believe that this rhetoric actually describes their potential salvation. Borrowing from the mindlessness of Louis Farrakhan and other spokespersons for what is marketed as "black self-help," many in the black community have essentially agreed that the "black poverty can be addressed only through black businesses." This reactionary formulation is championed in many black circles as a radical hypothesis. In effect, such arguments accept as legitimate the marginalization of the black poor from their rightful status as United States citizens. Instead of black poverty being the responsibility of the society at large, the black poor are reduced to wards of their ethnic group. Reagan could not have said it better![13] Not surprisingly, enterprising elements of the black middle and upper-middle classes will champion Kemp's formulations, for they will be the true beneficiaries.

Perhaps Martin Kilson's insightful analysis of the limitations of an earlier version of black capitalism needs to be dusted off. Kilson wrote:

Some professionals are adopting a Black Power ideological format not with the intent of preparing themselves for service to self-governing urban black communities but to make themselves more visible to the white establishment, which is not at all adverse to offering such persons good jobs as alternatives to Black Power. The more viable Negro businessmen are also simulating the Black Power advocates who have virtually no control over the use of their political style by the professional and business black bourgeoisie, which means the Black Power advocates will eventually lose the payoff potential of nationalist politics. If so . . . the Negro lower classes, whose riots legitimize Black Power, will be joined by the Black Power advocates in holding the bag—with nothing in it save a lot of therapeutic miscellany.[14]

The task before us as progressive intellectuals requires a brutal honesty that many of us may not be up to emotionally. It means, on the one hand, discarding romantic notions of the black poor. It also means being on the lookout for the seepage of American ideological naiveté into our formulations and practices. In effect, it means that we can no longer do intellectual business as normal, for if we authentically commit ourselves to the struggles of our most marginal citizens, we, too, will become increasingly marginalized. Their marginalization is so thoroughly accepted as part of the American landscape that attempts to breach the silence of their inhumane treatment will undoubtedly make one appear to be fanatical. There is no career reward within the academy for political engagement of this intensity. Moreover, of those blacks in the American academy who have risen to national prominence, none have done so as a result of their advocacy on behalf of the black urban poor.

Two months after the Los Angeles riot, the absence of significant public debate surrounding the events is quite deafening. Immediately following the termination of the rioting, commentators on numerous channels spoke about the neglect of urban areas during the Reagan administration. The condition of our nation's cities momentarily became a key issue. After trying, but momentarily failing, President Bush no longer seeks to demagogue the issue. On the other hand, progressives have not been able to sustain the riots as the backdrop for a discussion of a flawed democracy. Life in the republic continues as usual.

Notes

1. See Sari Horowitz and Paul Duggan, "3,000 Killings Later, a Culture of Violence Poisons Area," *Washington Post*, 29 December 1991, A1. The article contains an interview with a young black man who has lost fifteen friends to the violence of the streets.

2. See Keith Harriston, "Going to Jail Is 'Rite of Passage' for Many D.C. Men, Report Says," *Washington Post*, 18 April 1992, B3.

3. See William J. Wilson, *The Truly Disadvantaged: The Inner City, the Underclass, and Public Policy* (Chicago: University of Chicago Press, 1987).

4. For a thoughtful reflection on the problem of a growing nihilism in black urban communities,

see Cornel West, "Nihilism in Black America: A Danger That Corrodes from Within," *Dissent* (Spring 1991): 221–26.

5. In Elijah Anderson's description of life in a black inner-city poor neighborhood in Philadelphia, the nihilism and antisocial behavior are far more prevalent among the younger generation of blacks. The black elderly and middle-aged adults disproportionately function as the bearers of civility and humane values. See Elijah Anderson, *Street Wise: Race, Class and Change in an Urban Community* (Chicago: University of Chicago Press, 1990).

6. For a vivid discussion of the chaos and humanity present in an inner-city black ghetto, once again see Elijah Anderson, *Street Wise*. Also see Alex Kotlowitz, *There Are No Children Here: The Story of Two Boys Growing Up in the Other America* (New York: Doubleday, 1991).

7. For graphic depictions of this thug see Mike Davis, *City of Quartz: Excavating the Future in Los Angeles* (New York: Vintage, 1992).

8. Despite having fashioned an entire career on racist aggression toward blacks, Rizzo never dropped a bomb on a black neighborhood in Philadelphia. That honor was left to "His Honor" the black technocrat Wilson Goode.

9. Mike Davis, *City of Quartz*, 272.

10. For a trenchant critique of the limitations of the Bradley mayoralty on the lives of black and Hispanic inner-city Los Angeles residents, see Mike Davis, *City of Quartz*.

11. A picture of a stunned black businessman standing before his burning store appears on the cover of the newspaper *USA Today*, 1–3 May 1992.

12. For an interesting discussion of the ways that decay takes over an urban neighborhood, see Wesley G. Skogan, *Disorder and Decline: Crime and the Spiral of Decay in American Neighborhoods* (Berkeley: University of California Press, 1990).

13. For a discussion of the intersections between contemporary black-nationalist discourse and Reaganomics, see Jerry G. Watts, "Racial Discourse in an Age of Social Darwinism," *Democratic Left* 18, no. 4 (July–August 1990): 3–5.

14. Martin Kilson, "Black Power: Anatomy of a Paradox," *The Harvard Journal of Negro Affairs* 2, no. 1 (1968): 34.

16

Two Nations . . . Both Black

Henry Louis Gates, Jr.

Everyone knows there are two nations in this country, white and black, right? That's what the Kerner Commission Report said in 1968, and that's what the title of Andrew Hacker's best-selling sequel to that report says today. And for good reason. Track the statistics for public health, educational attainment, and income, and they all seem to point to the same thing: that African Americans are the ultimate unassimilables of the American mix, the pebble in the ethnic soup.

Peer a little closer, though, and this familiar image splits again. Even as the ranks of the underclass expand, a second nation within a nation has formed. The fact is, Afro-America's affluent elite is larger than it has ever been—a legacy of the post–civil rights era and just the kind of corporate and governmental programs of intervention that have fallen into such disfavor of late.

Now, most of the black communities' leaders, self-appointed or otherwise, are loath to acknowledge the existence of this class. They take it as part of their role to publicize the dire condition afflicting so much of black America. Why distract from the real problem? But here's the rub. Opponents of these post–civil rights era programs can then flatly declare that they have failed. How to explain the complicated truth: that for black America, these are the worst of times . . . and the best of times?

Today many black Americans enjoy a measure of economic security beyond any we have known in the history of black America. And yet, their very existence seems an affront to the swelling ranks of the poor. Nor have black intellectuals ever quite made peace with the concept of the black bourgeoisie, a group that is typically seen as devoid of cultural authenticity, doomed to mimicry and pallid assimilation. I once gave a talk before an audience of black academics and educators in the course of which I referred to black middle-class culture. Afterward, one of the academics in the audience, deeply affronted, had a question for me. "Professor Gates," he asked rhetorically, his voice dripping with sarcasm, "what *is* black middle-class culture?" I suggested that if he really wanted to know, he need only look around the room. But perhaps I should just have handed him a mirror: for just as nothing is more American than anti-Americanism, nothing is more characteristic of the black bourgeoisie than the sense of shame and denial that the identity inspires. What did we do to be so black and blue? You may well ask.

The truth is that black America has always been uncomfortable with the fact of its divisions, and none more so than the members of the elite themselves. Here's W. E. B. DuBois, black America's greatest intellectual, writing in 1903:

> Can the masses of Negro people be in any possible way more quickly raised than by the effort and example of [their own] aristocracy of talent and character? Was there ever a nation on God's fair earth civilized from the bottom upward? Never; it is, ever was and ever will be from the top downward that culture filters. The Talented Tenth rises and pulls all that are worth the saving up to their vantage ground. This is the history of human progress; and the two heroic mistakes which have hindered that progress were the thinking first that no more could ever rise save the few already risen; or second, that it would better the unrisen to pull the risen down.

So many things have changed since then, of course. That was a colored world then, back in 1903 when W. E. B. DuBois wrote his famous essay, "The Talented Tenth." It was a world that in some sense has shaped and nurtured many of us, a world in which both our purposes and our enemies were clear. We were to get just as much education as we possibly could, to stay the enemies of racism, segregation, discrimination. If we heard it once, we heard it a thousand times: Get as much education as you can, boy; nobody can take your education away from you. It was a world in which comporting ourselves with dignity and grace, striving to "know and test the cabalistic letters" (as DuBois put it) of the white elite and acknowledging and honoring those of us who had achieved were central to being a colored person in America.

We, too, were a people of the Book. When DuBois was the editor of *The Crisis* magazine, he published the portraits of black college graduates, lawyers, and doctors on its cover and in its pages. Being an athlete or an entertainer was fine and good, for DuBois, but these were not *serious* occupations. Law and medicine, education and scholarship—these were the pinnacles of achievement, these the province of the Talented Tenth.

I don't claim that we ever lived up to this idealized image. But at least these were the images, the ideals, that were presented to us. Only racism and segregation stood between our people and the fullness of American citizenship. If only we could secure our legal rights, the argument went, if only we could use the courts to strike down segregation; if only *de jure* segregation could be banished—then all else would follow, as day upon night. The world was simple then; our enemy an easy target.

And then the obvious obstacles tumbled and fell. *De jure* segregation was killed in the American judicial system. *Brown v. Board of Education* is such a great triumph of decades of legal scholarship, under the leadership of such stellar jurists as Charles Hamilton Houston, Thurgood Marshall, Constance Baker Motley—the list is long and noble—that its anniversary still has resonance in black America. So much went into the preparation of that brief before the Court—a rare collaboration between our legal practitioners and our scholars, between politicians and political activists, between whites and blacks, Jews and Gentiles, working together in an interracial compact that few of us can even remember, let alone imagine happening again. There can be little doubt that the period between 1954 and the passage of the Voting Rights Act of 1965 was the decade when the Negro felt more optimism than would be justified in any other decade in our century.

To be sure, the three years between 1965 and 1968 were bloody and turbulent ones—we could think of these years as framed by the assassinations of Malcolm X and Martin Luther King, or by the riots in Watts in 1965 and the riots just about everywhere in 1968, especially those surrounding the Democratic Convention in Chicago. And yet despite all this, the grandchildren of the Talented Tenth—those of us who had been trained to succeed, geared to prosper, adequately prepared by family and teachers to "cross over" into the white world once the walls of segregation came tumbling down—plunged headlong and joyously into the abyss of integration.

How have we fared since 1965? In so many ways, as I insist, our progress is astonishing, something we may need to be reminded of even in the wake of the Rodney King riots and the stark statistics that measure the gap within our community between the haves and have nots. The "black" community, as we knew it before 1965, simply does not exist any longer. And we do great harm to the truth when we pretend that the problems confronting the black underclass are identical to those confronting the black middle class. For a new crop of black youth, whose only experience has been of our affluent suburbs, Matty Rich's grim film of life in the projects, "Straight Out of Brooklyn," would have to be retitled

"Straight Out of Brookline." And who would ever have thought that any of us growing up would have considered enrolling our kids in "Jack and Jill"—not to advance them socially (as many of our parents hoped), but so that they would be with other black kids and learn about their ethnic heritage?

This is where we are in 1992, we members of the black middle class, the heirs of the Talented Tenth. We are isolated from the black underclass and yet still humiliatingly vulnerable to racism, in the form of random police harassment, individual racial insults from waitresses and attendants in stores, the unwillingness of taxi drivers to pick us up, systematic discrimination by banks and bank loan officers, wage discrimination in the workplace, and our perception of a "glass ceiling" in the corporate world. The questions that greeted our arrival at white colleges in the late 1960s and the 1970s—"Do you play basketball, football or baseball?" (translated: "Which sport got *you* to Yale?")—have been supplanted by more subtle forms of questioning about our right and ability to *hold* the positions for which we have worked so diligently. Far too often, white colleagues at school, in our mostly white neighborhoods, and in the workplace, see blackness as a sign of inferiority, our meal ticket into the middle class as an Affirmative Action quota. The most pernicious forms of racism—the stereotyping of an individual by the color of her skin—still pervade white America. And caught in this no-man's-land of alienation and fragmentation is the black middle class.

What do we do about this? What do we not do? First of all, it's time for the black middle class to stop feeling guilty about its own success while fellow blacks languish in the inner city of despair. Black prosperity does not derive from black poverty: Those who succeed are those whose community, whose families, *prepared* them to be successful. As Stanley Crouch and others remind us, the familiar exhortation in those days was to "get all the education that you can"—and we did. When I left home for Yale, virtually my whole hometown celebrated. "The community," as we put it, however sentimentally, wished us to succeed. Talking black, walking black, wearing kente cloth, listening to black music and filling our walls with black art—as desirable as these things can be in and of themselves—are not essential to "being black." You can love Mozart, Picasso, and ice hockey and still be as black as the ace of spades.

Second, we don't have to fail in order to be black. As crazy as this sounds, recent surveys of young black kids reveal a distressing pattern. Far too many say that succeeding is "white," education is "white," aspiring and dreaming are "white," believing that you can make it is "white." Had any of us said this sort of thing when we were growing up, our families and friends would have checked us into a mental institution. We need *more success* individually and collectively, not less.

Third, we don't have to pretend any longer than 30 million people can ever possibly be members of the same social class. After all, the entire population of Canada is 26 million. Canadians are not all members of one economic class. Nor do they speak with the one single voice of one single leader. We have *never* been members of a single social or economic class, and never will be.

How do we "fight the power" in a post–civil rights world in which Bull Connors and George Wallace are no longer the easy targets that white racists used to be? A world in which the rhetoric of the civil rights era sounds tired and empty? (If George Bush, Ross Perot, or anyone else had turned up at the March on Washington in April, and handed over a check for $500 billion to heal the ills of the inner city, I wonder if anyone there would have known what to do with it.)

The time has come for honesty within the black community. The causes of poverty within the black community are *both* structural and behavioral, as scholars as diverse as philosopher Cornel West at Princeton and sociologist William Julius Wilson at Chicago have insisted, and as most polemicists still shy from acknowledging. A generation of well-meaning social scientists has made the notion of "the culture of poverty" taboo, correctly observing that the concept, as originally introduced, ignored the economic and structural dimensions of the problem. But having acknowledged those dimensions, it's time to concede that, yes, there *is* a culture of poverty. How could there not be? How could you think that culture *matters* and deny its relation to economic success? In general, a household made up of a 16-year-old mother, a 32-year-old grandmother and a 48-year-old great-grandmother is not a site for hope and optimism. It's also true that not everyone in any society wants to work, that not all people are equally motivated. The commitment to redress a legacy of economic violence does not require a fantasy of economic egalitarianism.

Our task, it seems to me, is to lobby for those social programs that have been demonstrated to make a difference for those sufficiently motivated to seize these expanded opportunities. More important, we have to demand a structural change in this country. We have to take people off welfare and train them for occupations relevant to a twenty-first century economy. And while I'm sympathetic to such incentives as tax breaks to generate new investment in inner cities, youth apprenticeships with corporations, expanded tax credits for earned income, and tenant ownership of inner-city property, I believe we will have to face a reality. The reality is that our inner cities are not going to become oases of economic prosperity and corporate investment, and we should probably think about moving black inner-city workers *to the jobs* rather than wait for new factories to resettle in the inner city.

To continue to repeat the same old stale formulas—to blame, in exactly the same ways, "the man" for oppressing us all, to scapegoat Koreans, Jews, or even

Haitians for seizing local entrepreneurial opportunities that have, for whatever reason, eluded us—is to fail to accept moral leadership. Not to demand that each member of the black community accept individual responsibility for his or her behavior—whether that behavior assumes the form of gang violence, unprotected sexual activity, you name it—is another way of selling out a beleaguered community. It is to surrender to the temptation to act as ethnic cheerleaders ''selling woof tickets''—engaging in hollow rhetoric—from the suburbs instead of speaking the hard truths that may be unpopular with our fellows. DuBois dared to speak an uncomfortable truth when he addressed the responsibilities of the black elite. For them, the challenge awaits of healing the rift within black America, and the larger nation as well.

17

Learning to Talk of Race

Cornel West

———————————

What happened in Los Angeles this past April was neither a race riot nor a class rebellion. Rather, this monumental upheaval was a multiracial, trans-class, and largely male display of justified social rage. For all its ugly, xenophobic resentment, its air of adolescent carnival, and its downright barbaric behavior, it signified the sense of powerlessness in American society. Glib attempts to reduce its meaning to the pathologies of the black underclass, the criminal actions of hoodlums, or the political revolt of the oppressed urban masses miss the mark. Of those arrested, only 36 percent were black, more than a third had full-time jobs and most claimed to shun political affiliation. What we witnessed in Los Angeles was the consequence of a lethal linkage of economic decline, cultural decay, and political lethargy in American life. Race was the visible catalyst, not the underlying cause.

The meaning of the earthshaking events in Los Angeles is difficult to grasp because most of us remain trapped in the narrow framework of the dominant liberal and conservative views of race in America, which with its worn-out vocabulary leaves us intellectually debilitated, morally disempowered, and personally depressed. The astonishing disappearance of the event from public dialogue is testimony to just how painful and distressing a serious engagement with race is.

———————————

Cornel West's "Learning to Talk of Race" was first published in the 2 August 1992 edition of the *New York Times Magazine*.

Our truncated public discussions of race suppress the best of who and what we are as a people because they fail to confront the complexity of the issue in a candid and critical manner. The predictable pitting of liberals against conservatives, Great Society Democrats against self-help Republicans, reinforces intellectual parochialism and political paralysis.

The liberal notion that more government programs can solve the problems is simplistic—precisely because it focuses *solely* on the economic dimension. And the conservative idea that what is needed is a change in the moral behavior of poor black urban dwellers (especially poor black men, who, they say, should stay married, support their children, and stop committing so many crimes) highlights immoral actions while ignoring public responsibility for the immoral circumstances that haunt our fellow citizens.

The common denominator of these views of race is that each still sees black people as a "problem people," in the words of Dorothy I. Height, president of the National Council of Negro Women, rather than as fellow American citizens with problems. Her words echo the poignant "unasked question" of W. E. B. DuBois, who wrote:

> They approach me in a half-hesitant sort of way, eye me curiously or compassionately, and then instead of saying directly, How does it feel to be a problem? they say, I know an excellent colored man in my town. . . . Do not these Southern outrages make your blood boil? At these I smile, or am interested, or reduce the boiling to a simmer, as the occasion may require. To the real question, How does it feel to be a problem? I answer seldom a word.

Nearly a century later, we confine discussions about race in America to the "problems" black people pose for whites rather than considering what this way of viewing black people reveals about us as a nation.

This paralyzing framework encourages liberals to relieve their guilty consciences by supporting public funds directed at "the problems"; but at the same time, reluctant to exercise principled criticism of black people, they deny them the freedom to err. Similarly, conservatives blame the "problems" on black people themselves—and thereby render black social misery invisible or unworthy of public attention.

Hence, for liberals, black people are to be "included" and "integrated" into "our" society and culture, while for the conservatives they are to be "well behaved" and "worthy of acceptance" by "our" way of life. Both fail to see that the presence and predicaments of black people are neither additions to nor defections from American life, but rather *constitutive elements of that life.*

To engage in a serious discussion of race in America, we must begin not with the problems of black people but with the flaws of American society—flaws rooted in historic inequalities and longstanding cultural stereotypes. How we set up the terms for discussing racial issues shapes our perception and response to these issues. As long as black people are viewed as a "them," the burden falls on blacks to do all the "cultural" and "moral" work necessary for healthy race relations. The implication is that only certain Americans can define what it means to be American—and the rest must simply "fit in."

The emergence of strong black-nationalist sentiments among blacks, especially young people, is a revolt against this sense of having to "fit in." The variety of black-nationalist ideologies, from the moderate views of Supreme Court Justice Clarence Thomas in his youth to those of Louis Farrakhan today, rest upon a fundamental truth: white America has been historically weak-willed in ensuring racial justice and has continued to resist accepting fully the humanity of blacks. As long as double standards and differential treatment abound—as long as the rap performer Ice-T is harshly condemned while former Los Angeles Police Chief Daryl F. Gates's antiblack comments are received in polite silence, as long as Dr. Leonard Jeffries's anti-Semitic statements are met with vitriolic outrage while presidential candidate Patrick J. Buchanan's are received with a genteel response—black nationalisms will thrive.

Afrocentrism, a contemporary species of black nationalism, is a gallant yet misguided attempt to define an African identity in a white society perceived to be hostile. It is gallant because it puts black doings and sufferings, not white anxieties and fears, at the center of discussion. It is misguided because—out of fear of cultural hybridization, silence on the issue of class, retrograde views on black women, homosexuals, and lesbians, and a reluctance to link race to the common good—it reinforces the narrow discussions about race.

To establish a new framework, we need to begin with a frank acknowledgment of the basic humanness and Americanness of each of us. And we must acknowledge that as a people—*E Pluribus Unum*—we are on a slippery slope toward economic strife, social turmoil, and cultural chaos. If we go down, we go down together. The Los Angeles upheaval forced us to see not only that we are not connected in ways we would like to be but also, in a more profound sense, that this failure to connect binds us even more tightly together. The paradox of race in America is that our common destiny is more pronounced and imperiled precisely when our divisions are deeper. The Civil War and its legacy speak loudly here. Eighty-six percent of white suburban Americans live in neighborhoods that are less than one percent black, meaning that the prospects for the country depend largely on how its cities fare in the hands of a suburban electorate. There is no escape from our interracial interdependence, yet enforced racial hierarchy dooms us as a nation to collective paranoia and hysteria—the unmaking of any democratic order.

The verdict that sparked the incidents in Los Angeles was perceived to be

wrong by the vast majority of Americans. But whites have often failed to acknowledge the widespread mistreatment of black people, especially black men, by law-
enforcement agencies, which helped ignite the spark. The Rodney King verdict
was merely the occasion for deep-seated rage to come to the surface. This rage
is fed by the "silent" depression ravaging the country—in which real weekly
wages of all American workers since 1973 have declined nearly twenty percent,
while at the same time wealth has been upwardly distributed.

The exodus of stable industrial jobs from urban centers to cheaper labor markets
here and abroad, housing policies that have crated "chocolate cities and vanilla
suburbs" (to use the popular musical artist George Clinton's memorable phrase),
white fear of black crime, and the urban influx of poor Spanish-speaking and Asian
immigrants—all have helped erode the tax base of American cities just as the
federal government has cut its supports and programs. The result is unemployment, hunger, homelessness, and sickness for millions.

Driving that rage is a culture of hedonistic self-indulgence and narcissistic self-
regard. This culture of consumption yields coldhearted and meanspirited attitudes
and actions that turn poor urban neighborhoods into military combat zones and
existential wastelands.

And the pervasive spiritual impoverishment grows. The collapse of meaning in
life—the eclipse of hope and absence of love of self and others, the breakdown
of family and neighborhood bonds—leads to the social deracination and cultural
denudement of urban dwellers, especially children. We have created rootless,
dangling people with little link to the supportive networks—family, friends,
school—that sustain some sense of purpose in life. We have witnessed the collapse
of the spiritual communities that help us face despair, disease, and death and that
transmit through the generations dignity and decency, excellence, and elegance.

The result is lives of what we might call "random nows," of fortuitous and
fleeting moments preoccupied with "getting over"—with acquiring pleasure,
property, and power by any means necessary. (This is not what Malcolm X meant
by this famous phrase.) Postmodern culture is more and more a market culture
dominated by gangster mentalities and self-destructive wantonness. This culture
engulfs all of us—yet its impact on the disadvantaged is devastating, resulting in
extreme violence in everyday life. Sexual violence against women and homicidal
assaults by young black men on one another are only the most obvious signs of
this empty quest for pleasure, property, and power.

Lastly, this rage is fueled by a political atmosphere in which images, not ideas,
dominate, where politicians spend more time raising money than issues. The
functions of parties have been displaced by public polls, and politicians behave
less as thermostats that determine the climate of opinion than as thermometers
registering the public mood. American politics has been rocked by an unleashing

of greed among opportunistic public officials—following the lead of their counterparts in the private sphere, where, as of 1989, one percent of the population
owned thirty-seven percent of the wealth—leading to a profound cynicism and
pessimism among the citizenry.

And given the way in which the Republican party since 1968 has appealed to
popular xenophobic images—playing the black, female, and homophobic cards
and realigning the electorate along race, sex, and sexual-orientation lines—it is
no surprise that the notion that we are all part of one garment of destiny is
discredited. Appeals to special interests rather than public interests reinforce this
polarization. The Los Angeles upheaval was an expression of utter fragmentation
by a powerless citizenry that includes not just the poor but all of us.

What is to be done? How do we capture a new spirit and vision to meet the
challenges of the postindustrial city, post modern culture, and postparty politics?

First, we must admit that the most valuable sources for help, hope, and power
consist of ourselves and our common history. As in the ages of Lincoln, Roosevelt,
and King, we must look to new frameworks and languages to understand our
multilayered crisis and overcome our deep malaise.

Second, we must focus our attention on the public square—the common good
that undergirds our national and global destinies. The vitality of any public square
ultimately depends on how much we *care* about the quality of our lives together.
The neglect of our public infrastructure, for example—our water and sewage
systems, bridges, tunnels, highways, subways, and streets—reflects not only our
myopic economic policies, which impede productivity, but also the low priority
we place on our common life.

The tragic plight of our children clearly reveals our deep disregard for public
well-being. With about one out of five children living in poverty in this country
and one out of two black children and two out of five Hispanic children doing
so—and with most of our children ill-equipped to live lives of spiritual and
cultural quality, neglected by overburdened parents, and bombarded by the market values of profit-hungry corporations—how do we expect ever to constitute
a vibrant society?

One essential step is some form of large-scale public intervention to ensure
access to basic social goods—housing, food, health care, education, child care,
and jobs. We must invigorate the common good with a mixture of government,
business, and labor that does not follow any existing blueprint. After a period in
which the private sphere has been sacralized and the public square gutted, the
temptation is to make a fetish of the public square. We need to resist such
dogmatic swings.

Last, the major challenge is the need to generate new leadership. The paucity
of courageous leaders—so apparent in the response to the events in Los Angeles—

requires that we look beyond the same elites and voices that recycle the older frameworks. We need leaders—neither saints nor sparkling television personalities—who can situate themselves within a larger historical narrative of this country and world, who can grasp the complex dynamics of our peoplehood and imagine a future grounded in the best of our past, yet attuned to the frightening obstacles that now perplex us. Our ideals of freedom, democracy, and equality must be invoked to invigorate all of us, especially the landless, propertyless, and luckless. Only a visionary leadership that can motivate "the better angels of our nature," as Lincoln said, and activate possibilities for a freer, more efficient, and stable America—only that leadership deserves cultivation and support.

This new leadership must be grounded in grass-roots organizing that highlights democratic accountability. Regardless of whether Bill Clinton's cautious neoliberal programs or George Bush's callous conservative policies prevail in November, the challenge to America will be determining whether a genuine multiracial democracy can be created and sustained in an era of global economies and a moment of xenophobic frenzy.

Let us hope and pray that the vast intelligence, imagination, humor, and courage in this country will not fail us. Either we learn a new language of empathy and compassion, or the fire this time will consume us all.

Index

CONTRIBUTORS

Houston A. Baker, Jr. is Director of the Center for the Study of Black Literature and Culture and the author of the forthcoming *Black Studies, Rap, and the Academy*, University of Chicago Press, 1992.

Judith Butler is Professor of Humanities at Johns Hopkins University. She is author of *Gender Trouble: Feminism and the Subversion of Identity* (New York: Routledge, 1990) and co-editor with Joan Scott of *Feminists Theorize the Political* (New York: Routledge, 1992).

Sumi K. Cho is Assistant Professor of Political Science and Ethnic Studies at the University of Oregon.

Kimberlé Crenshaw is Professor of Law at the University of California School of Law, a Samuel Rubin Fellow at Columbia University School of Law, and one of the founders of Critical Race Theory, a movement bringing together critical scholars of race in law.

Mike Davis is a labor historian and author of *City of Quartz: Excavating the Future in Los Angeles* (New York: Vintage, 1991). The interview took place in late May 1992.

Thomas L. Dumm teaches American politics and contemporary theory at Amherst College. He is the author of *Democracy and Punishment* (Madison, WI: Univ. of Wisconsin Press, 1987), *Foucault and the Politics of Freedom* (Beverley Hills, CA: Sage Publications, 1993), and co-editor of *Rhetorical Republic: Governing Representations in American Politics* (Amherst, MA: University of Massachusetts Press, 1993).

Walter C. Farrell, Jr. is Professor of Educational Policy and Community Studies at the University of Wisconsin-Milwaukee where he also serves on the doctoral faculty in Urban Studies in the College of Letters and Science. He is a National Research Affiliate in the Center for the Study of Urban Poverty at UCLA. Farrell holds degrees in Geography from North Carolina Central University (B.A., 1967), Michigan State University (M.A. 1970, and Ph.D., 1974), and a postdoctoral Masters of Science in Public Health from the University of North Carolina at Chapel Hill (1980). His research focuses on the race and class underpinnings of the urban underclass and urban education and social issues. He has published widely in education, social-science, and public-health journals. Dr. Farrell was in Los Angeles during the rebellion.

Henry Louis Gates, Jr., is the W. E. B. DuBois Professor of Humanities at Harvard University. He is the author of *The Signifying Monkey: A Theory of African-American Literary Criticism* (New York: Oxford University Press, 1988) (winner of a 1989 American Book Award) and *Figures in Black: Words, Signs and the "Racial " Self* (New York: Oxford University Press, 1989). His most recent book is *Loose Cannons*, published in 1992 by Oxford University Press.

Ruth Wilson Gilmore is a lecturer, writer, and organizer based in Palmer Canyon, California. A member of the swelling ranks of the lumpenprofessoriate, she teaches part-time at the University of California-Los Angeles (Center for Afro-American Studies and English) and at the Claremont Colleges (Black Studies Department). Forthcoming works include "Decorative Beasts: Dogging the Academy in the Late Twentieth Century" (*California Journal of Sociology* special issue on education and the state, ed. Lourdes Arguelles and Gloria Romero, Winter 1992) and an edited collection of Stuart Hall's work on race, to be published by Writers and Readers and Verso.

Robert Gooding-Williams is Associate Professor of Philosophy and Black Studies at Amherst College. He has published essays on DuBois and Black Neoconservatism, and is currently completing a book, *Nietzsche's Pursuit of Modernism*, also to be published by Routledge, Chapman and Hall.

James H. Johnson, Jr., is Professor of Geography and Director of the Center for the Study of Urban Poverty at the University of California-Los Angeles. He holds degrees in Geography from North Carolina Central University (B.S., 1975), the University of Wisconsin-Madison (M.S., 1977), and Michigan State University (Ph.D., 1980). His research interests include the study of interregional black migration, interethnic minority conflict in advanced industrial societies, and urban poverty and social-welfare policy in America. He has published over 50 scholarly research articles and one research monograph and coedited four theme issues of scholarly research journals on these and related topics.

Elaine H. Kim is Professor of Asian American Studies and Faculty Assistant for the Status of Women at the University of California-Berkeley. Her book *Visions and Fierce Dreams: Lives and Work of Asian American Visual Artists* is forthcoming from Temple University Press; she is an editor of *Making Waves: Writings by and about Asian American Women* (Boston: Beacon Press, 1989) and the author of *Asian American Literature: An Introduction to the Writings and Their Social Context* (Philadelphia: Temple University Press, 1982). She is also the Associate Producer of *Slaying the Dragon* (1988), a television documentary on representations of Asian women in U.S. television and film and the co-producer of *Sa-i-Ku: From Korean Women's*

Perspectives, a video-documentary of Korean women's experiences of the L.A. crisis.

Melvin L. Oliver is Professor of Sociology and Associate Director of the Center for the Study of Urban Poverty at the University of California-Los Angeles. He received his B.A. (1972) in Sociology and Social Science from William Penn College in Iowa and his M.A. (1974) and Ph.D. (1977) in Sociology from Washington University, St. Louis. Professor Oliver's research focuses on interethnic minority conflict in advanced industrial societies; urban poverty, social stratification, and public policy in America; black social networks in cities; and minority-student adjustment and achievement in the American educational system. He is working with Thomas M. Shapiro on a monograph entitled *Black Wealth, White Wealth: Racial Inequality in Late 20th Century America*.

Michael Omi is a sociologist who teaches Asian American Studies and Ethnic Studies at the University of California-Berkeley. He is the co-author, with Howard Winant, of *Racial Formation in the United States: From the 1960s to the 1980s* (New York: Routledge, 1986).

Gary Peller is Professor of Law at Georgetown University Law Center and a co-chair of the Conference on Critical Legal Studies.

Cedric J. Robinson, Professor of Black Studies and Political Science at the University of California-Santa Barbara, received his B.A. from the University of California-Berkeley and his M.A. and Ph.D. from Stanford University. He has served as chair of the Political Science Department and Director of the Center for Black Studies at the University of California-Santa Barbara. His fields of teaching and research are modern political thought, radical social theory in the African diaspora, comparative politics, and media and politics. Dr. Robinson is the author of *Black Marxism: The Making of the Black Radical Tradition* (London: Zed, 1983) and *Terms of Order: Political Science and the Myth of Leadership* (Albany: SUNY, 1980). He is also the author of numerous articles on U.S., African, and Caribbean political thought; Western social theory; film and the press. His most recent articles are "Oliver Cromwell Cox and the Historiography of the West" (*Cultural Critique* 17, Winter 1990–91) and "C. L. R. James and the World System" (*The CLR James Journal*, Winter 1992). His current work includes *The Anthropology of Marxism* (in press), a monograph study of the historical and discursive antecedents of Marxism; and research into antifascism in Africa and the African diaspora in the 1920s and 1930s.

Jerry G. Watts is Associate Professor of American Studies at Trinity College, Hartford, Connecticut.

Cornel West is Professor of Religion and Director of the Afro-American Studies

Program at Princeton University. His book *Race Matters* will be published in the spring of 1993.

Patricia J. Williams is the author of *The Alchemy of Race and Rights*. She is Professor of Law at the University of Wisconsin and a board member of the Center for Constitutional Rights.

Rhonda M. Williams is a political economist now in the Afro-American Studies Program (joint with the Department of Economics) at the University of Maryland. As an Affiliate Faculty member for Women's Studies, she has both participated in and co-directed the Curriculum Transformation Project. Williams also serves as a member of the Board of Editors for the Maryland-based feminist journal, *Feminist Studies*. Prior to her employment at the University of Maryland, she taught at the New School for Social Research, Yale University, and the University of Texas at Austin. Williams's research continues to address theoretically and empirically the economic and social determinants of gender and race-ethnic employment and wage hierarchies in existing capitalist societies. She has contributed to recent scholarship on discrimination theory and the resurgent public dialogue on so-called cultures of poverty. Williams currently is analyzing the race and gender dimensions of economic restructuring.

Howard Winant teaches in the Sociology Department and directs the Latin American Studies Center at Temple University. He is the co-author, with Michael Omi, of *Racial Formation in the United States: From the 1960s to the 1980s* (New York: Routledge, 1986). He is also the author of *Stalemate: Political Economic Origins of Supply-Side Policy* (New York: Praeger, 1988), and of "Rethinking Race in Brazil" (*Journal of Latin American Studies* Vol. 24 No. 1 Feb. 1992).